Conspiracy Journal Presents

DEAD MEN TALKING

EXPOSING THE NEW WORLD ORDER CONSPIRACY AND THE EVIL AGENDA OF THE BROTHERHOOD OF ILLUMINATI

STRICTLY FORBIDDEN INFORMATION

Compiled By Commander X And The Committee Of Twelve To Save The Earth

DEAD MEN TALKING

**We denounce censorship and
support freedom of speech.**

GLOBAL COMMUNICATIONS
EX LIBRIS
POST OFFICE BOX 753
NEW BRUNSWICK, NJ 08903

DEAD MEN TALKING

Compiled by Commander X and The Committee Of Twelve To Save The Earth
This edition Copyright 2012 by Global Communications/Conspiracy Journal

Revised Edition

ISBN 1-60611-022-5
EAN 978-1-60611-022-5

Published by Global Communications/Conspiracy Journal
Box 753 · New Brunswick, NJ 08903

Staff Members
Timothy G. Beckley, Publisher
Carol Ann Rodriguez, Assistant to the Publisher
Sean Casteel, General Associate Editor
Tim R. Swartz, Graphics and Editorial Consultant
William Kern, Editorial and Art Consultant

THERE ARE FORCES AT WORK ALL AROUND US
By Commander X - For the Committee of 12

There are forces all around us who would like to do us in.

They are invisible. They are silent. They are cunning and they have no regard for you or your wellbeing despite what they might tell you.

We live in a great country...but there are utterly cruel beings at the center of our destruction who wish us to be slaves to their sinister thoughts and deeds. They want us to be part of their nefarious undertakings -- to take responsibility for that over which we have no control.

Here in this simple book we take on the task of revealing much and exposing all.

Be at peace for there is still hope. Pray that the outcome will be in our favor.

COMMANDER X

AN INSTRUCTIONAL NOTE:

EVERYTHING YOU THINK YOU KNOW IS A LIE—NOTHING IS TRUE

BREAKING DOWN DOORS

The doors and the houses and the people in them belong to the STATE. The police, who enforce the dictats of the STATE really don't need a warrant or any kind of "open container" or "suspicion of narcotics" pretext to break down your door and walk right into your abode.

If there is a house number, a street sign, a zip code attached to your house and/or name, it is all the permission the police need to break in and arrest you. A ZIP CODE is exactly the same as a military "kill box." It is a designated area to initiate military intervention. Period. If you have a driver license or a Social Security number, that alone is all the permission they need because by signing the license (a legal term), you agree to become the property of the STATE. Your birth certificate (a legal term) makes you property of the STATE, which then delivers the certificate to the Commerce Department, which sells or trades your life to foreign countries as promises to pay the National Debt. Your birth certificate will be endorsed just like a bank check. This makes you an indentured slave whether black, white, brown, yellow or red.

All these documents which bear your name as a STRAWMAN (ALL CAPITAL LETTERS) are covert contracts by which you agree to become property of the STATE; i.e., a slave of another person (lawyer/politician/barrister/king/queen/dictator). By signing a document bearing your name in all capital letters, you CAPITULATE or surrender to the person or agency from whom the letter originated. If you open a letter which bears your name as a STRAWMAN, you automatically agree to surrender yourself up to that person or agency. Jury duty. Letter from a lawyer. Letter from a business requesting payment, etc.

When a country or person capitulates after being defeated in war, all names upon the surrender document are capitalized. The STATE (an abstract entity) can only deal with other abstracts, not real persons. Hence, the STATE invents an abstract entity with whom or with which it can deal...the STRAWMAN. Corporations are abstract entities as in UNITED STATES OF AMERICA. This one just happens to be a bankrupt corporation because all the public treasuries have been plundered by the King's Agents Provocateurs (lawyers/politicians).

ObamaCare will establish another public treasury that will, likewise, be plundered by the politicians until it can no longer provide care for the millions who will be forced at the point of a gun to pay into it.

"Your Honor" and "Esquire" are titles of Nobility conferred upon American lawyers by the royal family of Great Britain, therefore making all who bear those titles agents of a foreign government. Their allegiance, if they have any, is to the royal family of England, the Windsors, (Saxe-Coburg-Goetha) not to Americans. Their primary purpose is to collect taxes and to secure oil and mineral rights for the King, which is required by a long-standing treaty with King George.

THE UNITED STATES OF AMERICA (one of the King's global businesses) is, by treaty, still a colony of Great Britain. The so-called "Constitution" of that corporation is nothing more than a set of by-laws written to govern how the King's colony should be established and run. It does not now, and never did, have anything to do with you, because you are not one of "the people." You are "property" (a legal term). A "citizen" (legal term). Got it?

Property has no rights, only the property owner has rights. Human property may be granted "privileges" (a legal term)," but never "rights" (a legal term)." You are not one of the "people;" you are property of the "people" and, therefore have no rights in their courts which, by the way, are really military tribunals established as STATES after Lincoln's War, the common law courts having been dissolved (by decree of the King of England) after the rightful sovereignty of the Southern states was destroyed.

CONTENTS

DEAD MEN TALKING

Forced Consent

Abraham Lincoln did not cause the death of so many people from a mere love of slaughter, but only to bring about a state of consent that could not otherwise be secured for the government he had undertaken to administer. When a government has once reduced its people to a state of consent—that is, of submission to its will—it can put them to a much better use than to kill them; for it can then plunder them, enslave them, and use them as tools for plundering and enslaving others. And these are the uses to which most governments, our own among them, do put their people, whenever they have once reduced them to a state of consent to its will. Andrew Jackson said that those who did not consent to the government he attempted to administer upon them, for that reason, were traitors, and ought to be hanged. Like so many other so-called "heroes," he thought the sword and the gallows excellent instrumentalities for securing the people's *consent* to be governed. The idea that, although government should rest on the consent of the governed, yet so much force may nevertheless be employed as may be necessary to produce that consent, embodies everything that was ever exhibited in the shape of usurpation and tyranny in any country on earth. It has cost this country millions of lives, and the loss of everything that resembles political liberty. It can have no place except as a part of a system of absolute military despotism. And it means nothing else either in this country, or in any other.

There is no half-way house between a government depending wholly on voluntary support, and one depending wholly on military compulsion. And mankind have only to choose between these two classes—the class that governs, and the class that is governed or enslaved. In this case, the government rests wholly on the consent of the governors, and not at all on the consent of the governed. And whether the governors are more or less numerous than the governed, and whether

DEAD MEN TALKING

they call themselves monarchists, aristocrats, or republicans, the principle is the same. The simple, and only material fact, in all cases, is, that one body of men are robbing and enslaving another. And it is only upon military compulsion that men will submit to be robbed and enslaved, it necessarily follows that any government, to which the governed, the weaker party, do not consent, must be (in regard to that weaker party), a merely military despotism. Such is the state of things now in this country, and in every other in which government does not depend wholly upon voluntary support. There never was and there never will be, a more gross, self-evident, and inexcusable violation of the principle that government should rest on the consent of the governed, than was the American Civil War, as carried on by the North. There never was, and there never will be, a more palpable case of purely military despotism than is the government we now have.

Lysander Spooner - 1808-1887

DEAD MEN TALKING

THE EXPOSIVE SECRETS OF MAJOR JORDAN'S DIARIES

American A-20 with Russian Star

Our gratitude and thanks goes to the Committee of Twelve for their valuable time donated to the compilation of this book. We've checked many sources and cannot find a publishing house now offering the book for sale. If you know of a source where people may purchase it, please let us know.

As time permits we'll add to the historical information surrounding the orchestration, implementation and tragic results of WWII. You will discover that major lies have been told, which proves once again the victors of war write the history.

In this case, as in all cases of war the 'victors' are never a nation, regardless of appearances, modern history books, or reporting by the media. Why? Because the real victors are the same group of international financiers who control the major publishing houses, education through all levels of learning, as well as the media. And let us not forget the major role the entertainment industry plays in the thought control process. Books, movies, games, videos, music. . . all of it geared to create the International Citizen/Slave.

Major George Jordan began his diary in 1942 when he became suspicious of US-sanctioned air shipments to the USSR. But he never expected to uncover a secret American WWII deal to give the Russians the raw materials and know-how to make atomic bombs!

The following is exerpted from the book, which will be published in full by Global Comminucations/Conspiracy Journal in late 2008.

DEAD MEN TALKING

From Major Jordan's Diaries © 1952 by George Racey Jordan, USAF (Ret.) with Richard L. Stokes. Originally published in 1952 by Harcourt, Brace & Company, New York Reprinted by American Opinion, 1961:

"MR BROWN" AND THE START OF A DIARY

Late one day in May 1942, several Russians burst into my office at Newark Airport, furious over an outrage that had just been committed against Soviet honor. They pushed me toward the window where I could see evidence of the crime with my own eyes.

They were led by Colonel Anatoli N. Kotikov, the head of the Soviet mission at the airfield. He had become a Soviet hero in 1935 when he made the first seaplane flight from Moscow to Seattle along the Polar cap; Soviet newspapers of that time called him "the Russian Lindbergh". He had also been an instructor of the first Soviet parachute troops, and he had 38 jumps to his credit.

I had met Colonel Kotikov only a few days before, when I reported for duty on May 10, 1942. My orders gave the full title of the Newark base as "UNITED NATIONS DEPOT No. 8, LEND-LEASE DIVISION, NEWARK AIRPORT, NEWARK, NEW JERSEY, INTERNATIONAL SECTION, AIR SERVICE COMMAND, AIR CORPS, U.S. ARMY".

I was destined to know Colonel Kotikov very well, and not only at Newark. At that time he knew little English, but he had the hardihood to rise at 5.30 every morning for a two-hour lesson. Now he was pointing out the window, shaking his finger vehemently.

There on the apron before the administration building was a medium bomber, an A-20 Douglas Havoc. It had been made in an American factory, it had been donated by American Lend-Lease, it was to be paid for by American taxes, and it stood on American soil. Now it was ready to bear the Red Star of the Soviet Air Force.

As far as the Russians and Lend-Lease were concerned, it was a Russian plane. It had to leave the field shortly to be hoisted aboard one of the ships in a convoy that was forming to leave for Murmansk and Kandalaksha. On that day the Commanding Officer was absent and, as the acting Executive Officer, I was in charge.

I asked the interpreter what "outrage" had occurred. It seemed that a DC-3, a passenger plane, owned by American Airlines, had taxied from the runway and, in wheeling about on the concrete plaza to unload passengers, had brushed the Havoc's engine housing. I could easily see that the damage was not too serious and could be repaired. But that seemed to be beside the point. What infuriated the Russians was that it be tolerated for one minute that an American commercial liner should damage, even slightly, a Soviet warplane!

The younger Russians huddled around Colonel Kotikov over their Russian-English dictionary, and showed me a word: "punish". In excited voices they demanded: "Pooneesh peelote!" I asked what they wanted done to the offending pilot. One of them aimed an imaginary revolver at his temple and pulled the trigger.

"You're in America," I told him. "We don't do things that way. The plane will be repaired and ready for the convoy."

They came up with another word: "Baneesh!" They repeated this excitedly over and over again. Finally I understood that they wanted not only the pilot, but American Airlines, Inc., expelled from the Newark field.

I asked the interpreter to explain that the US Army has no jurisdiction over commercial companies. After all, the airlines had been using Newark Airport long before the war and even before La Guardia Airport existed. I tried to calm down the Russians by explaining that our aircraft maintenance officer, Captain Roy B. Gardner, would have the bomber ready for its convoy even if it meant a special crew working all night to finish the job.

I remembered what General Koenig had said about the Russians when I went to Washington shortly after Pearl Harbor. He knew that in 1917 I had served in the Flying Machine Section, US Signal Corps, and that I had been in combat overseas. When he told me there was an assignment open for a Lend-Lease liaison officer with the Red Army Air Force, I was eager to hear more about it.

"It's a job, Jordan, that calls for an infinite amount of tact to get along with the Russians," the General said. "They're tough people to work with, but I think you can do it."

Thus I had been assigned to Newark for the express purpose of expediting the Lend-Lease program. I was determined to perform my duty to the best of my ability. I was a "re-tread", as they called us veterans of World War I, and a mere Captain at the age of 44 - but I had a job to do and I knew I could do it. The first days had gone reasonably well and I rather liked Kotikov. But there was no denying it: the Russians were tough people to work with.

As my remarks about repairing the bomber on time were being translated, I noticed that Colonel Kotikov was fidgeting scornfully. When I finished, he made an abrupt gesture with his hand. "I call Mr Hopkins," he announced.

It was the first time I had heard him use this name. It seemed such an idle threat, and a silly one. What did Harry Hopkins have to do with Newark Airport?

DEAD MEN TALKING

Assuming that Kotikov carried out his threat, what good would it do? Commercial planes, after all, were under the jurisdiction of the Civil Aeronautics Board.

"Mr Hopkins fix," Colonel Kotikov asserted. He looked at me and I could see now that he was amused in a grim kind of way. "Mr Brown will see Mr Hopkins, no?" he said, smiling.

The mention of "Mr Brown" puzzled me, but before I had time to explore this any further, Kotikov was barking at the interpreter that he wanted to call the Soviet Embassy in Washington. All Russian long-distance calls had to be cleared through my office, and I always made sure that the Colonel's, which could be extraordinarily long at times, were put through "collect". I told the operator to get the Soviet Embassy, and I handed the receiver to the Colonel.

By this time the other Russians had been waved out of the office, and I was sitting at my desk. Colonel Kotikov began a long harangue over the phone in Russian, interrupted by several trips to the window. The only words I understood were "American Airlines", "Hopkins", and the serial number on the tail which he read out painfully in English. When the call was completed, the Colonel left without a word. I shrugged my shoulders and went to see about the damaged Havoc. As promised, it was repaired and ready for hoisting on shipboard when the convoy sailed.

That, I felt sure, was the end of the affair.

I was wrong. On June 12th the order came from Washington, not only ordering American Airlines off the field but directing every aviation company to cease activities at Newark forthwith. The order was not for a day or a week. It held for the duration of the war, though they called it a "Temporary Suspension".

I was flabbergasted. It was the sort of thing one cannot quite believe, and certainly cannot forget. Would we have to jump whenever Colonel Kotikov cracked the whip? For me, it was going to be a hard lesson to learn.

Captain Gardner, who had been at Newark longer than I, and who was better versed in what he called the "push-button system", told me afterwards that he did not waste a second after I informed him that Colonel Kotikov had threatened to "call Mr Hopkins". He dashed for the best corner in the terminal building, which was occupied by commercial airlines people, and staked out his claim by fixing his card on the door. A few days later the space was his.

I was dazed by the speed with which the expulsion proceedings had taken place. First, the CAB inspector had arrived. Someone in Washington, he said, had set off a grenade under the Civil Aeronautics Board. He spent several days in the control tower, and put our staff through a severe quiz about the amount of commercial traffic and whether it was interfering with Soviet operations. The word spread around the field that there was going to be hell to pay. Several days later, the order of expulsion arrived. A copy of the order is reproduced in the centre section of this edition, a masterpiece of bureaucratic language.

I had to pinch myself to make sure that we Americans, and not the Russians, were the donors of Lend-Lease. "After all, Jordan," I told myself, "you don't know the details of the whole operation; this is only one part of it. You're a soldier, and besides, you were warned that this would be a tough assignment." At the same time, however, I decided to start a diary, and to collect records of one kind and another and make notes and memos of everything that occurred. This was a more important decision than I then realized.

Keeping a record wasn't exactly a revolutionary idea in the Army. I can still see Sergeant Cook, at Kelly Field, Texas, in 1917, with his sandy thatch and ruddy face, as he addressed me, a 19-year-old corporal, from the infinite superiority of a master sergeant in the regular Army: "Jordan, if you want to get along, keep your eyes and your ears open, keep your big mouth shut, and keep a copy of everything!"

Now I felt a foreboding that one day there would be a thorough investigation of Russian Lend-Lease. I was only one cog in the machinery. Yet because of the fact that I couldn't know the details of high-level strategy, I began the Jordan diaries...

THE "BOMB POWDER" FOLDERS

In my capacity as Liaison Officer, I began helping the Russians with necessary paper work and assisted them in telephoning to the various factories to expedite the movement of supplies to catch particular convoys. As Colonel Kotikov communicated with the many different officials in the Soviet Government Purchasing Commission, their names became more and more familiar to me.

Few of the American officers who came in casual contact with the Russians ever got to see any of their records. But the more I helped Rodzevitch and Colonel Kotikov, the more cordial they became. It became customary for me to leaf through their papers to get shipping documents, and to prepare them in folders for quick attention when they reported back to Washington.

At this time I knew nothing whatever about the atomic bomb. The words "uranium" and "Manhattan Engineering District" were unknown to me. But I became aware that certain folders were being held to one side on Colonel Kotikov's desk for the accumulation of a very special chemical plant. In fact, this chemical plant was referred to by Colonel Kotikov as a "bomb powder" factory. By referring to my diary, and checking the items I now know went into an atomic energy plant, I am able to show the following records, starting with the year 1942 while I was still at Newark. These materials, which are necessary for the creation of an atomic pile, moved to Russia in 1942:

Graphite: natural, flake, lump or chip, costing American taxpayers $812,437. Over thirteen million dollars' worth of aluminum tubes (used in the atomic pile to 'cook' or transmute the uranium into plutonium), the exact amount being $13,041,152. We sent 834,989 pounds of cadmium metal for rods to control the intensity of an atomic pile; the cost was $781,472. The really secret material, thorium, finally showed up and started going through immediately. The amount during 1942 was 13,440 pounds at a cost of $22,848. (On January 30, 1943 we shipped an additional 11,912 pounds of thorium nitrate to Russia from Philadelphia on the SS John C. Fremont. It is significant that there were no shipments in 1944 and 1945, due undoubtedly to General Groves' vigilance.)

It was about this time that the Russians were very anxious to secure more Diesel marine engines which cost about $17,500 each. They had received around 25 on previous shipments and were moving heaven and earth to get another 25 of the big ones of over 200-horsepower variety. Major General John R. Deane, Chief of our Military Mission in Moscow, had overruled the Russians' request for any Diesel engines because General MacArthur needed them in the South Pacific. But the Russians were undaunted and decided to make an issue of it by going directly to Hopkins who overruled everyone in favor of Russia. In the three-year period, 1942-44, a total of 1,305 of these engines were sent to Russia! They cost $30,745,947. The engines they had previously received were reported by General Deane and our military observers to be rusting in open storage. It is now perfectly obvious that these Diesels were post-war items, not at all needed for Russia's immediate war activity...

It is true that we never knew the exact use to which anything sent under Russian Lend-Lease was put, and the failure to set up a system of accountability is now seen to have been an appalling mistake. But could anything be more foolish than to suppose that the atomic materials we sent were not used for an atomic bomb which materialized in Russia long before we expected it? The British let us inspect their installations openly, and exchanged information freely. The Russians did not. Our Government was intent on supplying whatever the Russians asked for, as fast as we could get it to them - and I was one of the expediters. And when I say "our Government", I mean of course Harry Hopkins, the man in charge of Lend-Lease, and his aides. We in the Army knew where the orders were coming from, and so did the Russians. The "push-button system" worked splendidly; no one knew it better than Colonel Kotikov...

DEAD MEN TALKING

It had become clear, however, that we were not going to stay at Newark much longer. The growing scope of our activities, the expansion of Lend-Lease, the need for more speedy delivery of aircraft to Russia - all these factors were forcing a decision in the direction of air delivery to supplant ship delivery. It had long been obvious that the best route was from Alaska across to Siberia.

From the first, the Russians were reluctant to open the Alaskan-Siberian route. Even before Pearl Harbor, on the occasion of the first Harriman-Beaverbrook mission to Moscow in September 1941, Averell Harriman had suggested to Stalin that American aircraft could be delivered to the Soviet Union from Alaska through Siberia by American crews. Stalin demurred and said it was "too dangerous a route". It would have brought us, of course, behind the Iron Curtain.

During the Molotov visit to the White House, Secretary of State Cordell Hull handed Harry Hopkins a memorandum with nine items of agenda for the Russians, the first of which was: "The Establishment of an Airplane Ferrying Service From the United States to the Soviet Union Through Alaska and Siberia." When the President brought this up, Molotov observed that it was under advisement, but "he did not as yet know what decision had been reached".

Major General John R. Deane has an ironic comment on Russian procrastination in this regard:

"Before I left for Russia, General Arnold, who could pound the desk and get things done in the United States, had called me to his office, pounded the desk, and told me what he wanted done in the way of improving air transportation between the United States and Russia. He informed me that I was to obtain Russian approval for American operation of air transport planes to Moscow on any of the following routes in order of priority: one, the Alaskan-Siberian route; two, via the United Kingdom and Stockholm; or three, from Tehran to Moscow. I saluted, said 'Yes, sir', and tried for two years to carry out his instructions." (John R. Deane, The Strange Alliance, Viking, 1947, p. 78)

Where the US was not able to force Russia's hand, Nazi submarines succeeded. Subs out of Norway were attacking our Lend-Lease convoys on the Murmansk route, apparently not regarded as "too dangerous a route" for American crews. A disastrous limit was finally reached when, out of one convoy of 34 ships, 21 were lost. The Douglas A-20 Havocs, which were going to the bottom of the ocean, were more important to Stalin than human lives. So first we started flying medium bombers from South America to Africa, but by the time they got across Africa to Tiflis, due to sandstorms the motors had to be taken down and they were not much use to the Russians. Nor were we able to get enough of them on ships around Africa to fill Russian requirements for the big offensive building up for the battle of Stalingrad.

DEAD MEN TALKING

Finally, Russia sent its OK on the Alaskan-Siberian route. Americans would fly the planes to Fairbanks, Alaska; Americans would set up all the airport facilities in Alaska; Soviet pilots would take over on our soil; Soviet pilots only would fly into Russia.

The chief staging-point in the US was to be Gore Field in Great Falls, Montana. A few years before the war General Ralph Royce, who had been experimenting in cold-weather flying with a group of training planes called "Snow Birds", had found that Great Falls, with its airport 3,665 feet above sea level, on the top of a mesa tableland 300 feet above the city itself, had a remarkable record of more than 300 clear flying days per year, despite its very cold dry climate in the winter.

If you look at a projection of the globe centred on the North Pole, you will see that Great Falls is almost on a direct line with Moscow. This was to be the new and secret Pipeline. The Army called it ALSIB.

WE MOVE TO MONTANA

It was the coldest weather in 25 years when the route was mapped out. First of all, Major General Follette Bradley flew experimentally by way of the old goldfield airstrips of Canada. With the Russians he scratched out a route from Great Falls through Fairbanks, Alaska and across Siberia to Kuibeyshev and Moscow. It is the coldest airway in the world across the Yukon to Alaska and through the "Pole of Cold" in Siberia, but it worked.

Colonel (then Captain) Gardner, our trouble-shooter at Newark, was one of the first to go ahead to Montana. Then Lieutenant Thomas J. Cockrell arrived at Great Falls in charge of an advance cadre to make arrangements for the housing and quartering of troops of the 7th Ferrying Group of the Air Transport Command, which was moving from Seattle.

Gore Field was at that time known as the Municipal Airport of Great Falls. Although it had been selected as the home of the 7th, actual construction of barracks and other accommodations had not been started. The Great Falls Civic Center was therefore selected as a temporary home, with headquarters, barracks, mess-hall and other facilities combined under the roof of the huge municipal structure. The Ice Arena was also used as a combination barracks and mess-hall, and temporary headquarters were established in the office of Mayor Ed Shields and the offices of other city officials.

For nearly four months, the Civic Center remained the home of the 7th Ferrying Group, while contractors rushed construction of the barracks, hangars and other buildings which were to make up the post on Gore Field. The group completed its move up to Gore Hill early in November 1942. The 7th Group continued to supervise all stations and operations along the Northwest Route until November 17, 1942, when the Alaskan Wing of the Air Transport Command was established to take over the operations of the route to the north through Canada to Fairbanks, where hundreds of Russian pilots were waiting to take over.

Major Alexander Cohn arrived from Spokane to establish the 34th Sub-Depot for the Air Service Command. It was this depot that supervised the mountains of air freight that originated from all over the United States and poured into the funnel of this end of the Pipeline.

Colonel Gardner arranged for my transfer from Newark to Great Falls. My orders designated me as "United Nations Representative". Few people realize that although the United Nations organization was not set up in San Francisco until September 1945, the name "United Nations" was being used in the Lend-Lease organization as early as 1942, as in my original orders to Newark.

For the record, I want to quote my orders to Great Falls, with one phrase italicized. One reason for this is that in 1949 the New York Times printed the following statement of a "spokesman" for the United Nations: "Jordan never worked for the United Nations." I thereupon took the original copy of my orders in person to the Times, explained that this was an Army designation as early as 1942, and asked them in fairness to run a correction (which they did not do), since I never claimed to have "worked for the United Nations" and their story left the impression that I was lying. Here are my orders, with the original Army abbreviations.

Army Air Forces Headquarters, 34th Sub Depot Air Service Command Office of the Commanding Officer

Capt GEORGE R. JORDAN, 0-468248, AC, having reported for duty this sta per Par 1, SO No. 50, AAF, ASC, Hq New York Air Serv Port Area Comd, Newark Airport, N.J., dated 2 January 43, is hereby asgd United Nations Representative, 34th Sub Depot, Great Falls, Montana, effective this date.

By order of

Lt. Colonel MEREDITH.

These official orders activating my post were preceded on January 1st by a Presidential directive [see text box below]. This directive was addressed to the Commanding Generals of the Air Transport, Material, and Air Service Commands, through Colonel H. Ray Paige, Chief, International Section, Air Staff, who worked directly under General Arnold. This directive gave first priority for the planes passing through our station, even over the planes of the United States Air Force! It was extremely important in all my work. I quote from the crucial first paragraph:

DEAD MEN TALKING

"...To implement these directives, the modification, equipment and movement of Russian planes have been given first priority, even over planes for U.S. Army Air Forces..."

...The Russian staff had moved from Newark to Great Falls, with Colonel Kotikov still at their head. By this time I was on a very friendly personal basis with the Colonel. As human beings, we got on very well together. From the viewpoint of the usual Russian behavior toward Americans, it could even be said that we were on intimate terms...

HEADQUARTERS ARMY AIR FORCES WASHINGTON

January 1, 1943.

MEMORANDUM FOR THE COMMANDING GENERAL, AIR SERVICE COMMAND:

Subject: Movement of Russian Airplanes.

1. The President has directed that "airplanes be delivered in accordance with protocol schedules by the most expeditious means." To implement these directives, the modification, equipment and movement of Russian planes have been given first priority, even over planes for U.S. Army Air Forces...

By Command of Lieutenant General ARNOLD,

Richard H. Ballard Colonel, G.S.C. Assistant Chief of Air Staff, A-4

THE BLACK SUITCASES

After my return to Great Falls I began to realize an important fact: while we were a pipeline to Russia, Russia was also a pipeline to us.

One really disturbing fact which brought this home to me was that the entry of Soviet personnel into the United States was completely uncontrolled. Planes were arriving regularly from Moscow with unidentified Russians aboard. I would see them jump off planes, hop over fences, and run for taxicabs. They seemed to know in advance exactly where they were headed, and how to get there. It was an ideal set-up for planting spies in this country, with false identities, for use during and after the war.

It is hard to believe, but in 1943 there was no censorship set-up at Great Falls. An inspector more than 70 years old, named Randolph K. Hardy, did double work for the Treasury Department in customs and immigration. His office, in the city, was four miles from the airfield. He played the organ in a local church, and I was often told he was practicing and could not be interrupted. I took it upon myself to provide him with telephone, typewriter, desk, file cabinet, stenographer, interpreter and staff car.

DEAD MEN TALKING

Finally I was driven to put up a large sign over my own office door, with the legend in Russian and English: "Customs Office - Report Here". When Mr Hardy was not present, I got into the habit of demanding passports myself and jotting down names and particulars. It was not my job, but the list in my diary of Russians operating in this country began to swell by leaps and bounds. In the end I had the 418 names mentioned earlier.

Despite my private worries, my relations with Colonel Kotikov were excellent. I was doing all that I could do to expedite Russian shipments; my directives were clear, and I was following them out to the best of my ability.

Colonel Kotikov was well aware that a Major could do more expediting than a Captain. I was not too surprised, therefore, to learn that Kotikov had painstakingly dictated in English the following letter to Colonel Gitzinger:

Dear Colonel Gitzinger:

Capt. Jordan work any day here is always with the same people, Sub-Depot Engineering Officer, Major Boaz; 7th Ferrying Group Base Engineering Officer, Major Lawrence; Alaskan Wing Control and Engineering Officer, Major Taylor; Sub-Depot Executive Officer, Major O'Neill; and Base Supply Officer, Major Ramsey.

He is much hindered in his good work by under rank with these officers who he asks for things all time. I ask you to recommend him for equal rank to help Russian movement here.

A. N. KOTIKOV,

Col., U.S.S.R. Representative

When my permission finally came through, the gold oak leaves were pinned on my shoulders by Colonel Kotikov. This occasion was photographed and the picture is reproduced elsewhere in this book.

Now two other occurrences began troubling me. The first was the unusual number of black patent-leather suitcases, bound with white window-sash cord and sealed with red wax, which were coming through on the route to Moscow. The second was the burglary of morphine ampules from half of the 500 first-aid kits in our Gore Field warehouse.

The first black suitcases, six in number, were in the charge of a Russian officer and I passed them without question upon his declaration that they were "personal luggage". But the units mounted to ten, twenty and thirty and at last to standard batches of fifty, which weighed almost two tons and consumed the cargo allotment of an entire plane. The officers were replaced by armed couriers, traveling in pairs, and the excuse for avoiding inspection was changed from "personal luggage" to "diplomatic immunity".

Here were tons of materials proceeding to the Soviet Union, and I had no idea what they were. If interrogated, I should have to plead ignorance.

I began pursuing Colonel Kotikov with queries and protests. He answered with one eternal refrain. The suitcases were of the "highest diplomatic character". I retorted that they were not being sent by the Soviet Embassy but by the Soviet Government Purchasing Commission in Washington. He asserted that, whatever the origin, they were covered by diplomatic immunity. But I am sure he knew that one of these days I would try to search the containers.

They had grown to such importance in the eyes of the Russians that they asked for a locked room. The only door in the warehouse with a lock was that to the compartment in which the first-aid packets were kept. I put it at Colonel Kotikov's disposal. The couriers took turn about. First one and then the other slept on top of the suitcases, while his companion stood guard. Perhaps unjustly, I suspected them of stealing our morphine. They were the only persons left in the storeroom without witnesses.

At four o'clock one cold afternoon in March 1943, Colonel Kotikov said to me: "I want you dinner tonight." Then he doubled the surprise by whisking from his ulster pockets two slender bottles with long, sloping necks. "Vodka!"

The invitation was accepted with pleasure and also curiosity. For almost a year now I had associated with Colonel Kotikov and his staff, but I had never dined with them. As a matter of routine they lunched with us at the Officers' Club. But at night they disappeared, wandering off by themselves to other restaurants or the dining-room of the Rainbow Hotel, where they were quartered. So far as I knew, this was the first time they had bidden an American to an evening repast...

At the Officers' Club we had noticed that the Russians were extremely absent-minded about picking up bar checks. These oversights were costing us around $80 monthly, and we decided to remedy the situation. In the club were several slot-machines, for which the Russians had a passion. We decided to "set aside" one machine to cover their libations. Thanks to the one-armed mechanical bandit, we contrived after all to make them settle for their liquor.

Now, of a sudden, they asked me to dinner and were offering vodka, free, as an allurement. I could not help wondering why. Acting on a hunch, I excused myself from riding to town with Colonel Koticov in his Pontiac. I decided I would take my staff car, which had a soldier driver; in case of need, I preferred to have

DEAD MEN TALKING

mobility. I was directed to join the party at seven o'clock at a restaurant in Great Falls known as "Carolina Pines".

There was not much time, so I hastened to ask our maintenance chief whether the Russians were planning any flights. He answered yes; they had a C-47 staged on the line, preparing to go. It was being warmed up with Nelson heaters - large canvas bags, fed with hot air, which were made to slip over motors and propellers. (Winter temperatures at the airfield could be as severe as at Fairbanks, ranging from 20 to 70 degrees below zero. Oil would sometimes freeze as hard as stone, and two to four hours were required to thaw out an engine.)

The Russians wielded a high hand at the airbase, but I had one power they respected. Though Lend-Lease planes were delivered to them at Great Falls, they were flown by American pilots as far as Fairbanks. No American pilot could leave without clearance, and I had authority to ground any plane at any time. In my absence, permission was given by the Flight Officer of the Day. I called the control tower, gave the number of the restaurant, and issue a positive order that no cargo plane was to be cleared for Russia except by myself.

Occupied by these thoughts, I drove to "Carolina Pines"... The gathering consisted of five Russians and a single American, myself. Colonel Kotikov acted as host, and among the guests was Colonel G. E. Tsvetkov, head of the fighter-pursuit division of the Soviet Purchasing Commission...

With the vodka under our belts, we moved to chairs about the table. But at 8.30, when we were two-thirds finished, the waitress handed me a message in pencil. It notified me to call the control tower at once.

At a public telephone, in the corridor, I learned that the C-47 had warmed up and that a couple of newly-arrived couriers were demanding clearance. Without returning to the dining room, I threw on my great-coat, scuffled down the stairs and ordered the driver to race full speed for the hangars, four miles away.

It was mid-winter in Great Falls. Snow was deep on the ground, and stars glittered frostily in a crystal sky. The temperature that night was about 20 degrees below zero.

As we neared the Lend-Lease plane there loomed up, in its open door, the figure of a burly, barrel-chested Russian. His back was propped against one jamb of the portal. An arm and a leg were stretched across to the opposite side. I clambered up and he tried to stop me by pushing hard with his stomach. I pushed back, ducked under his arm, and stood inside the cabin.

It was dimly lighted by a solitary electric bulb in the dome. Faintly visible was an expanse of black suitcases, with white ropes and seals of crimson wax. On

DEAD MEN TALKING

top of them, reclining on one elbow, was a second Russian, slimmer than the first, who sprang to his feet as I entered. They were mature men, in the forties, and wore beneath leather jackets the inevitable blue suits of Russian civilians. Under each coat, from a shoulder holster, protruded the butt of a pistol.

It had been no more than a guess that a fresh installment of suitcases might be due. My first thought was: "Another bunch of those damn things!" The second was that if I was ever going to open them up, now was as good a time as any. With signs I made the Russians understand what I intended to do.

Promptly they went insane. They danced. They pushed at me with their hands and shrieked over and over the one English word they appeared to know. It was "deeplomateek!" I brushed them aside and took from my pocket a metal handle containing a safety razor blade which I carry in preference to a pocket knife.

Sensing its purpose, the lean courier flung himself face down across the suitcases, with arms and legs outspanned to shield as many as possible with his body. I dragged one of the containers from under him, and he leaped up again as I started to saw through the first cord. At this sight their antics and shouts redoubled.

While opening the third suitcase, I had a mental flash that brought sweat to my forehead. The Russians were half mad with fury and terror. They were on both sides of me, in front and behind. Supposing in desperation, one of them shot me in the back? There would be no American witnesses, and my death could be passed off as a "deplorable accident".

I called a Yank soldier who was on patrol thirty feet away. He crunched over through the snow. Bending down from the plane, I asked whether he had had combat experience. He answered that he had, in the South Pacific. I stooped lower and murmured:

"I'm going to open more of this baggage. I want you to watch these two Russians. Both are armed. I don't expect any trouble. But if one of them aims a gun at me, I want you to let him have it first. Understand?"

After a moment's thought, he looked me in the eye and said, "Sir, is that an order?" I replied that it was an order. He clicked the bolt of his rifle to snap a cartridge into the chamber and brought the weapon to ready. He was tall enough for his head to clear the doorsill. The muzzle was pushed forward to command the interior.

One courier jumped from the plane and sprinted for the hangars, where there were telephones. The other, his face contorted as if to keep from crying, began reknotting the cords I had severed. There was little trouble getting into the suitcases because the Russians had brought the cheapest on the market. They had no locks, but only pairs of clasps. All were consigned to the same address. The entry on the bill of lading read: "Director, Institute of Technical and Economic Information, 47 Chkalovskaya, Moscow 120, U.S.S.R."

I decided to attempt only a spot check - one suitcase, say, in every three. I examined perhaps eighteen out of fifty. Otherwise the search was fairly thorough, as I was looking for morphine. (Incidentally, none was found.) The light was so weak that it was impossible to decipher text without using a flash lamp. I had to take off my gloves, and my fingers grew numb with cold.

Using one knee as a desk, I jotted notes with a pencil on two long envelopes that happened to be in my pocket...

The first thing I unearthed made me snort with disgust. It was a ponderous tome on the art of shipping four-legged animals. Was this the kind of twaddle American pilots were risking their lives to carry? But in the back I found a series of tables listing railroad mileages from almost any point in the United States to any other.

Neatly packed with the volume were scores of roadmaps, of the sort available at filling stations to all comers. But I made a note that they were "marked strangely". Taken together, they furnished a country-wide chart, with names and places, of American industrial plants. For example, Pittsburgh entries included "Westinghouse" and "Blaw-Knox".

The next suitcase to be opened was crammed with material assembled in America by the official Soviet news organ, the Tass Telegraph Agency. A third was devoted to Russia's government-owned Amtorg Trading Corporation of New York. One yielded a collection of maps of the Panama Canal Commission, with the markings to show strategic spots in the Canal Zone and distances to islands and ports within a 1,000-mile radius.

Another was filled with documents relating to the Aberdeen Proving Ground, one of the most "sensitive" areas in the war effort. Judging by their contents, various suitcases could have been labeled under the heads of machine tools, oil refineries, blast furnaces, steel foundries, mining, coal, concrete, and the like. Other folders were stuffed with naval and shipping intelligence. There seemed to be hundreds of commercial catalogues and scientific magazines... There were also sheafs of info about Mexico, Argentina and Cuba.

There were groups of documents which, on the evidence of stationery, had been contributed by the Departments of Agriculture, Commerce and State. All such papers had been trimmed close to the text, with white margins removed. I decided that this was done either to save weight, or to remove "Secret", "Confidential" or "Restricted" stamps that might have halted a shipment, or for both

DEAD MEN TALKING

reasons...

Then I copied the legend: "From Hiss". I had never heard of Alger Hiss, and made the entry because the folder bearing his name happened to be second in the pile. It contained hundreds of photostats of what seemed to be military reports...

A suitcase opened midway in the search appeared to contain nothing but engineering and scientific treatises. They bristled with formulae, calculations and professional jargon. I was about to close the case and pass on when my eye was caught by a specimen of stationery such as I had never before seen.

Its letterhead was a magic incantation: "The White House, Washington". As prospective owner of an 80-acre tract along the shore of Washington State, I was impressed by the lordly omission of the capitals, "D.C.". Under the flashlight I studied this paper with attention. It was a brief note, of two sheets, in a script which was not level but sloped upward to the right. The name to which it was addressed, "Mikoyan", was wholly new to me. (By questioning Colonel Kotikov later, I learned that A. I. Mikoyan at the moment was Russia's No. 3 man, after Premier Stalin and Foreign Commissar Molotov. He was Commissar of Foreign Trade and Soviet boss of Lend-Lease.)

A salutation, "My dear Mr Minister", led to a few sentences of stock courtesies. One passage, of eleven words, in the top line of the second page, impressed me enough to merit a scribble on my envelope. That excerpt ran thus: "____ had a hell of a time getting these away from Groves."

The last two words should not be taken as referring to Major General Leslie R. Groves himself. What they meant, probably, was "from the Groves organization". The commander of the Manhattan Engineer District, later the Manhattan Project, was almost unique in the Washington hierarchy for his dislike and suspicion of Russia...

The first thing I had done, on finding the White House note, was to flip over the page to look for a signature. I penciled it on my envelope as "H. H." This may not have been an exact transcription. In any case, my intention is clear. It was to chronicle, on the spot, my identification of the author as Harry Hopkins. It was general usage at Great Falls and elsewhere to refer to him as "Harry Hopkins", without the middle initial.

I remember distinctly having had to remove that letter from a metal clip. It held two other exhibits - obviously the things which [someone] had such difficulty in "getting away from Groves". One was a thick map. When unfolded, it proved to be as wide as the span of my extended arms. In large letters it bore a legend which I recorded: "Oak Ridge, Manhattan Engineering District".

DEAD MEN TALKING

The other was a carbon copy of a report, two or three pages long, which was dated Oak Ridge. If it had a signature, I did not set it down. At the top of the first page, impressed with a rubber stamp, or typed, was the legend: "Harry Hopkins" followed by the title "Special Asst. Co-ordinator" or "Administrator". I gathered that this particular copy had been earmarked for Mr Hopkins. In the text of the report was encountered a series of vocables so outlandish that I made a memo to look up their meaning. Among them were "cyclotron", "proton" and "deuteron". There were curious phrases like "energy produced by fission" and "walls five feet thick, of lead and water, to control flying neutrons".

Probably no more than 200 men in all the country would have been capable at the time of noting down these particular expressions out of their own heads. The paper on which I made my notes was later submitted to the Bureau of Standards for a test of its age.

For the first time in my life, I met the word "uranium". The exact phrase was "Uranium 92". From a book of reference I learned afterward that uranium is the 92nd element in atomic weight.

At the time of this episode I was as unaware as anyone could be of Oak Ridge, the Manhattan District and its chief, General Groves. The enterprise has been celebrated as "the best guarded secret in history". It was superlatively hush-hush, to the extreme that Army officers in the "know" were forbidden to mention it over their private telephones inside the Pentagon. General Groves has testified that his office would have refused to send any documents to the White House, without authority from himself, even if it was requested personally by the President.

From the outset, extraordinary secrecy and security measures have surrounded the project," declared Henry L. Stimson, Secretary of War, in commenting on the first military use of the atom bomb. "This was personally ordered by President Roosevelt." Mr Roosevelt's orders, he innocently added, "have been strictly complied with."1

Yet Russians with whom I worked side by side at Great Falls knew about the A-bomb at least as early as March 1943, and General Groves had reason to distrust the Russians in October 1942! In common with almost all Americans, I got the first hint of the existence of the atom bomb from the news of Hiroshima, which was revealed on August 6, 1945 by President Truman.

I visited Washington in January 1944 to bring to the attention of the highest authorities what seemed to me to be treacherous violations of security in the Pipeline. I got exactly nowhere in the State Department or elsewhere. It was not until I heard the announcement of the atomic blast in Russia on September 23, 1949, that

DEAD MEN TALKING

I finally had the good fortune of meeting Senator Bridges and Fulton Lewis - but more of that later.

It was after eleven o'clock, and my checking job was virtually done, when Colonel Kotikov burst into the cabin of the plane. He wanted to know by whose authority I was committing this outrage [see previous issue] and bellowed that he would have me removed. I answered that I was performing my duty, and, just to show how things stood, opened two or three extra suitcases in his presence. I left the C-47 and with a nod of thanks dismissed my sentinel.

As I crossed the field toward the barracks, Colonel Kotikov fell in beside me. No doubt he reflected that he was in no position to force an issue. He may also have realized that I understood the gravity of almost nothing I had seen. All that mattered to him was getting the suitcases off to Moscow. Anxiously he inquired what I intended to do.

If I had known what I do today, I should have grounded the transport, but in the end it went on its way to Russia.

Colonel Kotikov asked me to open no more suitcases until instructions came from the War Department. He said he hoped he would not have to get me transferred. I expected to be fired, and went so far as to pack my gear. But I received no communication from the War Department, and gathered at last that Colonel Kotikov had made no complaint. Perhaps, I began to think, he did not dare.

I reported to Colonel George F. O'Neill, security officer of the 34th Sub-Depot at Gore Field, about the fifty suitcases I had examined. He was interested enough to pass the story on to his superior officer in Spokane. There was no reply, even after Colonel O'Neill made a second attempt. Apparently it was not considered good form to cast reflections on the integrity of our ally...

"DON'T MAKE A BIG PRODUCTION..."

One morning in April 1943, Colonel Kotikov asked whether I could find space for an important consignment of nearly 2,000 pounds. I said, "No, we have a quarter of a million pounds' backlog already."

He directed me to put through a call to Washington for him, and spoke for a while in his own tongue. Then he put a hand over the mouthpiece and confided to me in English, "Very special shipment - experimental chemicals - going through soon."

There was an interval of Slavic gutturals, and he turned to me again. "Mr Hopkins - coming on now," he reported. Then he gave me the surprise of my life. He handed me the phone and announced, "Big boss, Mr Hopkins, wants you."

DEAD MEN TALKING

It was quite a moment. I was about to speak for the first time with a legendary figure of the day, the top man in the world of Lend-Lease in which I lived. I have been careful to keep the following account as accurate in substance and language as I can. My memory, normally good, was stimulated by the thrill of the occasion. Moreover, the incident was stamped on my mind because it was unique in my experience of almost 25 months at Newark and Great Falls.

A bit in awe, I stammered, "Jordan speaking."

The male voice began at once. "This is Mr Hopkins. Are you my expediter out there?"

I answered that I was the United Nations Representative at Great Falls, working with Colonel Kotikov.

Under the circumstances, who could have doubted that the speaker was Harry Hopkins? Friends have since asked me whether it might not have been a Soviet agent who was an American. I doubt this, because his next remark brought up a subject which only Mr Hopkins and myself could have known.

He asked, "Did you get those pilots I sent you?"

"Oh yes, sir," I responded. "They were very much appreciated, and helped us in unblocking the jam in the Pipeline. We were accused of going out of channels, and got the dickens for it."

Mr Hopkins let that one go by, and moved on to the heart of things. "Now, Jordan," he said, "there's a certain shipment of chemicals going through that I want you to expedite. This is something very special."

"Shall I take it up," I asked, "with the Commanding Colonel?"

"I don't want you to discuss this with anyone," Mr Hopkins ordered, "and it is not to go on the records. Don't make a big production of it, but just send it through quietly, in a hurry."

I asked how I was to identify the shipment when it arrived. He turned from the phone, and I could hear his voice: "How will Jordan know the shipment when it gets there?" He came back on the line and said, "The Russian Colonel out there will designate it for you. Now send this through as speedily as possible, and be sure you leave it off the records!"

Then a Russian voice broke in with a demand for Colonel Kotikov. I was full of curiosity when Kotikov had finished, and I wanted to know what it was all about and where the shipment was coming from. He said there would be more chemicals and that they would arrive from Canada.

"I show you," he announced.

DEAD MEN TALKING

Presumably, after the talk with Mr Hopkins, I had been accepted as a member of the 'lodge'. From his bundle on war chemicals the Colonel took the folder called "Bomb Powder". He drew out a paper sheet and set a finger against one entry. For a second time my eyes encountered the word "Uranium". I repeat that in 1943 it meant as little to me as to most Americans, which was nothing.

This shipment was the one and only cash item to pass through my hands, except for private Russian purchases of clothing and liquor. It was the only one, out of a tremendous multitude of consignments, that I was ordered not to enter on my tally sheets. It was the only one I was forbidden to discuss with my superiors, and the only one I was directed to keep secret from everybody.

Despite Mr Hopkins' urgency, there was a delay of five weeks. On the morning of June 10th, I caught sight of a loaded C-47 which was idling on the runway. I went over and asked the pilot what was holding him up. He said he understood some kind of special shipment was still to come. Seven years afterward, the pilot identified himself to the press as Air Forces Lieutenant Ben L. Brown, of Cincinnati.

I asked Colonel Kotikov about the plane, and he told me the shipment Mr Hopkins was interested in had just arrived at the railroad yards, and that I should send a truck to pick it up. The consignment was escorted by a Russian guard from Toronto. I set down his name, and copied it later in my diary. It was Vladimir Anoufriev. I identified him with the initials "C.C." for "Canadian Courier".

Fifteen wooden cases were put aboard the transport, which took off for Moscow by way of Alaska. At Fairbanks, Lieutenant Brown has related, one box fell from the plane, smashing a corner and spilling a small quantity of chocolate-brown powder. Out of curiosity, he picked up a handful of the unfamiliar grains, with a notion of asking somebody what they were. A Soviet officer slapped the crystals from his palm and explained nervously, "No, no - burn hands!"

Not until the latter part of 1949 was it definitely proved, from responsible records, that during the war Federal agencies delivered to Russia at least three consignments of uranium chemicals, totaling 1,465 pounds, or nearly three-quarters of a ton. Confirmed also was the shipment of one kilogram, or 2.2 pounds, of uranium metal at a time when the total American stock was 4.5 pounds.

Implicated by name were the Lend-Lease Administration, the Department of Commerce, the Procurement Division of the Treasury and the Board of Economic Warfare. The State Department became involved to the extent of refusing access to files of Lend-Lease and its successor, the Foreign Economic Administration.

The first two uranium shipments traveled through Great Falls by air. The third was dispatched by truck and railway from Rochester, NY, to Portland, Oregon, and then by ship to Vladivostok. The dates were March and June 1943, and July 1944. No doubt was left that the transaction discussed by Mr Hopkins and myself was the one of June 1943.

This was not merely the largest of our known uranium deals with the Soviet Union, it was also the most shocking. There seemed to be no lengths to which some American officials would not go in aiding Russia to master the secret of nuclear fission. For four years, monopoly of the A-bomb was the cornerstone of our military and overseas policy, yet on September 23, 1949, long in advance of Washington estimates, President Truman announced that an atomic explosion had occurred in the Soviet Union.

In behalf of national security, the Manhattan Project during the spring of 1943 clapped an embargo on American exports of uranium compounds. But zealots in Washington appear to have resolved that Russia must have at all costs the ingredients for atomic experiment. The intensely pro-Soviet mood of that time may be judged from echoes in later years.

For example, there was Joseph E. Davies, Ambassador to the Soviet Union in 1936-39, and author of a book and movie of flagrant propaganda, Mission to Moscow. In an interview with the Times-Herald of Washington for February 18, 1946, he was quoted as saying, "Russia, in self-defense, has every moral right to seek atomic bomb secrets through military espionage if excluded from such information by her former fighting allies!" There also was Professor Harold C. Urey, American scientist, who sat in the innermost circle of the Manhattan Project. Yet on December 14, 1949, in a report of the Atlantic Union Committee, Dr Urey said that Major Jordan should be court-martialed if he had removed anything from planes bound for Russia.

When American supplies were cut off, the device of out-maneuvering General Groves was to procure the materials clandestinely from Canada. Not until 1946 did the commander of the Manhattan Project learn from the Un-American Activities Committee that his stockade had been undermined.

My share in the revelation was testimony under oath, leading to one conclusion only: that the Canadian bypass was aided by Mr Hopkins. At his direction, Lend-Lease issued a certificate of release without which the consignment could not have moved. Lend-Lease channels of transportation and Lend-Lease personnel, such as myself, were used. Traces of the scheme were kept off Lend-Lease books by making it a 'cash' transaction. The shipment was paid for with a check of the Amtorg Trading Corporation.

Because of the initial branch of the airlift to Moscow was under American control, passage of the chemicals across United States territory could not be avoided, in Alaska if not Montana. On account of that fact - the cash nature of the project - it was necessary to obtain an export license from the Board of Economic Warfare. Such a document, covering a shipment of American origin, was first prepared. It was altered, to comply with the Canadian maneuver, by some BEW official whose identity has been concealed by the State Department. As amended, the license was issued on April 29, 1943. Its serial number was C-1643180.

But two facts were forgotten: (a) public carriers use invoices, and (b) the Air Forces kept tallies not only at Great Falls but Fairbanks.

By diligent searching, freight and airway bills yielded incontestable proof that 15 boxes of uranium chemicals were delivered at Great Falls on June 9, 1943, and were dispatched immediately, in a Lend-Lease plane, to the Soviet Union.

The shipment originated at Eldorado Mining & Refining, Ltd, of Great Bear Lake, and was sent through Port Hope, Ontario. It was authorized by a Canadian arms export permit, No. OF1666. The carrier was the Chicago, Milwaukee, St Paul & Pacific Railway. Listed as consignee was Colonel A. N. Kotikov, resident agent of the Soviet Government Purchasing Commission at Gore Field, Great Falls.

The story behind the story is as follows. On February 1, 1943, Hermann H. Rosenberg of Chematar, Inc., New York City, received the first inquiry about uranium ever to reach his office. The applicant was the Soviet Purchasing Commission, which desired 220 pounds of uranium oxide, 220 pounds of uranium nitrate, and 25 pounds of uranium metal.

At that date Oak Ridge was under construction, but would not be in operation for another year.

Six days earlier the War Production Board had issued General Reference Order M-285, controlling the distribution of uranium compounds among domestic industries like glass, pottery and ceramics. A loophole was left by overlooking the export of such materials for war purposes. The Russians claimed that they had urgent military need for uranium nitrate in medicinal research, and for uranium oxide and metal as alloys in hardening gun-barrel steel. There was nothing for the US to do but grant an OK, since we did not want to imply that we were suspicious of Russia's request.

Uranium metal was unavailable. On March 23, at Rosenberg's instance, the S. W. Shattuck Chemical Co. of Denver shipped four crates, weighing 691 pounds, to Colonel Kotikov at Great Falls. The Burlington Railroad's bill of lading described the contents merely as "Chemicals", but it was accompanied by a letter from Rosenberg to Kotikov designating the contents as 220 pounds of uranium nitrate and 200 (not 220) pounds of uranium oxide. Since it was a Lend-Lease transaction, defrayed with American funds, no export license was required. The cargo was dispatched without friction along the Pipeline.

But the War Production Board, from which clearance had been sought, alerted the Manhattan Project. It was too late to halt the Shattuck sale. General Groves reluctantly approved it on the ground that it would be unwise to 'tip off' Russia as to the importance of uranium chemicals - a fact with which Moscow was only too familiar.

During the investigation, I was embarrassed by questions as to why tables of exports to the Soviet Union contained no mention of uranium. The Shattuck consignment was legitimate. It had been authorized by Lend-Lease, the War Production Board and the Manhattan Project.

Some months later I ran into John F. Moynihan, formerly of the Newark News editorial staff. A Second Lieutenant at the Newark Airport when I was there, he had risen to Colonel as a sort of 'reverse press-agent' for General Groves. His duty was not to foster publicity but prevent it.

"I heard you floundering about," he said, "and wished I could tell you something you didn't know. I was sent to Denver to hush up the records in the Shattuck matter. It was hidden under the phrase, 'salts and compounds', in an entry covering a different metal."

General Groves moved rapidly to stop the leak through which the Shattuck boxes had slipped. By early April he had formed a nationwide embargo by means of voluntary contracts with chemical brokers. They promised to grant the United States first right to purchase all uranium oxide, uranium nitrate and sodium uranate received by the contractors.

The uranium black-out was discovered by Rosenberg when he tried to fill another order from the Soviet Purchasing Commission, for 500 pounds each of uranium nitrate and uranium oxide. On April 23, 1943, Rosenberg was in touch with the Canadian Radium & Uranium Corp. of New York, which was exclusive sales agent for Eldorado Mining & Refining, Ltd, a producer of uranium at Great Bear Lake.

An agreement to fill the Soviet order was negotiated with such dispatch that in four days Rosenberg was able to report victory to the Purchasing Commission. The shipment from Ontario to Great Falls and Moscow followed in due course.

The Port Hope machination had the advantage, among other things, of by-passing the War Production Board, which was sure to warn the Manhattan Project if it knew the facts, but could be kept in ignorance because its jurisdiction ran only south of the border.

DEAD MEN TALKING

General Groves was advised at once of the Soviet application for 1,000 pounds of uranium salts. He was not disturbed, being confident the embargo would stand. After declining to endorse the application, he approved it later in the hope of detecting whether the Russians could unearth uranium stocks which the Manhattan Project had overlooked. American industries were consuming annually, before the war, upwards of 200 tons of uranium chemicals.

"We had no expectation," General Groves testified December 7, 1949, "of permitting that material to go out of this country. It would have been stopped."[2]

So far as the United States was concerned, the embargo held fast. The truth that it had been side-stepped by means of resort to Canadian sources did not come to the General's knowledge until three years later.

Another violation of atomic security was represented by the third known delivery to Russia, in 1944. It proved to be uranium nitrate. During May of that year, Colonel Kotikov showed me a warning from the Soviet Purchasing Commission to look out for a shipment of uranium, weighing 500 pounds, which was to have travel priority. The Colonel was soon returning home. As the climax of his American mission, he proposed to fly the precious stuff to Moscow with his own hands.

Disguised as a "commercial transaction" within American territory, the deal was managed by Lend-Lease. Chematar and Canadian Radium & Uranium were abandoned in favor of the Procurement Division of the Treasury Department, although the Treasury, under regulations, had no authority to make uranium products available to the Soviet Union.

Contractors were asked to bid, and the winner was the Eastman Kodak Company. Somewhere in this process, the expected 500 pounds shrank to 45. Eastman Kodak reported the order to the War Production Board as a domestic commercial item.

Whatever the motive, it was determined not to send the compound by air. After a Treasury inspection in Rochester, the MacDaniel Trucking Company drove it to the Army Ordnance Depot at Terre Haute, Indiana, arriving July 24. The shipment turned up in freight car No. 97352 of the Erie Railroad, and got to North Portland, Oregon, on August 11. By means of shifts not yet divulged, the uranium nitrate found itself aboard a Russian steamship, Kashirstroi, which left for Vladivostok on October 3. Colonel Kotikov, who had planned a triumphal entry into Moscow with a quarter-ton of "bomb powder" as a trophy, gave up the project in disgust on learning that the shipment would be only 45 pounds.

In charge of uranium purchases for the Manhattan Project in 1944 was Dr Phillip L. Merritt. Appearing January 24, 1950 before the Un-American Activities

Committee, Dr Merritt swore he was taken by surprise, a day earlier, on discovering for the first time that the Eastman Kodak order had been shipped to Russia by way of Army Ordnance.

General Groves was likewise uninformed. Asked as a witness whether it was possible for uranium shipments to have been made in 1944, he answered, "Not if we could have helped it, and not with our knowledge of any kind. They would have had to be entirely secret, and not discovered."3 He declared there was no way for the Russians to get uranium products in this country "without the support of US authorities in one way or another".4

The Soviet Purchasing Commission appears to have had instructions to acquire without fail 25 pounds of uranium metal, which can be extracted from uranium salts by a difficult process requiring specialized equipment. Supported or advised by Lend-Lease, the commission for a whole year knocked at every available door, from the Chemical Warfare Service up to Secretary Stimson. As a matter of fact, uranium metal was then non-existent in America, and for that reason had not been specified in the Manhattan Project's embargo or named as a "strategic" material.

Stimson closed a series of polite rebuffs with a letter of April 17, 1944, to the chairman of the Purchasing Commission, Lt General Leonid G. Rudenko. But Moscow was stubborn. Under Soviet pressure, the commission, or its American friends, had an inspiration. Why not have the uranium made to order by some private concern?

As usual, a roundabout course was taken. The commission first approached the Manufacturers Chemical Co., 527 Fifth Avenue, New York, which passed the order along to A. D. Mackay, Inc., 198 Broadway. By the latter it was farmed out to the Cooper Metallurgical Laboratory in Cleveland. According to Mr Mackay, neither he nor the Cooper concern suspected that their customer was the Soviet Union.

But Mackay reported the deal to the War Production Board, which warned the Manhattan Project. The latter's expert on rare metals, Lawrence C. Burman, went to Cleveland, it is related, and urged the Cooper firm to make sure that its product was of "poor quality". He did not explain why. But the metal, of which 4.5 pounds was made, turned out to be 87.5 per cent pure as against the stipulated 99 per cent.

Delivery to the Soviet Union was then authorized of a small sample of this defective metal, to represent "what was available in the United States". Actually shipped was one kilogram, or 2.2 pounds. The Purchasing Commission abruptly silenced its demands for pure uranium. But the powers that be found it suitable to omit this item, as well as the Rochester sale, from the 1944 schedule of exports to

DEAD MEN TALKING

Russia.

From the start, in contrast to the atmosphere prevailing in Washington, the Manhattan Project was declared by General Groves to have been "the only spot I know that was distinctly anti-Russian".5 Attempts at espionage in New York, Chicago and Berkeley, California, were traced to the Soviet Embassy. They convinced General Groves in October 1942 that the enemies of our atomic safeguards were not Germans or Japanese, but Russians. "Suspicion of Russia was not very popular in some circles [in Washington]," he stated. "It was popular in Oak Ridge, and from one month of the time I took over we never trusted them one iota. From that time on, our whole security was based on not letting the Russians find out anything."6

That the Russians found out everything from alpha to omega has been established by volumes of proof. Through trials in Canada, England and the United States there has been revealed the existence of an espionage network so enormously effective that Russia, scientists calculated, "should have been able to make a bomb considerably before September 1949". The network chief was the former Soviet Vice Consul in New York, Anatoli A. Yakovlev, who fled in 1946.

THE STORY OF THE "HEAVY WATER"

What is popularly known as "heavy water" is technically called deuterium oxide. It is in crystal form, not liquid.

In alleging medical and other grounds for its needs of uranium oxide and uranium nitrate, Russia had taken care to observe an appearance of truth, for such use is not unknown to therapeutics. It had been tried out in throat sprays and lent its name to Uranwein, a German specific against diabetes. Uranium oxide had been tested as an alloy for toughening steel, but it was found difficult to handle and had erratic results. Therefore when Moscow asked for heavy water, they let the cat out of the bag. Except for curious experiments in retarding plant growth, heavy water boasts only one useful property: it is the best of moderators for slowing down the speed of neutrons in nuclear reactions.

Records in evidence7 prove that on August 23, 1943, Hermann Rosenberg of Chematar received an application from the Soviet Purchasing Commission for 1,000 grams of deuterium oxide. The purpose stated was "research". A supplier was found in the Stuart Oxygen Co. of San Francisco, which shipped the merchandise on October 30 by railway express to Chematar's New York office. Rosenberg forwarded the consignment to the Purchasing Commission in Washington, which dispatched it on November 29, by way of the Pipeline, to Rasnoimport, USSR, Moscow U-1, Ruybjshova-22.

The order was packed with as much tenderness as if it had been a casket of jewels. Forty pyrex ampoules, each containing 25 grams, were enclosed in mailing tubes and wrapped in layers of cotton. The ampoules were divided in lots of 10 among four cartons, which were placed, with further precautions against damage, in a large wooden box. This was strapped and sealed. The overall weight was 41.12 pounds. The cost of the fluid content was that of expensive perfumes - $80 an ounce.

The export of heavy water to the Soviet Union was approved by a release certificate, No. 366, dated November 15, with the signature of William C. Moore, Division for Soviet Supply, Office of Lend-Lease Administration.

If General Groves had been consulted, the heavy water would not have left this country. Had it been known at the time, he said, that 1,000 grams were available, unquestionably he would have bought the treasure himself. He added, "If it had been pure."[8] That it was between 99.7 and 99.8 per cent pure was attested by an independent analysis made for Rosenberg in the laboratories of Abbot A. Hanks, Inc., San Francisco.

At the beginning of 1945, the Soviet Purchasing Commission placed with Rosenberg a second order for heavy water. Only 100 grams were sought. He applied once more to the Stuart concern, which expressed the 'liquid diamonds' to Chematar on February 7. One week later Rosenberg forwarded the parcel to the commission. Its subsequent adventures have not been traced. In August of the same year, Rosenberg was naturalized as an American citizen...

Was one kilogram of heavy water and were mere hundreds of pounds of uranium chemicals too insignificant for important use?

Specialists agree that the quantities delivered were inadequate for producing one A-bomb or even one experimental pile. They point out, however, that scarcely any fraction of a substance can be too small for laboratory research. The head of a pin could not have been formed with the first plutonium ever made. From 500 micrograms were determined most of the properties and the chemical behavior of an element which 18 months earlier had been entirely unknown.

On the presumption that 1,465 pounds of uranium salts were contributed to the Soviet Union, metallurgists estimate that they were reducible in theory to 875 pounds of natural uranium, which in turn would yield 6.25 pounds of fissionable U-235. But 4.4 pounds of the latter, or nearly two pounds less, are capable of producing an atomic explosion. Authority for this assertion may be found in the celebrated report which Dr Henry De-Wolf Smyth of Princeton University wrote at the request of General Groves and published in 1945.

The Shattuck and Eldorado purchases totaled 1,420 pounds. With their third requisition, the Russians expected so confidently to acquire another 500 pounds that papers to that effect were drafted and sent to us in Montana. If the full amount had been available, instead of 45 pounds, the aggregate would have been 1,920 pounds, or virtually one ton.

At his Paris laboratory, while chief of the Atomic Energy Commission of France, Frederic Joliot-Curie built an experimental pile to which he gave the affectionate name of "Zoe". It actually ran, though the wattage was feeble. The quantity of uranium crystals utilized, said Dr Joliot-Curie, was "something in the order of one ton".

It seems fair to take into account not merely what the Russians got, but what they tried to get. With Communist tenacity and ardent support from both White House and Lend-Lease, the Soviet Purchasing Commission strove again and again to obtain 8-1/2 tons each of uranium oxide and uranium nitrate, plus 25 pounds of uranium metal. The campaign started in February 1943, and persisted until the Russians were squelched by Secretary Stimson during April 1944.

There are memorable instances of what can be achieved with less than 17 tons of uranium powders. One was a model atomic pile which went into operation at Chicago University on December 2, 1942. "So far as we know," Dr Smyth recounts, "this was the first time that human beings ever initiated a self-maintaining nuclear chain reaction." With a power level of 200 watts, the device served as a pilot plant for the Hanford Engineer Works. The uranium supply available to them was six tons.

Even earlier, before the Manhattan Project was dreamed of, a group of scientists at Columbia University began a course of hazardous experiments under the leadership of two foreign-born savants, Leo Szilard of Hungary and Enrico Fermi of Italy. They were so ill-supported with cash that 10,000 pounds of uranium oxide had to be 'rented' at a nominal fee of 30 cents a pound from Boris Pregel, president of the Canadian Radium & Uranium Corp. of New York, who was later unjustly made a scapegoat by the press for the secret Canadian shipment.

Here was done all the preparatory work moving toward the eventual creation of the first man-made elements in history: neptunium-93 and plutonium-94. From the group's creative imagination rose in time the vast plutonium plant at Hanford, Washington, and, in a large sense, America's atom bomb itself. The materials of that triumph were not 17 but 10 tons of uranium compounds.

One of my lucky experiences was that of chancing upon the February 27, 1950 issue of the magazine, Life, shortly before my second appearance before the Un-American Activities Committee. I bore the copy with me to the witness chair. It contained an illustrated article on the atom bomb. I learned for the first time that a plutonium pile consists of giant blocks of graphite, surrounded by heavy walls of concrete and honeycombed with aluminum tubes. In these tubes, it was related, are inserted slugs of natural uranium, containing one per cent of U-235. The intensity of the operation was declared to be governed by means of cadmium rods.

Graphite, cadmium, aluminum tubes - where had I met these words before? In the Russian lists of Lend-Lease figures which I had added to the Jordan diary. Re-examining those pages, I discovered that during the four-year period 1942-45 we contributed to the Soviet Union 3,692 tons of natural graphite, 417 tons of cadmium metals, and tubes in an entry designating 6,883 tons of "aluminum tubes".

The figure for cadmium was arresting in view of its extreme scarcity in this country and because of the fact that it occurs, so far as we know, sparsely if at all in the Soviet Union. Under war stimulus, American production of cadmium rose from 2,182 short tons in 1940 to 4,192 in 1945.

It was interesting to find that in 1942-45 we shipped to Russia 437 tons of cobalt - a staggering amount when collated with American production, which was nothing before the war, and increased to 382 tons in 1942 and 575 in 1945.

That cobalt is valuable in the A-bomb for retarding radioactive emanations, and could be equally so in the hydrogen bomb, has been affirmed by a chemical engineer who was consultant to one of the war agencies. "Cobalt," says he, "was one of our highest scarcity materials. If I had known that so large a proportion was going to the Russians, I should have suspected them of being at work on the bomb." Incidentally, cobalt was the first item to be restricted by President Truman in the Korean emergency.

Almost as curious was the discovery that we shipped to Russia more than 12 tons of thorium salts and compounds. Two other elements alone, besides uranium and plutonium, are fissionable. They are protoactinium and thorium. The former may be disregarded because of its rarity in nature. But thorium, which is relatively plentiful, is expected by physicists to rival uranium some day, or even supplant it, as a source of atomic energy.

Then there were cerium and strontium, of which the Soviet Purchasing Commission obtained 44 tons. Both metals, along with cadmium, thorium and cobalt, figured in Colonel Kotikov's dossier on experimental chemicals. They are useless for atomic purposes. But Russian scientists may have been working their way through the rare earths and metals on a well-founded suspicion that something momentous was afoot in that group.

Everyone is aware, of course, that these elements have industrial or military functions unrelated to the atom bomb, but Russia had a very critical interest in procuring A-bomb components from America. Red scientists are said to have been the first in Europe to announce the theory of nuclear fission. As America discovered at a cost of billions of dollars, it is a far cry from setting down speculations on paper to putting them in practice at the dimensions imposed by modern war. Thus the Kremlin was frantically inquisitive about large-scale production techniques developed by the Manhattan Project...

One ground for minimizing my evidence is a claim that Russia had abundant uranium of its own, in connection with massive radium deposits in the former area of Turkestan, the Kazakh Republic and the state of Tannu-Tuva, north of Mongolia. More than 30 years ago, it is said, Soviet physicists worked out the correct formula for separating uranium from radium. On the other hand, as atomic experts are fond of pointing out, "You can never have too much uranium."

If a blunder occurred, such objections proceed, it was not the shipment of minor quantities of uranium compounds to the Soviet Union, but the publication of Dr Smyth's book, which told not only how to make a nuclear bomb but how not to make one. The chief atomic authority of Norway, Gunnar Randers, is cited as having pronounced that the indiscretion of this publication saved Russia and every other country two years of research. According to Professor Szilard, "one half of the atomic bomb secret was given away when we used the bomb, and the other half when we published the Smyth report." After the espionage trials, however, one may ask whether the Smyth revelations were not more informative to the American public than to the Politburo...

In any event, it is heartening to know that, on the whole, our uranium embargo stood firm. Moscow was prevented from winning its grand objective of 17 tons, in contrast to the delivery of 15 tons of uranium chemicals to Great Britain which the Manhattan Project authorized. The steadfastness of the General Groves organization against Russia was the more admirable in that it was challenged by Mr Hopkins, with the power of the White House behind him. After the Un-American Activities Committee closed its hearing on March 7, 1950, I was examined searchingly by Government investigators. They tried to lure me into admitting a possibility, however faint, that the person to whom I spoke might have been Edward R. Stettinius, Jr, who had died five months earlier on October 11, 1949.

My answer was that never once, during my two years at Newark and Great Falls, did I hear so much as a mention of Stettinius, though reference to Hopkins was daily on the lips of the Russians.

It is common knowledge that on August 28, 1941, Stettinius succeeded Hopkins as titular chief of Lend-Lease, and held the post until September 25, 1943, when the agency was merged with kindred bodies into the Foreign Economic Administration, with Leo A. Crowley as Administrator.

DEAD MEN TALKING

But even the official biographer of Mr Hopkins does not hesitate to write:

"Hopkins knew that policy governing Lend-Lease would still be made in the White House and that the President would continue to delegate most of the responsibility to him. Stettinius was his friend and they could work together - and that was that."9

Another effort to clear Hopkins was based on the supposition that he acted in ignorance of what it was all about. Even if he helped the Russians to get A-bomb materials, the implication ran, it was the unsuspecting tool of Soviet cunning.

The Hopkins papers for Mr Sherwood's book were organized by Hopkins' longtime friend, Sidney Hyman. A fortnight after my first broadcast he was quoted as affirming that, until Hiroshima, Harry Hopkins had not "the faintest understanding of the Manhattan Project" and "didn't know the difference between uranium and geranium".

On the contrary, Harry Hopkins was one of the first men anywhere to know about the atom bomb. Dr Vannevar Bush chose Hopkins as his intermediary for presenting to Mr Roosevelt the idea of the atom bomb. It was in consultation with Hopkins that Dr Bush drafted the letter, for Mr Roosevelt's signature, which launched the A-bomb operation on June 14, 1941! Where do we learn this? In the official biography by Mr Sherwood, on pages 154 and 155. Finally, on page 704 we are told that the head of a state, Winston Churchill, "was conducting this correspondence on the atomic project with Hopkins rather than with the President, and that he continued to do so for many months thereafter".

A witness on the topic, General Groves testified that to the best of his recollection and belief he never met Harry Hopkins, talked with him on the telephone, or exchanged letters or dealt with anyone claiming to represent him. But the General thought it incumbent to remark, "I do know, of course, that Mr Hopkins knew about this project. I know that."10

An early symptom of White House obsession for 'reassuring Stalin' has been described by General Deane. In letters to American war agencies, dated March 7, 1942, Mr Roosevelt ordered that preferential position, in the matter of munitions, should be given to the Soviet Union over all other Allies and even the armed forces of the United States. Then and there, decided the former chief of the US Military Mission to Moscow, was "the beginning of a policy of appeasement of Russia from which we have never recovered and from which we are still suffering"11...

DEAD MEN TALKING

Endnotes

1. Stimson, Henry L. and Bundy, McGeorge, On Active Service in Peace and War, Harper, 1947.

2. "Hearings Regarding Shipments of Atomic Materials to the Soviet Union during World War II", Testimony of General Groves, December 7, 1949, House of Representatives Committee on Un-American Activities, US Government Printing Office, USA, p. 941.

3. ibid., p. 945.

4. ibid., p. 900.

5. ibid., p. 948.

6. ibid., p. 947.

7. "Hearings...", Testimony of Hermann H. Rosenberg, January 24, 1950, p. 1035.

8. "Hearings...", General Groves, p. 954.

9. Sherwood, Robert E., Roosevelt and Hopkins: An Intimate History, Harper, 1948, p. 560.

10. "Hearings...", General Groves, p. 947.

11. Deane, John R., The Strange Alliance, Viking, 1947, p. 89.

THE WORLD OF ILLUSIONS

Fracturing Myths and Illusions

Hypocrites of the world, buoyed by their Evil essence, are, and have been, united in their ability to distort truth and reality on this plane ever since the take-over of this sector of the True Creation by the Evil Essence. You know this statement is true if you know anything about how the Media, Religions and Governments work.

Look at how distorted a picture has been presented to the "Free World" concerning activities around the September 11, 2001 attacks and the subsequent war. Examples to support my point abound. This deceiving attitude existed long before the personnel of Pearl Harbour were sacrificed to allow more expeditious programming of the human lemmings in the USA, long before Machiavelli put pen to paper, even long before the Sons of Darkness mocked the Jesus they murdered and then lied about his birth and death. Look how they mock the Truth by saying that "God so loved this (evil, depraved, condemned and doomed) world that He sent His Only Son as ransom (and to be spat upon, tortured and crucified so the demons could fill their bellies with the satisfaction of another murder!!)

This ability to deceive has been a trait of Evil since its nascent days.

But the True Reality is impinging on this corrupt, depraved plane of malevolent illusions as never before. Even as the evil ones point to the illusions they hope will support them, the very illusions they look to are fragmenting along with everything else which is fraudulent. I repeat: the lies no longer work. They will not work, for this is the time of truth, the time of accountability, the time of settling all scores. And there is no place those of injustice can escape to. Of course, such an assertion is most welcome to those who love Truth and Justice. It is the answer to their prayers. But to those of Evil, to those who have chosen Evil, to those who have created the deceiving illusions, to those who have denied the need for Truth and Justice, this is a threat to their very existence. Indeed, it is the announcement of their worst nightmare.

Myths and Illusions with which the Sons and Daughters of Darkness hope to deceive are many, but let me examine and dispel a few at random.

* 1.   The first illusional myth to be dispelled states that Jesus Christ will appear in the midst of the turmoil and introduce a period of one thousand years of peace.

Jesus was NOT the only Christ (anointed One). He, Jesus, had told us that He came with a sword - to cut away the evil ones from the viables. He said He, the Energy in Him, would return to judge all, and rescue those worthy of rescue. Judgement was always on the cards.

Those who deny such a Judgement by a Higher Energy - as do A Course in Miracles, and most New Age 'Doctrines', etc., - are mocking, Evil-created mechanisms which again are attempting to create self-deceiving Illusions! They will not work. They cannot work, for they are of Untruth.

For New Agers to say they forgive themselves and all others, and judge themselves worthy and therefore viable is not valid. Indeed we must all move on from transgressions, but with faith that the Higher Energy will decide! If we attempt to remove that privilege from the Higher Energy and make ourselves god as the New Agers do, we are in fact usurping the Power of the Judge and invalidating the process. The validity of the Process of Judgement is in having Faith that the Higher Energy will deal with True Justice with all of us. It is not up to lowly consciousnesses to say they forgive themselves and find themselves worthy. What that does is really eliminate the need for a real God.

Those who claim they are god are really using this mechanism of evil-created illusion making, but deep down in their hearts they know they are lying. And this becomes obvious when they are confronted by my words. They panic and scatter like ants set on fire. Why is that? It is because their evil cover, given by their self-deceiving illusions, is blown away by the energy in these words.

If they still want to argue they are god, let them explain how they created Black Holes; let them explain how they created the forces controlling meiosis; let them explain how they created the chromatic processes in retinas. They cannot, can they? But they would be able to if they were "god", right? They are not "god", they are evil, self-deceiving fools.

The Christ Energy is an Essence, not an individual. The Essence has come. It has judged and is evacuating those who are viable. It has judged and marked those who are not viable, so that they will be sent to the transmutation vats when this physical dimension is DESTROYED totally!

Even our lower minds tell us the likelihood of peace in the near future is zero. The talk is of war and more war. Those who were not terrorists before are now contemplating such a profession in response to the gross injustices that have been forced upon them by recent events. All manner of personnel are lining up to fight what they see as the good fight for justice. Countries are about to fragment from the smell of war. Pakistan at present is the most obvious example. And bombs everywhere are being primed to explode. They too have a consciousness.

Bombs and their terror are creating the scope for future generations of assassins and martyrs. Humanity has learned nothing from the theft of Palestine.

Do you think those poisoned by spent uranium are contemplating one thousand years of peace as they see their children die with deformities and malignancies from the radiation?

And just where would the one thousand years of peace be staged? It cannot be Earth or this Solar System, for they are primed for destruction. The homeostatic controls are no longer working. Within a generation this earth would be uninhabitable even if it were to last that long.

Uncontrollable AIDS, Mad Cow Disease, Ebola, diseases and genetic mutations from the poisons purposely planted in Chemtrails and genetically Modified Foods - thanks to the aliens who want to eradicate a major portion of Humanity - will devastate the Earth's population that is left after the Nuclear Bombs have had their turn.

Previously I had told you that all must leave the physical for that is the Plan of Correction. There will be no more time, hence, there cannot be One Thousand Years of Peace!

The Christ Energy has been here on the planet. What do you think did the assessment and organized the evacuation of viables, if not the Christ Energy? E.T.?

What do you think has allowed the exposure of all corruption, all Evil? What do you think allowed the Beast to be unleashed so that it would pursue its well-known path of destruction which would end as self-destruction?

All these have been the work of the Christ Energy using the Power provided by the True Love of the Mother of Creation - a Power maliciously and forcefully denied by the Yarwehnians and Jehovians. And that too was from the creation of other self-deceiving illusions by the sycophants of Darkness.

* 2   The Second Illusional Myth to dispel states that Nibiru, the twelfth

DEAD MEN TALKING

Planet is approaching and the Creators of Humanity will set all things right.

Let the fools who have been deceived by this evil-spun illusion of idiocy dream on. They shall be rudely awakened soon enough by the knowledge of the non-existence of this planet Nibiru, and by knowledge that the creators of the biological aspects of humanity have been here all the time and are even now plotting mechanisms of genocide with which to diminish the numbers of their too-successful experiment.

* 3   The third myth is that this planet Earth is a classroom in which souls are to learn and develop.

Think back for a moment to when you were young, and loving and caring and so innocent. What have you learnt in the years since childhood? What have you acquired? You have learned how much evil there is in the world. You have learned how few people can be really trusted. You have acquired emotional scars you never asked for. The fools who can program themselves to not think about this will not agree, but the fact is you learned all about evil and how it messes things up. You may have been programmed to commit evil. Is that what a classroom is for? Is that proper development?

Most non-demonic geriatrics - unless they have lost their marbles - are sour, paranoid sceptics who see life as a waste of good years. Depression is very high among the elderly, as is suicide. Is that because they learned to be godlike in classroom earth or because they developed into future little gods? Not on your Neddy. It is because they are bruised by the burden of evil they have had to endure.

Make no mistake about it, this planet is a jail for maximal suffering and energy exploitation of those with good energy. Of course it suits those who exploit and gain the energy - because they have none of their own - to a tee! They are the demons who tell you this is a classroom. For them it is, for with each lifetime they learn how to exploit more efficiently.

Just one other point which I have mentioned often: Why would a real god create souls so imperfect that they would need to come to a crappy place like this to learn anything? Is this god incapable of something better? The systems on earth are atrocious. The exploitation is never-ending. Does one really need to be raped, abused, exploited, robbed, subjected to all sorts of injustices, etc., just to learn living? Sure, these things do not happen to everyone, but they do to the majority. Everyone suffers in one way or another. Those of evil deny it is so.

Even those who are apparently successful learn to cheat better. They learn to subdue and disadvantage others so they can finish on top of the pile. And don't deny this; don't say that it is not so. A cursory glance at all the powerful and rich families in the world will reveal they gained their wealth by cunningly evil exploitation. How do rich nations become a lot richer if not by exploitation of the weaker ones and their resources?

Each creature is a murderer or a meal for another. These bodies are continually breaking down. The degree of mental illness in the world should tell you no one is really enjoying this so-called learning classroom, except the demons who gain energy from all the pain, suffering and misery, even though they themselves appear to be caught up in the same processes.

Look back over the centuries. Apart from multiplying like bacteria out of control, humanity has learned nothing but to be more violent, more efficient in killing large numbers and to be more efficient in exploiting people, animals, the seas, the vegetation and Earth itself, bringing everything to the point of non sustainability of life. In truth, collectively, Humanity has learned how to destroy more, and more quickly, and how to self destruct. What a classroom! It truly is spitting into the eye of the creator of this atrocious system, and that is all such a creator deserves!

In the near future I will write about the myths that Humanity is an ontologically homogenous entity and that Humanity is in control of its own destiny.

A brief examination of 'A Course in Miracles'

Since posting the first essay on this topic I have received quite a deal of material, some of it psychiatric advice, which made me smile, coming as it did from the most inept and ignorant of the readers. It is amazing what they see in my words - concepts that are nowhere in sight but which incite them to ridiculousness. They are reactions to the energy of the words, of course. Hence, as the ones of Truth are buoyed and sustained by the writings, those of Darkness writhe in anguish at the very thought of what it could all mean. They are confronted and disarmed by the words, and they realize they are exposed in all their ontological nakedness. This they do not like, for it reveals what they really are. They are exposed in the Light, and their hypocrisy, deceitfulness and dank evil are exposed as never before. They are traumatised by the exposure, thinking they would never be found out. But then recovering somewhat, they write the drivel that makes me laugh, confirming ever so speedily that they are suffering the effects of the terminally mad. (Jerry Attrick says I've been laughing so much I am in danger of developing a waist line. Well, small danger anyway!)

The most vile of the respondents have been adherents of A Course in Miracles (ACIM). At first they present with the false sugary sweetness of trained deceivers. But their façade does not last long with me. Soon enough they turn into the ghastly demonic beasts awakened beings now known so well.

DEAD MEN TALKING

Let us examine this Course again. I have done so in the past, but, it is important, and I will spend a few minutes on it again. The story told is that the information in ACIM was dictated to a Zionist in New York, supposedly by Jesus. You know the Christ Energy of Jesus and Zionism are ontological opposites from what I have revealed. Hence, how could that be? The fact is that Jesus did NOT dictate this nonsense. Ramtha did. You remember him - the one who claims he was the biggest bastard of them all, and still is!

Having read ACIM cover to cover, and every word therein, I must admit it is of compelling subtlety. It appeals to the ego as it aggrandises it, ever so apparently innocently and harmlessly, luring it with words such as love, compassion and forgiveness. It creates an illusion of Peace while claiming to dispel the illusion of Evil and Ignorance. In fact, by doing this, it creates a greater illusion, masking as it does, the reality of the War of Essences, the existence of Evil, the destructiveness of Evil, the need for a Higher Energy to judge, the need to separate the sheep from the goats, the need to fight back for all the injustices, humiliations and exploitations those of Goodness are burdened with.

And it lays the blame of personal failure, not on this demonic system and its sycophants, if there is personal failure, but totally on the individual, who is blamed for the failure to dispel the reality of Evil. It makes Evil an abnormality in the eye of the beholder, and if that beholder happens to perceive Evil, demons, injustice, etc., s/he, the beholder, is blamed for being incompetent and ignorantly imprudent. The beholder is blamed for perceiving incorrectly according to ACIM, when, in fact, s/he has impinged upon the truth of existence. In fact, as you well know, empirically and experientially, the truth is opposite to what ACIM teaches.

Some say it is a good course because it eradicates conflict and friction. That is the whole point of its evilness. In a struggle, if one side's propaganda can make the other side put down its weapons and not fight, the war is over, is it not? If one side convinces the other to give up, are the ones who laid down their arms then not defenceless victims to be exploited at will by the evilness of the deceivers? Indeed they are. This is what ACIM tries to do. By denying Evil and the need to fight it to the very end, it tries to disarm those with energy so that they can be exploited mercilessly.

Let me dwell for a moment on the assertion that this level with obvious Evil is illusional, with no real Evil at all, as postulated by ACIM. It manages to allay the need to fight Evil by saying it does not exist, that this is some sort of godly play in which we are ignorantly experimenting in all sorts of ways, and do not realize that this is so. Once we will realize it, according to ACIM, we will be happy with all circumstances everywhere on the globe, and just let things be, knowing soon enough we, one and all, will return to a godly state, with no judgement. Hence, according to this book, ultimately there is no need to be responsible for our actions, no need to be accountable. Ultimately there is nothing to forgive, so it says. "Your brother has done nothing to forgive"! it asserts.

This state of affairs suits the evil ones admirably, and they beam with joy at such thoughts, for it means they can exploit at will, and not worry about it. They forgive themselves and everyone else on a superficial outer mind level and appear to live guilt-free. But their self-justification, their self-deception are temporary and illusional. The sense of forgiveness in these people is contained in the evil concept from ACIM that ultimately there is nothing to forgive!

These thoughts are only on a superficial outer mind level, for the moment they meet my words they are traumatized. You see, deep down they know they are deluding themselves, and my words drag them back to a reality they had hoped they could deny forever. But they cannot. It catches up with them. That is why they are distraught.

But, let's examine their beliefs from ACIM a little closer. If there is no Evil, and this whole mess is just playfulness of ignorant little children who have strayed a little, ever so innocently, then all things are validly godly and not condemnable, according to ACIM, is that not so?

Now, a firm believer in ACIM, like Oprah Winfrey, for example, should be able to not only accept the following scenario, but be happy that it is just a leela, as the Hindu say, a playful prank by godly children who really do no wrong. Hence, if she is assaulted one dark night by five men and raped repeatedly, after which her breasts are cut off, her uterus is perforated with a broomstick or rifle thrust vaginally, and she has her eyes gauged out, everything should be OK, according to the no-Evil brigade.

According to ACIM, it is only god's children at play, and the rape, torture and maiming are only illusional pranks of godly children. Let us say she had a harmless and defenceless four year old child and she, too, received the same treatment after having her two harmless and defenceless puppies smashed against the walls until they die in excruciating agony, giving out wails and screams that tear the heart of any who truly know justice and love, and who are unfortunate enough to hear the sounds which include the fearful supplications for mercy, but then become the sorrow-filled whines of self-pity, involuntary canine whimpers seeking release from such Evil-imposed pain, seeking a speedy physical death from the insufferably unjust injuries.

I have depicted these gory scenes on purpose, namely to demonstrate the gruesomeness of Evil. In the moments of tragedy, humans react in a similar fashion, as they are forced to bear the full brunt of Evil. Under such circumstances they find it very hard to deny that Evil exists. Tell them then that Evil is an illusion! They will not agree.

In such a devilish scenario, can Oprah keep smiling and remain calm and happy using the notions of ACIM? I doubt it. Can you? You see, such evil assertions only work when the hypocrites are free from being victims themselves. Such scenarios occur everywhere around the world, constantly with and without war. Especially now they are occurring with the "war" in Afghanistan. The assailants go further there, of course. They murder their victims. Are adherents of ACIM still happy and laughing? If they are, they deserve to be called fools!

And yet, ACIM insists on total forgiveness, and, in total contradiction, it ends up by saying one must believe that there is ultimately nothing to forgive. Even in such cases as above, it states that "your brother, has done nothing that needs forgiveness"!

Here is the direct quote from its textbook: "Forgiveness is knowing that your brother has done nothing for you to forgive."

How many can truly live with that in the scenario described above?

ACIM claims it wants to dispel guilt. But this direct quote demonstrates how dastardly it imposes the burden of guilt : "The sin and guilt we fail to forgive in others remains in us as well."

So, if a victim has not forgiven the demons and has not embraced the sordid cruelty of hell, s/he is also just as guilty. How perverse! Of course, rehabilitation is one thing. We should never accept Evil. If we do, we not only condone it, but eventually use it freely with misperceived impunity. How would it ever be eradicated under those circumstances? That is the whole point of why ACIM presents this scenario. Being from Evil, it does not want the eradication of Evil.

Also, realize that Judgement and Forgiveness are not for humans to dispense. There is a God for that. And to have imposed on oneself the sin and guilt of another just because one cannot accept the demonic behaviour of another is the ultimate injustice dispensed by Evil, and this makes a mockery of those who truly seek Justice and Fairness.

Ultimately, as I said, it accuses those who see Evil of being incompetently misperceiving the status quo. It claims the perception of those who see Evil (that is, see truly) needs to be changed, and that they need to block out the vision of the Reality of Evil for according to ACIM, that is a misperception. According to ACIM, true perception (that is, being spiritually blind) is the perception it wants its sycophants to have. Now, isn't that Evil? Of course it is!

So, back to the quote: "Forgiveness is knowing that your brother has done nothing for you to forgive." If that is the case, what is the point of struggling against the impurity and devilishness of this plane? There would be no point. We could act as despicably as we could imagine, knowing we do nothing wrong in that case. But we know Right from Wrong, don't we? We know there is a line between Goodness and Evil. Even in demons who try to deny this Principle, it is ingrained into the substance of every unit of consciousness, whether it be theomorphic or counterfeit. And that is where the fear of those who chose Evil comes from.

One more quote: "What you see in another is you." This surely is given by Ramtha to scare the guts out of any who perceive truly. If not fully awakened to the Truth, when they see the demonic essence in some, they tend to remember this threat which naturally makes them shut off their inner vision, for who wants to be a demon? Of course it is nonsense. It is another way of scaring the adherents into submission. And this comes after the Oneness is stressed, the quote from ACIM being that we are all equal (in ontological terms). Believing that, any who see demonic essences in others think there is something wrong with them, rather than thinking they are perceiving truly. Quite an effective evil plot, hey?

Another point stressed by ACIM which needs to be dispelled is the one stating that it is we, 'humans', who are the cause of any evil, even illusional evil, with all its confusion, conflict and suffering to be found in the world. According to it, once we stop perceiving it, it will simply disappear, as will all the pain, suffering and misery. Ha!

Children play a game of covering their eyes to make danger and fear supposedly disappear. That is exactly what ACIM wants adults to do: stop seeing Evil and it will disappear. Fat chance! This is not just a childish prank. It is a very serious and pernicious aspect of Evil which really is spiritual cancer. Always remember that perniciousness left untreated is fatal in the end.

I repeat, ACIM wants adherents to be spiritually blind. That is the function of Evil. That is why Evil is called Darkness and Ignorance! ACIM is Evil, make no mistake about that whatsoever. Ignorance in these circumstances is bliss, but only until the self-deceiving illusion lasts. Once it is broken, as it is with these words, the bliss vanishes, and the reality of the cruelty of Evil comes as a stark reminder to both its victims and those who need to pay the ultimate price, if in fact, they have chosen Evil as their essence..

It is no coincidence that most adherents of ACIM are middle class Westerners, especially in the more affluent states of the USA. ACIM was tailor-made for such places as California and Colorado, and for those who are blind to the horrors of this world.

There is a pragmatic point to what I am revealing. Watch how these hypocrites react once the suffering reaches their doorstep, as it will soon enough with the spread of overt, destructive and openly malicious Evil throughout the West, and the USA in particular, in the next few months. Watch how the word 'forgiveness' will disappear from their vocabulary once the others of Evil start to hit them.

My personal experience has been that these people who claim there is no Evil are the most evil of all. When I lectured to them, and they felt most uncomfortable about having been reminded that they are accountable to a Higher Consciousness, and after having told me repeatedly there was no Evil, they would, quite contrarily, call me evil for having disturbed their artificial mind shelters of delusional tranquillity. Can you beat that? So, they did believe in Evil all along, hey? It is just that it suits them to pretend when left alone, so that they can continue sucking dry any unaware "good energy" being they meet.

I admit some of the adherents of ACIM and other New Age garbage are victims, trapped by the lure of the promise of some temporary peace of mind from the opiate effect of these false philosophies. And some of these have had the evil spell broken with my words. I say that in all modesty and have many who would aver to the fact they have been pulled out of the abyss of darkness, in which these false philosophies placed them, by the words in our books, website, etc.

Finally, realize that the Truth is no whore. It cannot be used and abused to please one and not another. Truth is immutable. Hence, no matter what people think when it pleases them, eventually Truth will emerge victorious.

* The Truth is that there is Evil.

* People do suffer from Evil.

* There is Superior Consciousness that judges.

* Some, who have squandered countless chances to be in the Light, all due to their own fault, have been judged to be worthless failures and are to be transmuted.

* There has been a Celestial Error and a raging Battle of Essences.

* There are demons and ones who have chosen Evil.

* There is occurring a rectification of this abomination.

* There is a happy ending for those of Love, Peace and Justice!!

Indeed, from the truthful perspective, 'A Course in Miracles' should be renamed 'A Course in Mockery!'

***

DEAD MEN TALKING

A World in Crisis

A time to rethink the definition of Reality

Whether you want to believe it or not, you and every other individual on Earth is being affected by a process of unique change. Indeed, this is a Generation of Uniqueness, a generation of massive change; a generation of fragmentation of many things, a time of sorting out, a time of finality. You, like everyone else, are going to have to rethink the paradigms of normality which you have accepted since the Age of Reason, and which you have modified, knowingly or unknowingly, in order to make sense of a world which seemed to accommodate you as the years passed in your life.

But suddenly, especially with events unfolding since the time of the bombing of the World Trade Towers, nothing seems the same in our minds. Suddenly there are forced upon many minds, very aware ones and less aware ones, many issues and fears which shatter the laboriously moulded paradigms of normality we hoped would see us to the end of our lives. One of the fears encroaching on minds is the fear that whatever paradigms of normality we had, they are now not sufficient. Suddenly the world makes less sense; suddenly the guard rails we used to set our minds at ease in times of crises are no longer there. Suddenly we feel vulnerable as never before. It is as if a massive mental earthquake has shattered our inner being and we are on shifting mental ground, trying to make sense of that which is no longer familiar.

Our vulnerability is not just physical, as with the threats of attacks from known and unknown quarters, nor just financial with threats of loss of jobs, loss of financial stability and independence. It is not even the thought of war alone, for many of us have lived with the reality of multiple wars ever since the 1940s. Our vulnerability lurks in the mind as we see the fragmentation of the life we thought was stable and would remain so. Our vulnerability comes from seeing the fragmentation of other nations, institutions, traditions, foundations and organizations we thought would never fail us.

What we are witnessing, and what is causing the fears in minds which do not fully understand the shift in reality is the inevitable breakdown of the false reality in which we have lived ever so illusionally. The Virtual Reality of this dimension is fracturing.

Why I call this a Virtual Reality, why it is fracturing, and what is to replace it are the very realizations individuals have to make in order to maintain mental health in this time of unprecedented change.

The Process of Realization of the Falsehood of this dimension is painful. However, the process is the only process which will give hope to the desperate. It is the only process which will allow an understanding of what is happening and an understanding of why the True Gnostics called this dimension the Plane of Hypocrisy, the Plane of Dishonesty, of Illusion, and, as I have described, as the Plane of Programming, Pollution and Indoctrination.

To be more specific, it is painful to realize that the Media upon which many of us have relied on for facts of what is going on in the world is but a tool for programming the masses; a tool to convey any Untruth which those in charge, whom elsewhere I have called the Archons, want to convey to the masses who are indeed used as milking cows to do the Archons bidding. They do this bidding by being exploited of their money, time and energy by the many systems we find in modern society. They do this by being programmed to fight wars for the reasons the Archons give them. They do their bidding by killing whenever, and wherever they are asked to do so, under the cover of many so-called ideals, used dishonestly and most evilly. In due course, I shall give examples of this. However, here I want to make the point that this has been the mechanism on this Earth for a long, long time, in order to fool, program and exploit the masses. It is in this century especially that the Media has played such a worldwide role.

But now, as all things fragment, even the Media is becoming ineffectual compared to previous times. Like all other systems, it is disintegrating and those who had been its victims previously are awakening, not only to its disintegration, but also to its ineffectiveness. At the same time, minds are awakening to the programming that they previously received via the Media and are now growing more and more angry at this tool of the Archons.

In previous eras, Religion served a similar purpose as the Media to program the masses, and fight wars in the name of this god and that god. It still does today, as we can see with the evolution of Jihads against Western Countries, and the nonsense of Jew versus Muslim in the Middle East, Catholic verses Protestant in Northern Ireland, Hindu versus Muslim on the Indian subcontinent, Christian versus Jew in many parts of the world, etc.

It is going to be a painful process now to realize that what we learned at our mother's knee as children about our religion, about Jehovah, etc., is false and ridiculous. Sure, all religions have, or had, some of the seeds of Truth at some time when they first evolved, but by an intentionally EVIL process, these truths have been so corrupted that the Religions are now useless in providing any truth about the Truth-filled Emerging Paradigm of the New Dimension. That is why religions now have no idea of what is going on. That is why they are unable to provide any insight or hope to struggling minds caught in the stresses of incredibly massive changes on Earth. The corrupted and very convoluted texts of pseudo-Christianity, texts such as the Book of Revelation, although based on Gnostic writings, are now useless in defining anything worthwhile with which people could remain mentally aware. If they did provide anything worthwhile, the majority would not be traumatized as they really are. They are awakening to the fact that they have been lied to, even with their Religious Instruction, and this is causing mental anguish as they seek the reality behind the falsehood.

The awakening mind will see that extant religions have been used to keep individuals programmed, exploited and trapped in the Illusion of this pseudo-reality. Religions have been efficient tools of bellicosity which, with the never ending suffering of wars, has yielded much energy to the evil system to sustain itself. I realize that some of the assertions I make in this short essay may appear esoteric, and hence readers are referred to my early books for fuller explanations.

And so it is also with Science and Government. Minds are awakening to the trickery they have been subjected to. The tricks no longer work. The lies no longer work, again for the same reason - namely, fragmentation is occurring in every sphere of human endeavour, and what kept the people programmed the way the Archons wanted in the past is no longer working, for it is fragmenting.

I have often called Science a fraud. Its explanations appear to work on this level, but in fact, its real fraudulence is seen as it acts, via bluff, to create a false paradigm of reality. As such, it has been a tool of the Evil Archons to keep minds trapped in the illusion. Here are some examples. One of the greatest of its evil tricks which Science performed is the one which dismisses the need for another energy - let's call it ESSE (essential, special, spiritual energy) for the moment - which is essential for existence beyond the physiological processes which Science describes ever so well and fraudulently. The ancient Sanskrit scholars called this energy 'prana'.

This trick of Science then negates the spiritual component to existence without which nothing could work in the physical, not even the smallest unit - the atom. What is an atom? Does it have consciousness? Science says no. Of course it has consciousness. What is it made of? A nucleus and electrons. What are electrons? Matter? Energy? Particles? Waves? Science does not know. Where do electrons get the energy to keep spinning around the nucleus? There must be a source, otherwise they would collapse. The power of centripetal and centrifugal forces, of velocity, and of attraction and repulsion are instigated, but these forces need energy to function. Where do they get their energy? Science does not know. It is ESSA (prana). What else? But science scoffs at this for it denies a spiritual component. And yet, its explanation of the simplest complete building block of matter is incomplete without the spiritual component. The basis of all matter - even this evil-created, corrupted matter in this dimension has a spiritual basis. All things have, and this is what all individuals are in the process of finding out as this world in crisis fragments inexorably.

Not convinced that Science bluffs with its picture of Reality? How about the notion that 98% of matter in this universe is Dark Matter? What function does it serve? Why can we not see it? Does it serve some other life forms? What? Am I suggesting the possibility of other lifeforms? Indeed, I am! But Science will have none of that, because Science has given us a false paradigm of Reality.

When Science cannot explain, it bluffs right along. Consider Quantum Mechanics and the disappearance of particles in an accelerator. Where do they go? How can they disappear and reappear? What are they really made of? Can you not conceive the fact that they may be subunits of consciousness which manifest in and out of dimensions? Science cannot, because it does not really have room in its false paradigms for consciousness outside of the physical and it cannot accept multiple dimensionality!

Governments - institutions which can be as corrupt and evil as anyone can imagine, when they are examined closely - are being seen more and more for what they are today, especially with the actions cited as involving terrorism, cleansing of nations of terrorists, etc. The lies are not working. People are seeing through the rhetoric of Government, of leaders, of demagogues and despots as never before.

Thus it is that now, in this unprecedented time, individuals are beginning to question everything - Religion, Science, the Media's honesty, the honesty of Governments and leaders, etc. It is what they are finding which is causing so much mental stress. They realize they are being lied to. They are realizing the basis of existence in this illicit dimension is Falsehood, and they do not like it. And they are internally rebelling. Soon they will rebel physically as well. But no matter what actions they take, they will be left with the need to find the paradigm of Reality if they are going to avoid the chasms of Terminal Madness which await those who cannot make the jump.

Questioning the status quo and finding it is illusional, of falsehood, is not enough. One must gain access to facts of Reality which will allow the emergence of the paradigm of Truth in which one can mentally survive. As I said, the process is painful, for much of what we accepted as normal must be dismissed as illusional. And for most there is a degree of urgency, for the final fragmentation is upon us.

The path to finding the True Reality, the reality into which we are now being hurled, as we witness the disintegration of that which we thought was valid, but which is being exposed as obviously fraudulent, as each hour passes, poses the questions of "Why? Who? When? and How?".

Why is this a fraudulent reality? Why is it a Virtual Reality? Who set it up? Why is it being shattered? Who gained from its existence? Why do the Archons treat us this way? Of what benefit is it to them? Why are we kept pretty much in the dark? Why have institutions such as Religion, Science, Governments become corrupt and a virtual conspiracy against the 'common man'? Why is recorded History so much bunkum?

The answers to these questions, which are readily available in the Realm of Gnosticism, are essential components for the basis of realizing the New Reality which is emerging. Although individuals do not need to know every last detail of what is involved, an outline will be helpful in understanding what is going on, why this is a world and realm of fraudulence, why it is being allowed to disintegrate, and to be actively eradicated, why some are seen as sons and daughters of Darkness and why some will disappear into an abyss of irreversible madness.

That the basis of all existence depends on a spiritual component, so vehemently denied by materialistic science, will become obvious now as never before. It is in the ability to shift awareness to that component which will allow minds to make fuller realizations at this time of physical disintegration.

And so, as minds travel from this fast-fragmenting, material world of illusion to a new reality, questions will arise of what a human actually is, how humanity was formed, and by whom. There are valid answers. The answers which the Archons of Falsehood have provided in extant Science, Religion and History will be seen to be deficient as the false paradigm collapses. In the transition of awareness from the false to the true reality, concepts which many may not have considered will need to be integrated.

These concepts include the following:

* the emergence and continued existence of the essence of Evil;

* the existence of an evil pseudo-creator (known by True Gnostics as Jehovah who is also Satan) of this corrupt dimension and its matter;

* the existence of counterfeit beings and of this counterfeit reality which is breaking down;

* the existence of other lifeforms, some much more advanced than humanity;

* the interaction of these with humans;

* the existence of galactic wars;

* the ubiquitous battle of Good against Evil;

*   the necessary assessment for viability and worthiness of all units of consciousness;

*   the existence of consciousness in all living and so-called 'non-living' expressions.

(Just to diverge a little - it has been a great crime committed against the True Reality that humans have been conned by evil Archons into killing animals for fur, food or fun. Lack of awareness of the existence of consciousness in spheres such as the Earth, the Moon, the Sun, has allowed, particularly in Earth's case, the profane abuse of it leading, certainly, to murderous and suicidal endings. I realize these statements may be subjected to ridicule by the fools. But, knowing ridicule is the baneful tool of the stupidly ignorant, I plough on, knowing such stupidly ignorant fools will soon no longer be part of any reality whatsoever.)

Knowledge of these concepts allows an understanding of what is going on, and the concepts facilitate the acceptance that this is a period of Correction of a Spiritual Error which occurred long, long ago; that this is a period of sorting out, of re-establishing a Divine Order, with True Justice in a valid paradigm of Truthful Reality.

The concepts allow the understanding, which will comfort minds, that Correction necessitates the elimination of that which was corrupt, counterfeit, of falsehood and of Evil, so that the basis of the True Reality now emerging will be one of honesty, not deceit.

And so it is that the process we are now witnessing will, per force, require the permanent removal of all things, be they material or spiritual, which are of the Corruption, of the Counterfeit, or of the Falsehood which fooled us for so long. These aspects will perish forever via a process of transmutation in due course. What we are seeing now in the physical, with the breakdown of many systems, with the disintegration of what we thought was a stable biosphere, with the lashing out of evil intent, is nothing more than the process of elimination of the unwanted. It is a process which must occur. No material thing will survive this process, for every material thing, your physical body and mine included, is of the evil essence which must be eradicated.

Viewed rationally, this process of elimination should not produce fear except to those who have acted with evil to sustain the illusion. They fear, for now they are in the process which judges them and finds them wanting. And they know this means permanent removal from existence. This they fear.

You have known since you attained the Age of Reason that some day you would physically die. Only a fool would think otherwise and deny that is so. Alas, there are many fools among us. Be that as it may, an understanding that many other facets, apart from the physical, make up our existence will allow a smoother transition from this collapsing reality to the one awaiting. With realizations to be made, knowing that nothing of value is lost, that the evil-created, unwanted physical is being discarded, individuals can detach from the process of disintegration and focus on the coming reality which will be of True Peace and Justice.

Without the realizations I speak of, without the knowledge I am revealing, without the detachment from the horror now obvious in the world, individuals will be overcome with anxiety, hysteria, paranoia and fear of physical decay. They will not cope; rather they will succumb to the Terminal Madness of the Physical Endtime. If that is the case, they have only themselves to blame.

The Beast Unleashed

The next few months will leave no one on the planet in any doubt about the existence of Evil, and the fact that Evil has been allowed to overrun the plane, purposely, so that it will entrap itself in a process of self-destruction.

Horror, terror and destruction will be witnessed by all, as the illusion fragments, as Evil plies its trade which has always been destruction, causing pain, suffering and misery to its trapped victims. What is different now is the fact that Evil will be unable to limit its madness, and its destruction of everything it over-runs. Its very nature of hypocrisy, deceitfulness, dishonesty, cupidity and hate will be exposed as never before in the history of this planet. Even those Sons and Daughters of Evil who for so long appeared to relish the energy gains they made from the exploitation of others will now be filled with terror as they realise they are caught in an unstoppable process which will claim them physically, mentally and spiritually. And as they see their end coming, they will lash out even more angrily with hate and venom, at themselves and all whom they can corner, for their nature of hate and anger will be exposed as never before.

Indeed, the vile Beast has been unleashed - to do itself in, and annihilate all its sycophantic progeny in the process! It is being allowed to show its true colours, and its essence of utter Evil which forms it.

Bombs will fall as Terror from darkened skies. Germs released ever so maliciously, along with chemicals of warfare, will pervade the air, soil, water, bodies and minds of all caught in this maelstrom of Malignity. And knowing not where to turn next, the Beast, in all its Terminal Madness, represented by the Archons, the leaders of most nations, will do what it does best: destroy. Already we are being given a glimpse of that in Central Asia. Not long now before the Beast in all its forms, being unable to restrain itself, and being aware of its entrapment, will escalate its destructive power to bring the physical world to an end.

That the Beast with the essence of Evil is made up of parts such as Archons,

DEAD MEN TALKING

and various groups of aliens present as consciousnesses in all classes of consciousness, is but detail, not essential to the understanding of the process of annihilation unleashed upon this Earth by those various parts of the Beast.

Every segment, every aspect of the Beast, regardless of its physical manifestation, will be caught in its own process of decay and self-destruction. It has always harboured hate in itself for all things, including itself. While it had victims from which to extract energy, it contained its self hate somewhat. But now, unleashed, it will hate all things with the zeal of demons doomed to die.

When utter hopelessness looms on the horizon of minds already undergoing decay due to Terminal Madness, as is occurring world-wide in non-viables, the path of destruction is the only path open to such minds.

For now, Archons appear to be playing the game of eradicating their enemies for material spoils, with wars that are ever-widening in their stance. But soon enough, they will realize that they, as part of the unleashed Beast, have actually been cornered and labelled as failures and will be transmuted once they self-destruct in the physical plane. When they realize this fully, they will reel headlong into the Abyss of Despair, and discharge all their venom here, there and everywhere, indiscriminately, so as to show the rest that they know they are doomed.

This time of madness in the Unleashed Beast has already begun. The fullness of the fury is no further away than 12 to 18 months according to my reckoning.

* Now shall all see the corruption, deceit, and evil manipulation which has kept us tightly sealed in this Truth-destroying illusion.

* Now shall we all see the despicable modus operandi used by the Archons, as leaders of government, as captains of cartels, to keep us trapped and exploited.

* Now shall we gleefully see their evil mechanisms being exposed, and fractured hopelessly as is their hope of escaping True Justice.

The fires of Hell will be no hotter as nuclear bombs rain down accompanied by the laments of the damned. Verily will there be wailing and gnashing of teeth.

Protect yourself now so that your emotional body will not react too forcefully, sending you too into the anguish of Horror and Despair. Remember the emotional body was created by Evil to be incorporated into these physical bodies for the purpose of allowing illicit extraction of energy from the Centres of Consciousness which are forced to use these bodies while expressing on the physical plane.

Anticipate the use of the most vile forms of warfare. Expect the ruthlessness of demons to be seen everywhere, just as we saw in the butchering of apparently innocent people in East Timor and Indonesia when vigilantes indiscriminately chopped heads off terrified victims with machetes.

Expect to see Hypocrisy reach new heights of malediction as Archons dressed in their finery talk about protecting their commercial interests as they bomb defenceless women and children, as they force starvation on ever-increasing numbers, as they drop incendiary bombs to burn the flesh of those they really consider inhuman.

It is they with the bombs and the malicious power to starve others, and the willingness to practise genocide as they wish, who are inhuman (contrary to the accepted sense of being human which means being aware of others, being cultured, and caring for fellow humans). They are demons from the depths of Hell, and there shall they return to await transmutation.

Unfortunately, those of us still in the physical will have to witness this destructive act by the Beast now unleashed. But we can be buoyed by the fact that nothing of value is lost in the process. All that is being eradicated is Evil and those consciousnesses who have chosen Evil over Good. We can be buoyed by the fact that this is a necessary step in the Corrective Process being applied to this illicit, counterfeit pseudo-reality which is Jehovah's corrupt world of Deceit, Dishonesty and Despair.

****

How the Unleased Beast will act

And so, if the Beast is going to self-destruct, it will need to vent its anger, its lusts and greed, totally uninhibited by any restraints. The end of the process is what is important - its total self-annihilation.

In accordance with this, it will wage war wherever and whenever conditions suit it. It will drop bombs on all whom it perceives as its enemies, and it will do so without reason, citing its ability to do so as reason enough. And by doing this, it will incite many others to oppose it, leading to confrontation and more violence, friction and murderous war. But, being self-absorbed with its own power and importance, the Beast will pursue the path of self-destruction regardless of the signs along the way that it is doing just that.

Former matters of pretence, such as caring for others, caring for Democracy, equanimity, freedoms of speech, action, choice, will all be abused. The power of the Beast, which when unleashed and unrestrained it finds inebriating and self-adsorbing, will be misused to crush those less powerful, even if in a true ontological sense those others are but extensions of its own being. What else would one expect of a Beast?

The circle of destruction will increase inexorably, each blunder being replaced with many more, and the Beast will continue unashamedly, feeling initially exhilarated by its ability to cause so much destruction, suffering and anguish.

But, the Law of Diminishing Returns will apply. Unlike former times when ruthlessness and destruction yielded an abundance of energy upon which to feast, the Beast will now find little energetic rewards for its labours. Enraged, it will expend even more effort to cause even more destruction and suffering. Is that not what we are seeing even now?

And members of its own corpus, struck by the ferocity of attacks, will retaliate with the excessive manner of madness. From within the breast of the beast will explode the vials of venom it has harboured for a long time. It will turn on itself, and all segments which it sees even in its own ranks as untrustworthy, and attempt to destroy them quickly. The Process of self-annihilation has the essence of paranoia as well as the Delusion of Grandeur and Invincibility. Thus will the Beast pursue the path of all despots, the difference this time being the fact that it will totally achieve its aims of destroying others, and itself, as a final outcome!

So, what is the Beast which will physically destroy this world and all physical expressions in it? It is the essence of Evil with the Mind of Malignity which, as parts and projections of the consciousness of Darkness, resides in all the Classes of Consciousness in this counterfeit, and illicit, Universe. Unleashed, it will now destroy itself, all its parts, all the things which it created from the energy it stole from the Sector of the True Creation which it invaded.

Let it ignite the last and most fatal conflagration which will consume all the Profanity. Let it singe and burn; let it engulf all it hates in flames as its True abode, Hell, is engulfed. Let it express that unlimited hate and let all of Truth, Love and Justice witness the fate of Evil, and the fact that this hate of Evil's is hate for all things, including itself.

None who form the Beast - and this includes all the evil beings in human bodies, as well as all others who have chosen evil - will escape the process. Regardless of previous pretence, they will now show their true nature. They will exhibit the venom and hate of demons. Fear not; they are the Shadows of Darkness; chimeras of a soon-to-be dispelled illusion, a mocking parody of malevolence which has formed a false facade to hide the Truth from the trapped beings of Honesty.

Let it all happen and fear not, for it must happen. This spiritual cancer must be obliterated in order to restore spiritual health. Fear not the passing of the physical which was a trap for the True Souls from the very beginning. Rejoice instead at the success of the Corrective Process which promises an Evil-free state to Viables, for an eternity.

Finally, know that parts and projections of the Beast are to be found in every country, in every race, subscribing to every religion and belief on the globe. They are present, as the consciousnesses, in all sections of Humanity everywhere. They are in the Military, in Religious Orders, in Governments, in the Media, in teachers, labourers, housewives, doctors, lawyers, architects, children, etc., etc. In fact, parts and projections of the Beast are in the Mineral Kingdom, the Vegetable and Animal Kingdoms, as well as the Human, Devic, Galactic and Universal Kingdoms. And that is why aspects of these Kingdoms are manifesting the aggressive violence of the Beast Unleashed. That is why we see insanity in them. That is why all these aspects are fracturing and self-destructing.

****

Do not for one moment think that Evil is based solely in any one group of people or in just any one country.

Evil is an essence, created by Jehovah, the Grand Deceiver, the Usurper, the Demiurge, and is present in every facet of Humanity, regardless of genetic make-up and geography.

But, of course, in this evil system, in mockery to Honesty, in claiming all are equal in respect to ontological essence, some possess more of the Spirit of Devilry, depending on what portion of the Demonic Hierarchy they were created after the Celestial Error occurred.

So, each one of Evil has its degrees, none of which True Justice please. And that is why now each will in turn Erupt, to be judged, and in its demonism burn. Unfairly you think I explain this Blight? Not so, once you know removed has been the Light. And the few Warriors still on the plane are here by right To witness that all of Evil's schemes destructively ignite.

Only Time will force one and all to see what I write And what's here as described is in the future sight, And also that the End of the exploitative Night, Created by the Darkness, certainly not the Light, Is the work of Love and Justice, in Their right.

DEAD MEN TALKING

THE REALITY OF LOVE

LOVE CONQUERS ALL!!

Love is one of the Essences of the Divine Energy.

It is the Love of Truth, Justice and Peace, and the Love for fellow Theomorphs and viables which has allowed Rescuers to descend to this level, this abominable Hell, in order to rescue those who are worthy of rescue.

* It is Love which has empowered the Rescuers, and sustained them, as they battled the Forces of Darkness.

* It is Love which has allowed them to persist in the face of ridicule, derision and gross abuse.

* It is Love which allowed Jesus to suffer the humiliation of being spat upon, tortured and crucified, even as He showed nothing but Love and Compassion to those whom He had come to assist.

* It is True Divine Love which has allowed all Rescuers, even the less well-known ones, apart from Rama, Krishna, Moses, Zoroaster, Manichaeus, Mohammed, etc., to bear the brunt of the brutes, the dastardly acts of the beasts who were, and are, the progeny of Darkness.

* It is Love which has almost completed the evacuation and the Liberation from Darkness of those worthy to be rescued.

True Love has showered all living things with Its Essence. It has poured onto all segments of Consciousness in all Levels of Consciousness, as the Love of a True Mother would.

But alas, those of Darkness did not respond, and still do not respond, for they are incapable of responding to True Love, and that is the Crux of the Problem of Evil.

Evil does not respond to True Love.

56

DEAD MEN TALKING

Evil Beings - including evil humans, do not respond to True Love.

If they could respond, they would embraced Truth, Justice and Peace. But by nature, Evil is the very opposite. It stands for the Deceit of Untruth, for Injustice by which it can exploit others, and for bellicosity, friction, violence and war, without which it cannot entrap and exploit.

Make no mistake about it, it is True Love which has allowed this Clearing of the Planet that is now in progress, the Evacuation of Viable Consciousnesses, the Correction of this Celestial Error.

Those who have chosen Evil, and those who are of the Evil Essence and refused to change have remained in a space where they are unable to respond to True Love. And hence, they cannot grasp Truth, Justice and Peace. Is this not obvious as we examine the activities around the fragmenting planet carefully?

Think about this Essence of True Love. It is not the essence of Emotional Love which is a programming of these evil bodies by an evil mechanism. Emotional love is exploitation. It is hormonally induced in most circumstances. It is the love which allows a mother to accept its neonate for the purpose of suckling it. It is the force which allows copulation and propagation of species. Once its phase is finished, nothing remains. In fact, it can be replaced by the opposite essence on this evil plane - Hate! That could never be so with True Love.

Emotional Love is not true giving. It has a sucking gradient of taking, an expectation of selfish reward. No one shows emotional love without the expectation of a return, and of a selfish fulfilment of that expectation. All too often we see that when one in an emotional relationship refuses to give further, the relationship collapses, for the expectations of gain are no longer met in the other.

Emotional love is a vector of drainage; it sets up dissatisfaction, for it is accompanied by the fear of loss. It is irrational when allowed to grow excessively, for it becomes an obsession with phobic outlines, and it poisons the body so that often many have described it as a disease.

Allowed to fester, emotional love leads to selfishness, cupidity, paranoia and violence.

*   It is emotional love of one's country that allows programming of citizens to destroy others.

*   It is emotional love of one's religion which allows zealots to massacre in the name of their god, to pursue murderous Crusades and Inquisitions in order to satisfy the lust induced by that emotional love.

*   It is the unfaithfulness induced by emotional love and its lust which al-

lows the massive scars, and sometimes violence and anarchy which we all know so well in "matters of the heart", so-called.

* It is emotional love which spawns hate of that which does not fall in the shadow of that emotional love. Compare that with True Love which is universal, all embracing, non-directional, not expecting of a selfish reward, and you will see the differences.

These things could never occur with True Love.

Look at those who shared emotional love which has soured into the bitterness of all too common acrimony. What are they when the phase ends? In most cases are they not victims of ill-will towards that which they previously exploited under the illusions of emotional love? Would that ever occur with Real, True Love? "Never!" is the answer!

Sex may or may not come into the equation of emotional love. But sex, too, is a programming which ebbs and flows with the incitement of evil influences.

True Love dispels the ego, for with such Love one becomes part of all others who express it, whereas emotional love panders to the ego, and builds it up in defiance to all others, making the self more deserving in an evil-induced process of alienation to others.

Emotional love separates the majority, even as it claims it unites the objects of desire, and causes, not harmony and unity, but dissention.

Emotional love is the agent of self-aggrandisement, of separation, of ego-mania, of alienation from the all-encompassing Divine Energy. What else would one expect from an Evil-created mechanism?

So, having written all that, where do the spiritual and intellectual jerks stand when they claim my words and message are unloving?

They stand in the pit of despair, for my work shows clearly that it is True Love which has conquered Evil and set the Spirit of Viables free.

It is nothing but True Love, for Truth, Justice and eventual Godly Peace, which is allowing me, and all others in this rescue work, to stand up to the abuse and ridicule of the jerks until we have totally rescued those deserving of rescue.

And as clear proof that this is so, I cite the many thousands upon thousands whom I know personally who have been touched by the True Love of these words and message.

It is only those of Darkness, who cannot respond to the Essence of True Love, who see no love in these words and message. They are blind to Love. How then can they see it? It is their spiritual blindness which is at fault, not the words and message.

It is True Love which will set things right. It is the Light of True Love which banishes the Darkness.

Do not let the Sons and Daughters of Darkness bluff you out of this knowledge. They who say they can see no love here are for once telling the truth, for indeed, they are blind to the Essence of True Love, just as they are to all the Essences of the Divine Energy.

Hence, they do NOT share the other essences which include the Power of Truth, Honesty, Wisdom, Peace, Perseverance against adversity, and the Glory of an Evil-free Eternity!

*

DEAD MEN TALKING

DEAD MEN TALKING

THE SECRET BROTHERHOOD
AND THE MIND CONTROL AGENDA

THE BROTHERHOOD AND THE MANIPULATION OF SOCIETY

Ivan Fraser and Mark Beeston

Who controls the past, controls the future: who controls the present, controls the past

(from '1984') George Orwell

INTRODUCTION

From the moment our senses first register the presence of our parents we are being shown the way that life apparently is. Through no fault of ours or theirs, our parents begin the programming process as their views of life, shaped by their education, employment and the media are imposed on us. Formal education through schools, colleges and universities continues the systematic indoctrination where the 'correct' views and interpretations of science, history and society result in exam passes and the ability to 'get on' in life. Alternative views and the rejection of establishment education lead to supposedly lesser jobs and a struggle against economic poverty. Our entire understanding of the world and current affairs is filtered through the mass media, interpreted by journalists and so-called experts. Their views become our views simply because we are not offered any alternatives. To overcome daily problems within society we turn to elected representatives of our community. We give our decision-making abilities to these few people who are increasingly remote, as local council power is removed to national government and ever more to Europe.

Our experience of life is determined by the framework around our society. The basic premise is that the goal of each individual should be to become a minute part in the global machine of consumerism led by Western multinational corporations and banks. Every other consideration is subordinate to the prime motivation of profit. Obviously, those in the positions of influence – politicians, bankers, corporate executives, media moguls – have been, according to their own definition, 'successful' within the System, so have an interest in maintaining the status quo at all costs. This framework shapes every aspect of our life through education, the media, health care, cultural and sporting events, religion etc.

With these framing conditions in place, the System regulates itself: individuals with attitudes that suit the perpetuation of the System achieve status and influence within it; those who accept the establishment rules soon find ways to impose those rules; those who are blind to the exploitative realities of consumerism attain positions to promote it. Regardless of how the framework came to be imposed, the truth is that the same attitudes control education, media, governments and banks and therefore exert an irrepressible influence over every aspect of our lives, our thoughts and opinions.

The vast majority of the world's population are merely sheep happily following the herd. Whatever is broadcast in the media as being desirable to the masses suddenly and miraculously becomes desired by the masses. Whatever our neighbour owns or achieves becomes the object of great envy and we lust to acquire what we believe to be ours by right. Thus, when we are shown a solution to a problem, any old solution to anything which interferes with our need to follow the latest trends, we accept it without question and cease to seek any further for ourselves. Problems abound and so do solutions; but it is the easiest and most profitable proffered option which is seized by the majority whilst the minority are trampled underfoot in the stampede to acquire the latest object of idolatry. And just like sheep who follow blindly and without question the direction of the herd, we are led through the gates of a pen to be confined at the shepherds convenience until it is time for the final journey, once again without hesitation and happy in the knowledge that we are with the 'in-crowd', through the gates of the slaughterhouse

However, this framework has not been constructed by chance or appeared by accident. It is a deliberate policy which has been implemented over the centuries and continues with ever more sinister repercussions today. It is the identities of these shepherds, their methods and motivation with which the following chapter is concerned.

Since Biblical times, the esoteric knowledge, outlined briefly in this book, has been largely withheld from the majority of people throughout the world. Initially, this information was the remnant of Atlantean knowledge but was gradually dispersed and further diluted by cataclysmic events such as the Great Flood. Throughout the ages, lost information has been returned to the collective consciousness of mankind via prophets and channellers. Great Mystery Schools, such as the Essene order, set themselves apart in order to carry forward this knowledge via carefully selected initiates. These initiates were the mystics and magi as well as the scholars, healers and philosophers, such as Pythagoras, who, it is said, was very much influenced by the Druid culture.

Secrecy was maintained by these orders to avoid persecution and to prevent the very powerful information from falling into the hands of those who would use it for imbalanced reasons. Knowledge was concealed within myth and fable, often passed between generations by word of mouth alone, as in the case of the Celtic Druids. Any written documents were careful ciphered, with the keys to the code known only to selected initiates. Covens formed throughout the world and maintained secrecy through secret signals and codes which would reveal their meeting places. This practice persists today amongst secret orders such as occultists and Freemasons etc..

Eventually, a large number of sects, which were initially sub-divisions of essentially the same orders, began to lose sight of the original purity of their doctrines. Gradual misinterpretation of codes and myths as well as the uprising of egotistical desires caused many of the groups to become separated in their intent; some of these have developed into cult organisations and religions. Luciferic influence has seen to it that most dogmatic religion owes more to misunderstanding of basic truths than anything else. Differences are amplified and seen as more important to followers of such creeds than the common ties between them – all due to misinterpretation of the same fundamental knowledge. All of the world's major religions share a pagan origin but have gradually moved their sights further and further to the left of the centre where Truth inevitably lies.

Despite this, some of the purer mystery schools have survived through the ages in areas all over the world. The ancient Egyptian magicians, the ancient Greek philosophers, the Celtic Druids, American Indian shamen, Australian aboriginal shaman and oriental magicians have all possessed arcane knowledge pertaining to the true nature of Creation. Initiates were often revered as holy men by the laity and were spared the distractions of daily life in order to keep alive the flames of the inherent magic of life.

However, within certain of the more secretive societies, the Luciferic consciousness has managed to take hold with disastrous consequences for mankind.

For millennia, human history has been a chronicle of the power struggle of man against man and of man against nature. In his over-physical five-sense-perception state, that which man could acquire for himself as an individual has been the main motivating factor, often seen as essential for survival. Survival has been perceived as for the fittest, the most powerful, the wealthiest and this has perpetuated imbalance all the way to its most bitter conclusions which are war, bondage and persecution. Domination through conflict and might over meekness has seen aeons of feudalism and social hierarchy in the worst possible expressions.

To perpetuate their claim of deserved superiority over the masses, the rulers of the past have explored innumerable ways to achieve their goals, both subtle and violent. One method has been recognised as being the most effective and has been employed by the ruling aristocracy throughout the world since pre-history right up to the present day through governments, businesses and monarchies. That is, by keeping the masses in ignorance of their true potential and power; to keep them at a low level of education, preoccupying their minds away from who they truly are from birth; to manipulate them via a systematic education programme, in all areas of their existence, into channelling their lives in pursuit of handing over power to their rulers. If this can be done in such a way that the masses have no recourse and believe this condition to be the only way to live, then they will be highly unlikely to challenge the status quo.

The present System has been engineered throughout the ages by these imbalanced secret societies in order to perpetuate their wealth and power. It is they who designed the System and it is only they who know every individual link in the chains which have kept us in bondage for millennia. Today we have a global network of secret societies, initiates into the 'Mysteries', whose only motivation is to serve the Luciferic consciousness. How many times have we heard such phrases as 'It's the money men who really rule the world', but how many of us realise the accuracy of this sentiment and its full implications?

Armed with vast amounts of wealth and esoteric knowledge, the negative secret society network has flourished as the aristocracy of the world. Power, wealth and information has been gained and maintained via warfare, exploitation, and especially in the last century, through control of the world's economic systems. Collectively these organisations, led by the self-appointed global Elite, have become known as the 'Brotherhood'.

These days, initiation into the various secret societies which form the Brotherhood is relatively easy. Potential initiates are hand picked and invited to join certain exclusive clubs, such as the Freemasons and certain mutually beneficial business cartels which are merely Brotherhood front organisations. Candidates are tempted with the promise that, once accepted into the organisation, many personal advantages would be on offer: improved career prospects with promotion easier to achieve, more prosperous lifestyles and obstacles to success would be made to disappear. In other words this mutually beneficial 'old-boy network' would take care of its own.

The only way for the Brotherhood to prosper is to keep the world in ignorance of who they really are. By convincing people that they are little more than robots, they can use those robots to perpetuate their power base. Power always seeks power and will never stop until all power is focused solely in the hands of the most ambitious.

In the last century, with the acceleration in technological development, particularly in terms of communication, the Elite have sought to realise their ambitions more swiftly with more blatant and definable aims: the creation of a World Government; a world currency and bank; a world army; the control of public opinion culminating in a microchipped population connected to a central computer; the destruction of any alternatives to their System; and to make huge amounts of money in the process. This sinister plan by the Elite has become popularly known by researchers as the New World Order.

The situation within the hierarchy of the Elite is necessarily complex as the activities are concealed behind a large number of front organisations of varying degrees of secrecy. Everything is based upon the pyramid principle with the very few Elite at the apex as the All-Seeing-Eye and ultimate controllers right down to those at the bottom who, in the largest numbers, have no idea about the true agenda which is being ministered to them from above. Through the levels of initiation from the bottom to the top, only the most ambitious and ruthless are filtered out to occupy more and more select positions of power and knowledge of the ultimate agenda. This is further enforced at each step of the pyramid by the process of COMPARTMENTALISATION which is the operation of the 'need to know' principle; this way even those upon the same level of the pyramid know very little of their fellow initiate's business and role within the overall plan. The vast majority of people working to further the Elite's aims of a New World Order, do so unknowingly but others whose names constantly recur will have a pretty good idea of what is happening.

The USA was founded by the Elite for the very reason of executing the plan to control the world. It is this nation which is the hub of its wheel of influence. Christopher Columbus and his voyage was backed and financed by the Brotherhood, with his ships' sails bearing a red cross on a white background, the symbol of the Knights Templar (the chivalric order who went on to become the Freemasons etc., whose symbol is the red rose or cross upon a white background which represents blood and semen in Satanic ritual). Almost a century before Columbus, the Templars had reached North America and had already begun trading with and exploiting the native nations there. Since its 'discovery', the history of the USA has been the history of ethnic cleansing, imposition of power, slavery, mass exploitation and the worship of wealth. The U.S. president, generally accepted as the most powerful man in the world, is a slave to his prime allegiance, the Brotherhood. Even he is probably not a top-level member as it is wiser to hide behind the tools of corruption in anonymity and to pull the strings in this way.

I do not seek to condemn these people for their beliefs – everyone should be free to develop their own belief system – but I feel that they are seriously misguided in the ways they seek to impose them on the majority and conceal the truth. They have allowed themselves to become slaves to and also the major implementers the Luciferic consciousness which has taken this planet to the brink of destruction.

Presenting the information concisely is a difficult operation due to the complexity of the interconnections between people, organisations and events. I have attempted to simplify the situation into a manageable amount but it remains merely the tip of the iceberg. It should be remembered also that nothing is black and white, no one is 'good' or 'evil' – such simple distinctions are part of the manipulation which encourages us to judge our neighbours in order to create conflict.

THE MAIN MANIPULATING GROUPS

Freemasonry

The basic recruitment of members to further the Elite's plans is through the secret society network of Freemasonry which is the latest incarnation of the Christian/military order known as the Knights Templars who gained staggering riches and a wealth of esoteric knowledge during the Crusades, in which the 'righteous' Christians were dispatched to the Holy Land with free reign to slaughter the Jews and Moslems in a series of campaigns between the 11th and 13th Centuries.

The vast majority of members are on the first three rungs of the thirty-three level hierarchy and have no idea of the hidden agenda.

Once initiated into the lowest level – the first of thirty three degrees – vows are taken to pledge allegiance to the society above all else. Most initiates are willing to do this as the temptation of power, wealth and knowledge is hard to refuse. It is hinted that there are penalties to pay for betraying their society and revealing its secrets but at this level the organisation is viewed by its members as little more than a secretive social club with a morality based upon chivalry. Certain of what appear to be esoteric secrets are revealed to them upon initiation as a 'taster' for what is to come as long as the initiate remains faithful to the order. Money is then paid by the initiate in order to progress to the second degree through a ceremony involving the revelation of yet further secret knowledge with the promise of more to come at each stage.

Initiation into higher degrees requires increasingly larger sums of money and still the clues keep coming; promises of wonderful arcane knowledge are continual yet the actual knowledge revealed remains encoded and only serves to whet the appetite. No one is ever given the full scenario, only pieces of what appears to be a picture of the most awesome significance. As more and more is revealed and the higher up the ladder the initiate is allowed, the greater are the personal perks provided and doorways opened in terms of career and social status. Moreover, the warnings against transgression of the secret society's rules become blatant and more sinister at each step.

It is impossible to achieve high levels of initiation within Freemasonry unless one is hand picked by those of the higher degrees. In order to do this, one must meet their criteria of wealth, status, social class and character type. By the time the twentieth degree is reached a minimum of professional level income is required to fund progression through the system. The result of this financially dependent progression is that the top level members of the Brotherhood elite are among the richest, and most powerfully influential people in the world. They are also responsible, directly and indirectly for most of the money/power based crime such as the illegal drugs industry, political assassinations, Satanism and mind control which goes on every day, all round the world.

At the apex of the pyramid of the Brotherhood are the select few who actually know the full agenda of the organisation. These privileged elite have become known as the 'Illuminati', which is Latin for 'illuminated ones'. All other members (nearly five million world-wide) are ignorant of the true purpose of their individual organisation as a front for the Illuminati. Only the most suitable are selected to rise in the ranks, those recognised as being wealthy, ambitious and corrupt enough to perpetuate the ultimate goal which is world domination. No one but the Illuminati actually knows anything of importance and therefore cannot betray the game plan. Everyone else provides a front, a smoke screen of ignorance and misinformation and all must offer complete obedience to the will of their organisation or be banished (or worse). The same thing also happens in our universities whereby particularly talented scholars are approached with magnificent offers of wealth and status in order to follow unofficial secret research programs into such topics as UFOs, psychic warfare and advanced energy sources.

Betrayal of the Brotherhood is the worst crime possible in the eyes of its members and is ultimately punishable by death. The Brotherhood is all powerful: all top level members of the police and military forces around the world are placed there through the Brotherhood as Brotherhood tools. Judges and lawyers, media moguls, businessmen and politicians are recruited so that no member of the Brotherhood elite is ever in danger of being held accountable by the System for any crime or misdemeanour. The Brotherhood can, and quite literally does, get away with murder because it is also the law which opposes it. If a non-Brotherhood member should slip through the net and achieve high status then there are ways to ensure that such people are unable to achieve their full potential. For example,

DEAD MEN TALKING

I doubt if Prince Charles will ever fulfil his right of kingship as he has publicly refused to enrol with the Freemasons. It infiltrates every area of our society at all levels, but at the top, in the highest social and monetary bracket, the Brotherhood prevails almost in total. It is the single largest vehicle for the perpetuation of the Luciferic consciousness on Earth.

One of the ways by which the faithfulness of members is ensured, especially in the higher levels is by the insistence that the initiated give details of their most intimate secrets to the organisation, so that if any transgression of the rules were to occur then this information would be revealed and used to publicly destroy the individual concerned. As an example of this, one Masonic branch, the Skull and Bones Society, centred around the Harvard and Yale universities, was founded on opium money, is blatantly racist, has some particularly bizarre rituals including an initiation which includes lying in a coffin with a ribbon tied around the genitalia whilst masturbating and shouting out one's greatest sexual fantasies. It boasts amongst its members (who, remember, swear complete allegiance to the society above all other commitments) George Bush, Percy Rockefeller, Winston Lord (one time CFR chairman) and nine members of the board of the Morgan Guaranty Trust (see House of Rothschild).

Also associated with Freemasonry within the Elite's own hierarchy are other esoteric societies such as the Grand Orient Lodges, the Knights of Malta, the Knights Templar, P2 and the Black Nobility.

The Brotherhood owns the law, they own the military, they own the oil companies, pharmaceutical companies and just about everything which provides fuel for the status quo. It sets the standards for education, it sets the curriculum, it plants seeds via the media and education systems of what will later become, through tender nurturing, power hungry, dis-satisfied, spiritually unaware slaves to their System. If it was not so sinister it would be purely perfect in its all encompassing design.

While the first three degree Masons and Round Table members are raising money for charity and enjoying relatively harmless social events, their superiors in the Craft are organising wars, drug pushing, co-ordinating assassinations, mind-control, raping and murdering young children in Satanic abuse and formulating plans for world domination.

History has convinced me that it is possible to get away with virtually any crime as long as it is on a large enough scale.

The U.S. presidents, also thirty-third degree Masons, are financed into the position not as leaders of men but as a tool of the Brotherhood. All allegiance come secondary to the bonds within their secret society, on pain of death. Political systems are also a front for the Brotherhood elite. Not as representatives of the people, elected by the people, for the people, but as tools of and for the Brotherhood. Science is controlled to the benefit of the elite, wars are created and manipulated to the benefit of the elite. Every time a bomb is dropped or a tank built, ultimately it is the multi-national businesses who profit, especially the oil industries and world bankers. All is Brotherhood controlled. The scale of the manipulation in all areas of the status quo is almost immeasurable and for this reason virtually unbelievable to most prisoners of the System.

The Round Table

The Round Table was established in the 1891 as a Masonic-like secret society to manipulate events to lead to a centralised global government. The leading lights were Cecil Rhodes, whose wealth largely derived from the exploitation of South African diamond reserves, and Alfred Milner, a Rothschild agent who took over after the death of Rhodes. Financial backing also came from the Rockefellers. Groups were established throughout the world, working behind the scenes through a co-ordination of world banks in order to bring pressure on governments to promote the New World Order.

As well as Milner, who effectively controlled Lloyd George's War Cabinet during the Great War, members in the first half of this century included Arthur Balfour (then Foreign Secretary, later Prime Minister and whose Balfour Declaration created the State of Israel); Lord Astor who owned The Times; and Nathan Rothschild, Governor of the Bank of England. After WW1, the Round Table was instrumental in the formation of the League Of Nations, the forerunner of the Elite-controlled United Nations.

Rhodes' legacy includes a bequeathal of funds for the financial sponsorship of selected overseas students who attend Oxford University to be sold the New World Order. These 'Rhodes Scholars' include Bill Clinton.

The influence of the Round Table and that of the various groups it has spawned is prevalent today, although the majority of members will have no idea of what they are involved in.

Royal Institute of International Affairs (RIIA)

One of the more public Round Table creations is the Royal Institute of International Affairs which is based at Chatham House in London and was formed in 1920 by the Anglo/American delegations from the Treaty of Versailles meetings. Prominent in the British delegation was Alfred Milner. The RIIA's patron is the Queen of England.

Supposedly, the RIIA is a 'think tank' but in effect it determines British policy.

DEAD MEN TALKING

And yet, its membership list is never divulged and it is shrouded in secrecy. Information that has been obtained reveals that its current joint presidents are Lord Carrington (former Foreign Secretary, director-general of NATO and close business partner of Henry Kissinger), Lord James Callaghan (former Foreign Secretary and Prime Minister) and Lord Roy Jenkins (former Chancellor of the Exchequer and president of the European Commission).

Funding is derived from its corporate members which is a vast list including government departments, petrochemical companies (who also fund its Environment Programme!), merchant and high street banks, newspapers, television stations, the Church of England, Amnesty International ...etc..

Council on Foreign Relations (CFR)

In 1921, funded by the Rockefellers, the RIIA founded its American wing – known as the Council on Foreign Relations. As its membership is marginally more public than its British counterpart it is clearly seen that anyone who has had any influence on American or global politics ever since has been a member of the CFR. This includes 14 of the last 18 US Secretaries of State; the previous eight CIA directors; the majority of presidential and vice-presidential candidates including Eisenhower, Nixon, Carter, Mondale, Ford, Nelson Rockefeller, Bush and Clinton.

The Bilderberg Group (Bil)

This was convened for the first time in May 1954 by Polish socialist Joseph Retinger, a major voice behind the European Union. Also instrumental in its creation was Prince Bernhard of the House of Orange in the Netherlands (former German SS officer an spy via chemical company I.G. Farben and who later became chairman of Shell Oil). It was to be a group of leading politicians and their advisors, executives from media, banking and multinational corporations, educationalists and military leaders who would meet to discuss the global future by addressing matters of critical importance in an off-the-record manner so that the distractions of politics could be kept out of the way.. The group has since met annually in strict secrecy and despite the considerable high level media representation in the group the meetings are never reported.

Leading the group is an unelected steering committee, the chairman of which since 1991 has been Lord Carrington. Members outside this committee probably do not know the agenda towards which the group is working and are merely invited to be sold the public face of the New World Order for them to expound its virtues in their areas of influence.

The Trilateral Commission (TC)

Also known as the 'Child of Bilderberg', this group was founded by David

DEAD MEN TALKING

Rockefeller in 1972-73 to covertly unify the policies of the US, Europe and Japan. Jimmy Carter's presidency was their first major coup with the president and many members of his administration being Trilateralists, including Zbigniew Brzezinski, his national security advisor and the first director of the Trilateral Commission.

THE MAIN PROTAGONISTS

House of Rothschild

The Rothschild empire was founded by Mayer Amschel Bauer (born 1743 in Frankfurt) with money embezzled from a German prince, William IX, who had in turn stolen the money from soldiers he was supplying to the British in the American War of Independence.

Nathan, the son of Bauer (now Rothschild), set up the London branch and established the banking interest, N.M. Rothschild and Sons, which also had branches in Paris, Vienna, Berlin and Naples. Control passed through Nathan's son Lionel to Nathan Mayer Rothschild who became Governor of the Bank of England, was awarded a peerage in 1885 and was a member of the Round Table. At this time (1886-87) Randolph Churchill (Winston's father) was Chancellor of the Exchequer, funded by the Rothschilds and a close friend of Nathaniel Rothschild.

Other notable family members include:

* Lord Victor Rothschild, the alleged '5th man' in the KGB spy ring, who was in charge of the 'Regulation 18b' prosecutions under Winston Churchill whereby a person could by arrested and imprisoned merely 'on suspicion'. He was head of Edward Heath's policy unit (1970-74) and allegedly head of an unnamed subversive organisation designed to manipulate the introduction of a Federal Europe. He was also once a governor of the BBC. * Baron Edmund de Rothschild was instrumental in the 'debt for equity' schemes whereby Third World countries gave up 'environmentally sensitive' land as a payment for debts. * Evelyn de Rothschild is the current chairman of N.M. Rothschild and is a member of the board of the Daily Telegraph, owned by the Hollinger Group.

Associated Companies/Families

Since the late 1800s, business interests in America have been largely represented by Kuhn, Loeb and Co and controlling interests are often concealed by companies with 'City' or 'First City' in their names e.g. First City Financial Corporation of Vancouver, First City Development Ltd.

The operation is largely co-ordinated through Rothschild Inc (New York) and PowerCorp, a Canadian company with strong links to the Hollinger Group.

The Rothschilds are allegedly behind the Morgan Empire which derives from the London based George Peabody and Co which became J.S. Morgan and Co in 1864 on the death of Peabody (a Rothschild agent). Control passed to J.S. Morgan's son, John Pierpont Morgan, and the company acquired its present name of J.P. Morgan. The Morgan Empire now includes General Electric and all its subsidiaries, Morgan Guaranty Trust, National Bank of Commerce...etc..

The House of Rothschild also has strong connections with the Warburg banking family which includes Paul and Felix, who were instrumental in the setting up of the US Federal Reserve System, and their brother Max who ran the German interests.

Rockefeller Empire

The Rockefeller Empire is based on oil, largely the Standard Oil company set up by John D. Rockefeller in 1853. (Part of this is now more familiar as Exxon and Esso.) Its influence on the political arena has been fairly open and obvious.

J.D. Rockefeller III set up the Population Council in 1952 which, ever since, has been advocating zero population growth in the US. In 1972 this sentiment was echoed by Lawrence Rockefeller (CFR, Bil, TC) who was appointed by Nixon to lead a commission into population growth.

When Ford became president as a result of Nixon's resignation in the aftermath of Watergate, Nelson Aldrich Rockefeller became vice-president (1974-77). A member of the CFR, he had formerly been part of the US delegation at the creation of the UN.

A key family member is David Rockefeller who is head of the Chase Manhattan Bank, was chairman of the CFR (1946-53), is an omnipresent Bilderberger and creator of the Trilateral Commission.

Percy Rockefeller is on the board of the Morgan Guaranty Trust and a member of the Skull and Bones Society.

The Rockefellers donated money for the construction of the League of Nations headquarters in Geneva and donated the land in New York on which the UN headquarters are built.

Associated Companies/Families

The companies in which the Rockefellers have a controlling interest include Chase Manhattan Bank, Standard Oil (Esso/Exxon), National City Bank, Hannover National Bank, United States Trust Company, Equitable Life and Mutual of New York.

Cousins of the Rockefellers are the Dulles brothers who were appointed to the US State Department during World War I, participated in the Treaty of Versailles meetings, became part of the RIIA/CFR network and had connections throughout US, English and German banking. John Foster Dulles, very much in favour of a 'super race' and a prominent supporter of Hitler, became Secretary of State at the same time as his brother Allen was head of the CIA.

Dr Henry Kissinger

A member of the Council on Foreign Relations, Trilateral Commission, leading Bilderberger and head of Kissinger Associates (with Lord Carrington), Henry Kissinger is also connected with the RIIA, the Chase Manhattan Bank, the Rockefeller Foundation and is international advisor to the Hollinger Group. His public offices include being Head of the State Department and National Security Council under Nixon (1969). Kissinger was the leading international diplomat in the events that precipitated the Vietnam conflict and the Yom Kippur war between Egypt/Syria and Israel and yet was awarded the Nobel Peace Prize in 1973. He is also a member of the Alpine Freemasons Lodge in Switzerland and was (is?) possibly a leading figure in P2.

ECONOMIC CONTROL

Moves towards the New Word Order have been aided by the development of the current banking and economic system. As I have said before, it does not take a leap in imagination to realise that, at present, those who own the money in the world, control the world. And this is exactly how the Brotherhood has achieved its extensive influence.

During the middle ages, when wealth was measured in riches, property and treasure – in gold especially – the Brotherhood, mainly in the guise of the Templars, managed to set themselves up as high level money lenders and repositories for wealth of the rich. Over time a system was devised whereby IOU tokens were supplied which represented the gold in store, instead of moving the cumbersome treasure itself. It was realised that vast sums could be made by the Brotherhood by lending out – in the form of paper representations of wealth – more than they actually had and charging interest on this wealth which did not exist. The returns were real wealth and gold as interest on worthless paper. Eventually, the world's gold reserves fell into the hands of the Brotherhood who initiated a now world recognised system of paper bartering which merely represented the wealth which lay in the vaults of these mega-wealthy few. Thus was created the system which rules the world today – known now as a respectable business it is the system called banking.

Since Babylonian times usury – the lending of wealth at interest – has been one of the main causes of war and empire building. Nations such as Persia and Rome became great due to their massive debts incurred by lending money from wealthy nations. Later, unable to return the wealth, but rich and with great armies funded by this borrowed wealth, they soon realised a need to conquer these lending nations in order to nullify their debts. This was also the reason for the introduction of taxes, a global system which is in use right up to today.

The charging of interest inflates the prices of goods as a large percentage of an item's cost is spent in servicing the debts of the suppliers/ manufacturers/ distributors etc. The greater the debt, the higher the price. Banks use this high 'rate of inflation' to justify raising interest rates in order to discourage borrowing. This serves to create more debt on the existing loans and further reduce the amount of money in circulation. Economic depressions and booms are simply created by the banking institutions at will, by controlling the amount of money and credit in circulation.

Banks extend their influence to every aspect of life by manipulating the stock markets to gain controlling interests in multinational companies. For example, a company seeking expansion is refused a loan by a bank. The value of the shares fall, the bank buys them before changing its mind and granting the loan.

In order for a nation to prosper on a global economic basis it must borrow from private money lenders other people's money and money which does not exist in real terms, to pay for the implementation of its policies and then take real wealth back out of the nation's hands, plus interest, in order to pay back the debt. At the same time people are borrowing from the same banks to pay their taxes, their mortgages (other money lent at interest!) and to maintain the lifestyle they feel they deserve. This means that the banks can never lose. All wealth in circulation around the world, in effect, either belongs to them, is owed to them or will eventually be dragged into their vaults via the banking system. In 1993 the UK paid £24.5 billion in interest, more than twice that in the education budget!

And yet, there is nothing to stop governments from printing their own money and lending it interest free. Abraham Lincoln did so – just before he was murdered by John Wilkes Booth (allegedly a Rothschild agent) and J.F. Kennedy had proposed to revive government printed money just before he too was removed in the same way.

The Elite-controlled banking system is partly co-ordinated through the Bank of International Settlements in Switzerland and handled in individual countries by the national central banks which are either private banks (e.g. US Federal Reserve) or privately controlled banks under a facade of nationalisation.

In England, the national bank was established in 1694 by the new King William of Orange, manoeuvred into place by the Orange Order which is directly controlled by the Black Nobility. It was a private venture under the House of Rothschild which has maintained its influence since nationalisation.

The US Federal Reserve System was manipulated into place by the Elite bankers in 1910 through the efforts of Paul and Felix Warburg and Colonel House. The imposition of a Federal Income Tax required an amendment to the 16th constitution and therefore needed the agreement of 36 states. It was never actually ratified as only two states agreed but Congress was lied to and the bill was passed as 'law'.

In 1985 the fact that all US Federal Tax collection has been illegal was acknowledged when a court granted a total refund to a businessman on this basis. As a letter from the Commissioner of the Internal Revenue Service to his regional directors says:

'… every tax paid into the Treasury since 1913, is due and refundable to every citizen and business'. However, he advised that 'we will not publish or advertise this finding' and 'you are to destroy this memorandum'.

Today we see the British government asset stripping in virtually every area of our society and promising great improvements in standards of living and health care whilst standards continue to fall and we wonder where all of the money is going to. The answer is simple, they are not selling the nation's assets to release money for the nation's good, they are taking it to pay the national debt.

And why, in a world so rich in resources, are there people dying in their millions in second and third world countries through war and starvation? Again, it is because these private companies, the banks, would rather keep these nations in debt to the tune of billions of pounds than allow them the chance of developing their own societies to a healthy level. At present these nations need to borrow money to produce goods to sell to other nations in order to raise the money to pay back the banks at interest whilst their people starve and die. Many researchers have come to the conclusion with which I agree, that this is a deliberate policy of the Illuminati; to destroy the poorer nations through famine, disease and manipulated war in order to take total control of their lands which are often rich in mineral wealth. The penalty for not being able to pay debts is the loss of property and land, whether through an inability to pay one's mortgage or an inability to pay one's national debt.

In reality, very few people are almost entirely responsible for the vast majority of negativity and suffering in the world. It is an ingenious system which has us all at its mercy. The great god 'Banking', together with its spin off deities of 'Economic Growth' and 'Gross Domestic Product', has seen to it that the majority of the world's nations are drowning in an ocean of debt whilst the minority elite are floating on staggering amounts of wealth. It makes little secret of its origins either: the symbol of the Illuminati for the Brotherhood, the 'All Seeing Eye' which sits inside a triangle/pyramid, is the symbol which adorns the U.S dollar bill.

Whilst the world is controlled by the economics of banks and whilst survival depends upon lending money at interest, there will always be rulers and the ruled and a need for war. This is because there will always be vastly more money in circulation than there is actual wealth to back it up; and when the borrowers run out of money to pay their lenders they have merely two choices: to become enslaved to their debtors or to conquer them. It is for this reason that the bankers must maintain their position of ownership over the military, law, oil, pharmaceuticals, media and education etc..

In order to maintain this position of absolute power, the world's borrowers must be kept in ignorance of the truth of the situation which is that they are little more than slaves to their lenders. True history, which is the story of billions of individuals, including their manipulation, must not be taught. Indeed, it most certainly is not. The history books are full of kings and queens, 'goodies' and 'badies', wars and conquered nations, when they should more accurately be described as the chronicles of greed and wealth. For the System to survive it must also suppress true science, true history and the full exploration of spirituality.

Steps towards a Global Bank

The World Bank This lends money to finance projects in the Third World to meet the needs of the multinationals. By financing projects which are totally irrelevant to the needs of the local people; the local economy is destroyed and rainforests are decimated. This conveniently adds to the environmental 'problem' (see later).

Bill Clinton nominated the current president of the World Bank – James Wolfensohn from the Schroder Bank, Population Council, Bilderberg Steering Committee, CFR and business partner of the Rothschilds.

International Monetary Fund (IMF) When poor countries get into Elite-engineered financial trouble, the IMF intervenes to offer more loans (thereby increasing the debt) on the condition that the Elite's policies are followed e.g. giving up land, which should be used to grow crops to feed the country's population, to produce luxury cash crops instead, which are exported at cut down prices to the multinationals.

Free Trade Agreements such as GATT, NAFTA and APEC are promoted as 'good' things, showing close co-operation between the peoples of the world. In fact, 'free' trade serves to make all countries reliant on global consumerism dominated by the multinationals. With no tariff on imported goods there is no financial protection for home production, so Third World countries become dependent on imported goods. Land and people in the developing world are therefore open to exploitation by global companies, and industries in the developed countries can be undermined at will.

European Monetary Union The most obvious stepping stone to a global bank and currency is the move by the European Union towards a centralised bank and single currency. Despite the apparent debate, this has already been decided upon with the UK's supposed opt-out clause in the Maastricht Treaty being over-ruled by another.

Also in the Maastricht Treaty are details of the control of the European currency and the reserves of each member state by six members of the Executive Board of the European Central Bank who, through their eight years of guaranteed security of tenure, 'may not seek or take instructions from Community institutions...or any other body'.

Control of Food One of the more unbelievable examples of corporate exploitation of particularly the Third World is the systematic destruction of natural agricultural seeds, replacing them with patented genetically engineered ones. According to UN estimates, 75% of genetic diversity in agricultural crops has been lost this century and in England, 1500 'unapproved' seed varieties have been withdrawn. The situation now is that, instead of using native seed varieties, Third World countries must pay royalties to the multinational companies for genetically engineered seeds, which have been distributed and chemically produced by the same corporations, and which are useless in a Third World environment. As a result the same people control the actual food that we can eat – 90% of all food trade is in the hands of five multinationals: 50% are controlled by Unilever (who's chairman, Paul Rykens was at the heart of the formation of the Bilderberg Group) and Nestlé alone.

POLITICAL CONTROL

Underpinning the Elite's control of the political systems throughout the world is the philosophy of 'divide and rule'. This manifests in many ways on different scales, e.g. the Cold War between Eastern communism and Western capitalism; managed conflicts in the oil rich Middle East (aided by the creation of Israel after World War I); the illusion of choice in apparent democracies. To achieve this, the same organisations finance and covertly encourage sides that are portrayed as being opposites.

Wars are used to abruptly change political systems, so are seldom fought for the simplistic 'good versus evil' reasons declared publicly. Instead, they are deliberately engineered to further the progress to the New World Order. After all, as decided by the Carnegie Endowment for International Peace (one of the tax-exempt foundations established by the Carnegie, Rockefeller and Ford families) wars are the 'most effective way to alter the lives of an entire people'. They also make vast amounts of money for the armaments companies and the banks who lend money to governments.

Such control has been going on for centuries through the Knights Templars who could 'make kings', the manoeuvring of particular Royal Houses into power throughout Europe in the 15th-17th centuries, the French Revolution, the American War of Independence etc.. In this century the manipulation is demonstrable but, because it is clandestine and apparently contradictory, the situation is very complex. However, a brief look at the events from the First World War onwards reveals the true motivation behind major events and the organisations/people behind them.

Behind the First World War/Russian Revolution

In 1914 the Austrian Archduke Ferdinand, who had received death threats from Freemasons, was killed (at the second attempt) by a Serbian secret society. This was used as an excuse for Austria, backed by Germany, to declare war on Serbia, backed by Russia and France. Rasputin (the peasant mystic who gained favour and thereby actual political power in the house of Nicolas II because of his apparent ability to heal the crown prince Alexis' haemophilia), who effectively ran the administration in Russia, could have averted the war but was temporarily removed by an assassination attempt which occurred at almost exactly the same time as the murder in Serbia.

In Germany, Kaiser Wilhelm's Chancellor was Bethman-Hollweg, a cousin of the Rothschilds and his personal banker was Max Warburg. The German newsagency, Wolff, was owned by the Rothschilds who also had a controlling interest in Havas and Reuters, the French and British newsagencies. Britain entered the war against Germany and America did likewise in 1917, as was always planned; the ostensible reason of the sinking of the (arms carrying) Lusitania (which knowingly sailed into German patrolled waters) was merely a publicity stunt to 'outrage' the American people and so give them the impression that they had entered the war through choice. The Carnegie Endowment for International Peace which, despite its name, had manipulated America into the war, consequently telegraphed the US President Woodrow Wilson requesting that he 'see that the war did not end too quickly'.

To remove Russia from the war, Germany openly supported the Russian Revolution by funding Bolshevik propaganda and safeguarding Lenin's passage through Germany. However, it was also co-ordinated by the Rockefellers and Rothschilds (via Kuhn, Loeb and Co) who funded both Trotsky and the anti-Bolshevik reaction in America. Trotsky himself was most probably a German who left the US in 1917 on a passport arranged by President Wilson. Final details were arranged in a 24 man Red Cross mission to Russia in 1917 – a 'medical' mission in which only seven were doctors, the others being leading financiers including William Boyce Thompson, head of the Federal Reserve Bank of New York. With the Bolsheviks successfully installed, media opposition in Britain and America was suppressed and agents dispatched to control diplomatic and intelligence reports.

After the war, the treaty negotiations were held at Versailles, hosted by Baron Edmund de Rothschild. Accompanying Lloyd George was Alfred Milner and the US delegation with Wilson included Colonel House, Max and Paul Warburg, the Dulles brothers and Thomas Lamont of J.P. Morgan. The Treaty of Versailles served three main purposes: it spawned the League of Nations which was the first attempt at world government drafted by House with its Genevan headquarters built with Rockefeller money; it confirmed the State of Israel creating instability in the Middle East; and it created the financial situation to lead inevitably to a second war through which the New World Order could consolidate its position. This was achieved through setting German reparations at a level to cripple the new German republic and by returning all economies to a gold standard which affected all the European countries who were already in serious debt to the American banks, especially to J.P. Morgan.

The Second World War

Through the 1920s and '30s, loans from Wall Street financed German rearmament and the rise of Hitler. One German company which benefited substantially from these loans was I.G. Farben which by 1939 had become the biggest chemical manufacturer in the world, and enabled Germany to become self-sufficient in rubber, petrol, oil and explosives. (This company used the inmates of Auschwitz as slave labour at their massive chemical plant during the war and are estimated to have worked at least 25,000 inmates to death; others were killed in their drug testing program. In the Nuremberg Trials after the war twelve of I.G. Farben/Germany's top executives were sentenced to minor terms of imprisonment for slavery and mistreatment offences whilst many others were acquitted. None of the Americans who also sat on the same board as the convicted were ever tried as a war criminal). On the supervising board of I.G. Farben was Max Warburg and on the board of American I.G. Farben were US and German bankers, friends of Roosevelt and members of Nazi intelligence. Rockefeller's Standard Oil assisted I.G. Farben's programme of research into making oil from coal (which Germany had a plentiful supply of). I.G. Farben were Hitler's major financial backers along with US money channelled through the German subsidiaries of General Electric Company (GEC), International Telephone and Telegraph (ITT) and Ford.

Having supplied the loans to rearm Germany, repayment was demanded in cash causing the German economy to crash, ensuring Hitler could seize power with popular support of his economic solution. In the same year, 1933, Franklin Roosevelt took the American Presidency in a remarkably similar situation, offering a 'New Deal' type solution in the wake of serious economic depression. Both Hitler and Roosevelt were advised by people connected with the American-German cartels and the Bank of International Settlements.

Meanwhile, Britain had adopted a policy of appeasing Germany. This was promoted by the PM Neville Chamberlain as advised by Round Table members such as Lord Halifax, Lord Lothian, Leopold Amery and the Astors (who owned The Times). In order to be self-sufficient through a lengthy war, Hitler's Germany needed the resources of Czechoslovakia, so the British government continued promoting appeasement until Austria and then Czechoslovakia were taken in 1939. The Bank of England then relinquished the £6 million of Czech gold deposited in London to the conquering Nazis. The erstwhile appeasers (Milner, Lothian, Astor and Amery) turned on Chamberlain and on the ensuing wave of pro-war opinion Churchill swept to power. There is evidence to suggest that before Churchill became Prime Minister coded messages passed between him and Roosevelt which confirm that the war was a premeditated set-up. On taking office Churchill immediately appointed Victor Rothschild to implement 'Regulation 18b' to imprison, without trial, anyone suspected of opposing the war.

Thus, the protagonists were in place – Roosevelt, otherwise known as the Knight of Pythias, a 33rd degree mason and member of the Ancient Arabic Order of Nobles of the Mystic Shrine; Churchill, a freemason who had several meetings with the esoteric guru Aleister Crowley; and Hitler who, with Himmler, Goering and Hess, were steeped in the esoteric traditions of groups such as the Thule Society, the Vril Society and the Edelweiss Society, all of which preached anti-Semitism and a Master Race. Occult symbolism and ritual pervaded Nazi Germany from the swastika to the Nuremberg rallies and the organisation of the SS.

World War II was fought to the game plan laid down by the Elite. Despite Roosevelt's assurances to the contrary, American entry into the war was a foregone conclusion and was engineered by the Council on Foreign Relations who advised that the US adopt an anti-Japanese stance in the China-Japanese war, including a trade embargo and refusal of entry into the Panama Canal. Roosevelt knew Pearl Harbour was to be bombed from eight independent intelligence sources and 'fortunately' the cream of the US navy was not in the harbour on the day of the bombing. The invasion of Britain by Germany was not part of the plan so, despite having the ideal opportunity after Dunkirk, Hitler did not cross the channel. However, the Elite's script required the creation of an apparent east/west divide, so as the Allies swept victoriously into Germany, they allowed the Soviet Union to extend to and divide Berlin.

DEAD MEN TALKING

During the war, the American-German cartels made fantastic amounts of money. Their German factories were left amazingly unscathed amidst the bomb devastation, and after the war the same people were appointed by Roosevelt to supervise the fate of German industry. These decided that German industry could only continue if the German people accepted full responsibility for Nazism, thus diverting public scrutiny away from the truth.

At the farcical Nuremberg Trials only insignificant German directors of the cartels were tried and few found guilty. Elsewhere at the trials defendants were barbarically tortured and, due to a change made by a professor at the Carnegie Endowment for International Peace in April 1944, 'following orders' was not an admissible defence. The major Nazi leaders were probably smuggled out of Germany to South America and the scientists responsible for their advanced rocket and mind-control technology were re-situated in prestigious posts in major colleges, universities and NASA in the US. This relocation and infiltration spanned forty years and was known as Operation Paperclip. These scientists are still in positions of influence and are involved in covert high-tech mind-control experiments for the Central Intelligence Agency (CIA) and Defence Intelligence Agency (DIA) which are under National Security Agency (NSA) known as Operation MK-Ultra (see Who We Are – Mind Manipulation).

The outcome of this was just as planned by the Elite with the public crying out for any means to prevent future wars. Many of the solutions offered by politicians have been moves towards global government and the centralisation of power.

The United Nations

This was created to solve future disputes by words, not war, but was in fact one of the main reasons that the Second World War was fashioned. The UN had been created by the Council on Foreign Relations as early as 1941, four years before its official foundation by representatives of more than 50 countries. The US delegation to the founding meeting in San Francisco, June 1945, included 74 members of the CFR.

The majority of people working for the UN are genuinely seeking to bring peace to the world. However, it is one of the main vehicles for world government and world army and all six UN Secretary Generals have promoted New World Order type attitudes.

More and more areas of our lives are being globalised through UN organisations under different excuses for international jurisdiction—the World Health Organisation, UN Population Fund, UN Environment Programme, UNESCO (for education, science and culture).

DEAD MEN TALKING

European Union

The three trading blocks of Europe, the Americas and Asia-Australasia are the stepping stones through which government is being centralised before global control.

NAFTA (North Atlantic Free Trade Agreement), which has recently been extended, and APEC (Asia-Pacific Economic Co-operation) look set to follow the example of Europe which is developing from a trade co-operative to a United States of Europe.

The European Economic Community (EEC) was largely the brain-child of Jean Monnet and Joseph Retinger (a founder of the Bilderberg group). It was funded by loans devised by Monnet and the CFR and was formally created in 1957 by the Treaty of Rome, drafted by Monnet and the CFR. If any country showed a reluctance to join, the US pro-Europe position was made very clear to the 'offending' country.

The EEC has since become the European Community and now the European Union. Monetary union has been confirmed by the Maastricht treaty and the situation moves ever closer to a Federal Europe. In 1980, the EC drew up a map of regions within a proposed Federal Europe. England did not feature as an administrative unit and the regions defined in the former Yugoslavia are those which have since been created by the recent war. The public have always been kept in the dark about the extent of the union, with Prime Ministers Heath, Wilson and Callaghan all accepting the renunciation of sovereignty and incorporation into a Federal Europe. Margaret Thatcher served her economic purpose with Reagan in the 1980s but her resistance to European Union ensured her downfall in 1990. Her demise was decided upon by the 1989 meeting of the Bilderberg group.

In the June 1995, Bilderberg meeting, attended by Norman Lamont and William Waldegrave, John Major was threatened with a similar fate if he didn't back a Federal Europe. The leadership challenge by John Redwood, supported by Lamont, was based on their alleged opposition to Federalisation. Major conveniently won and purged his Cabinet of anti-federalists.

The Illusion of Democracy

Centralisation of power would not be accepted by the public if it was imposed directly; but by offering an apparent choice in the democratic elections of Britain and the US, people are sold the illusion that actions of politicians are accountable to the majority.

In America, presidencies are won through money, so those who control the financial resources dictate who becomes president and the president is then under obligation to those who funded him. The apparent differences between Republicans and Democrats are a façade as epitomised by George Bush, the Republican President 1989-1993, and Bill Clinton, the current Democratic President. Both are members of the Council on Foreign Relations and the Trilateral Commission; both are 33rd degree masons; both support GATT, NAFTA, centralisation and economic growth at the expense of humanity and the environment; and both are heavily involved in drug trafficking, child abuse, murder and the Iran-Contra affair.

In the British 'democracy' a person's allegiance to a political party is largely dictated by income and image. The majority of constituencies are 'safe seats' because due to the affluence, or otherwise, of an area the people automatically vote Conservative or Labour, respectively. Any candidate who toes the Elite line can be easily installed in parliament through these seats and subsequently MPs are instructed how to vote by their party. Those who attempt to be individuals and not support their party on certain issues face sanctions, whereas those who are willing to do as they are told advance rapidly. MPs are bribed to ask questions on behalf of certain companies, they often have external directorships and consultancies and on leaving government they often move into top commercial posts. For example, Lord Wakeham, who was instrumental in the privatisation of the electrical industry, became a director of N.M. Rothschild who had made a fortune from the privatisation. Other directors of N.M. Rothschild include Norman Lamont (former Chancellor), Lord Armstrong (one of Thatcher's cabinet secretaries during privatisation), Clive Whitmore (Home Office permanent secretary) and Frank Cooper (Ministry of Defence permanent secretary).

As early as 1940 Harold Wilson was preaching a centralised Federal Europe and outlined a plan of infiltration of the Labour and Conservative parties to form a centre party of moderates which could brand any genuine opposition as extremists. The plan also included the destruction of the British manufacturing industries. Between 1964 and 1975, Wilson (Labour) was Prime Minister, except when he was replaced in 1970-74 by his Bilderberg colleague Edward Heath (Conservative). The two of them ran down British industry, limited MI5 investigational powers and moved towards European Union. Wilson was aided by Lord Victor Rothschild as the head of his Central Policy Review Staff, and his Chancellor Denis Healey (Bilderberger, TC, RIIA).

Today, all political parties agree on the major issues—Major, Blair and Ashdown are all in favour of European Union, a single currency and bank, Maastricht, GATT and Western consumerism.

DEAD MEN TALKING

THE WORLD ARMY

A world army is to be achieved through the manipulation of conflicts leading to extra military powers for the United Nations Peacekeeping Forces. Meanwhile, NATO is expanding to absorb more countries of the Eastern bloc and operate outside its designated areas. Eventually these will fuse to form a world army to enforce the New World Order. The Gulf War was a major step along the path, as it was fought with NATO funding under a UN banner. Just prior to the conflict, closer co-operation was called between the countries of the former Soviet Union and NATO in order to extend the alliance beyond the North Atlantic and Europe

The Gulf War

Iraq, in an attempt to recover from the expensive eight year war with Iran, had been seeking to control its own oil reserves – independence which the Western oil companies could not allow. So, as well as being of importance to the Elite's long term goals of a world army, the conflict was engineered to effectively destroy Iraq both economically and in terms of its population.

Saddam Hussein had been installed in 1968 on the back of CIA support for his Baath party. In November 1989, US loans to Iraq were guaranteed providing that the money was used to buy US farm produce. Instead, as expected, Hussein used the money for arms and defaulted on the loans. The US taxpayer is now picking up the bill for rearming the 'enemy'. This US funding was done through the Atlantan branch of the Italian government bank, Banco Nazionale del Lavaro (BNL), which loaned $5 billion. Loans from the BNL to Iraq for arms purchases were organised as early as 1984 by Kissinger Associates. Some of the Iraqi arms were bought from Britain in illegal sales which implicate the British government. This possibly includes the Midland Industrial Trade Services, allegedly the secret arms running wing of the Midland Bank, which was introduced to the Iraqis by Kissinger Associates.

Having armed Iraq, America needed an excuse to invade. This opportunity came through covertly supporting Kuwait's obstinate insistence to make economic recovery difficult for Iraq by over-producing oil and keeping prices low. In July 1990, whilst assuring Hussein that his administration had no interest in an 'Arab-Arab conflict, like your border disagreement with Kuwait', Bush reached agreement with Gorbachev that Russia would not intervene if America invaded Iraq. Kuwait was invaded by Iraq in August 1990 and Bush started talking about economic sanctions against Iraq. Saudi Arabia was convinced by the Americans that it was under threat and under this pretext US forces were dispatched to protect Saudi Arabia. These were later joined by British and French troops to create a UN army.

DEAD MEN TALKING

One month before the UN invasion of Kuwait/Iraq, a US army report detailed the destruction of Kuwait, the firing of the oil wells and which companies would be involved in the lucrative rebuilding of Kuwait and extinguishing the fires. In the ensuing bombing, Iraqui industry, and therefore its post-conflict economy, was destroyed and hundreds of thousands of people have died, either as a direct result of indiscriminate bombing or in the ensuing poverty and deprivation.

Through the Gulf conflict, the phrase 'New World Order', used by Bush in a victory speech, was used by all and sundry to describe this unprecedented global military co-operation. Public approval for this type of intervention has been amplified by the manipulation of Yugoslavia to show inadequacies in the current UN Peacekeeping force, as first highlighted by their ineffectiveness in Rwanda and Somalia. As none of these trouble spots adversely effect the oil trade, an operation on the scale of the Gulf War is not required. Incidentally, there is already a joint UN/NATO Allied Rapid Reaction Corps whose existence was justified by the failure of the UN in Yugoslavia.

The Supposed ET Menace

The need for a world army is also being sold to the public as a defence against UFOs, for planetary security against aggressive extra-terrestrials. This has been achieved through a massive cover up of genuine ET contact and UFO sightings.

ETs of both positive and negative intent for humanity are visiting this planet – they have been for millennia – and have possibly established underground bases on Earth. By working with these ETs, Elite science is far more advanced than conventional science would have us believe. Free energy, anti-gravity technology, advanced mass mind manipulation techniques are all under the control of the military in highly secretive and sinister underground centres like Area S-4 in Nevada, the Dulce facility in New Mexico, RAF Rudloe Manor (Wiltshire) and Mount Weather near Washington DC. The 'non-existence' of such technology enables the issue of UFO/ET interaction to be plagued with disinformation. The propaganda machine ridicules true sightings, while high publicity awaits encounters where people are subjected to terrifying experiments at the hands of ETs. However it is very probable that such incidents are in fact carried out by the military and intelligence services using technology the general public are unaware of in order to create the desired response of fear and the demand for global defence. However, I believe that a proportion of abductions are occurring to individuals who have agreed – perhaps before incarnation – to being involved in such ET experiments which are monitoring the human race in such areas as pollution effects on the body and genetic evolution etc.. Abductee reports include a programme of implantation and removal of foetuses for the purpose of cross-breeding humans and aliens.

DEAD MEN TALKING

One further sinister twist to the tale of ETs is that certain people who have been victims of Satanic and paedophilic abuse have, as part of the process of regaining suppressed memories, uncovered images of ETs over-laid on the memories of abuse by people. Mind control is a central part of the process of Satanic abuse whereby the brain is compartmentalised through severe trauma, assisted by drugs and Electro-Convulsive-Treatment. In this way it is possible to bury memories of events a long way behind implanted ones. This is the same technique used by the intelligence agencies to create perfect lone assassins.

POPULATION CONTROL

Eugenics

One of the most alarming of the Elite's doctrines is that of eugenics – controlling human reproduction in order to reduce the number of those that the Elite perceive as inferior to create a 'master race' with 'desirable' genetic characteristics. Eugenics had its highest public profile in Nazi Germany but the policies began a long time before Hitler and are continuing to the present day.

The philosophy was pioneered by Thomas Malthus in the 18th/19th centuries who sought to encourage disease and child mortality in the poor. So-called Malthusianism has since been adopted by different organisations for a variety of excuses. After various eugenics policies in the US states in the late 19th century, including the compulsory sterilisation of the mentally ill and 'undesirables' in Indiana, the Rockefellers established a eugenics research centre in New York. They were supported in this venture by the Harrimans, another family of manipulators.

The First International Congress of Eugenics was held in London in 1912 and was attended by a certain Winston Churchill. By 1917, fifteen US states had eugenics laws to sterilise epileptics, the mentally ill and regular criminals. On the agenda of the Third International Congress in 1932 was the 'problem' of African-Americans which, according to the delegates, revealed a need to sterilise to 'cut off bad stock'. At this meeting were several Nazis, including Dr Ernst Rudin, who had been enabled to attend by the Hamburg-Amerika Shipping Line, owned by the Harriman and Bush families. On returning to Germany, Rudin, who was funded by the Rockefellers, supervised the policy of sterilising those who were retarded, deaf, blind or alcoholics.

Between 1941 and 1943, at the same time as the 'master race' mentality in Hitler's Germany was being condemned by the rest of the world, 42,000 people were sterilised in the US. Five years later the Sterilisation League/ Birthright Inc. established a eugenics centre in North Carolina which began a project to forcibly sterilise young children who were considered to have a low IQ. This was part funded by the Gray family, close friends of the Bush's. After the war, John D.

DEAD MEN TALKING

Rockefeller III and John Foster Dulles campaigned against the extension of the non-white populations and in 1952 launched the Population Council. This still exits and is still advocating zero population growth in the US, family planning in the developing sector and the expansion of the Club of Rome's 'Malthusianism'. (See later for details of the Club of Rome.)

Eugenics policies are funded by the World Bank which, at the Rio summit, pledged to double the money available to population control. Birth control is now forced on the developing countries through fear of economic sanctions.

The extent of the population control towards which the Elite are striving was revealed in the 1962/63 'Report from Iron Mountain' , a secret study group into controlling population without war. It sought completely artificial procreation to supersede the 'ecological function of war'. This was to include total control of contraception via water supplies and essential food stuffs so babies could only be conceived by those to whom a carefully controlled antidote had been administered. Such a system was apparently already under development... 35 years ago!

George Bush is a major voice in the eugenics movement and is surrounded by like-minded people – Boyden Gray (his legal advisor) and William Draper III (head of fundraising for his 1980 presidential campaign). Draper's grandfather had unsuccessfully urged eugenics policies on Eisenhower before convincing Johnson to adopt them. In 1969 Bush was involved in hearings into the 'dangers of too many black babies' and when he became ambassador to the UN in 1972 he arranged for the Association of Voluntary Surgical Contraception (formerly the Sterilisation League) to extend its policy of sterilising young children with 'low' IQ to non-white countries. This was further extended when Bush became president in 1988.

Engineered Wars

War is one of the most effective ways of culling an 'undesirable' population as Thomas Ferguson, a member of the Office of Population Affairs, explains:

'to reduce the population quickly you have to pull all the males into the fighting and kill significant numbers of fertile, child-bearing age, females.'

From his position of 'shuttle' diplomat, Henry Kissinger has successfully engineered conflict throughout the world. In Vietnam, the war was caused by the movement of hundreds of thousands of people from the north to the south – a move forced on them by the Saigon Military Mission, created by the CIA in 1954. With no food, they resorted to theft, and by labelling the bands 'the Viet Cong' a problem was created. Under the pretext that they were controlled by the Khmer Rouge, the north Vietnamese were severely bombed. According to estimates, 30-500,000 Cambodians died in the bombings, when in fact China was the power behind

DEAD MEN TALKING

North Vietnam, supported by Kissinger with US/China liaisons headed by George Bush. The Khmer Rouge reacted, as expected, and took Cambodia, murdering 32% of the population. During the war, the CIA station in Saigon co-ordinated Operation Phoenix which reportedly murdered 40,000 Vietnamese on 'suspicion' of working for the Viet Cong – that is, they could read and write. Two of the US commanders in the conflict were Maxwell Taylor and William Westmoreland, both members of the Population Crisis Council and Draper Fund.

The Yom Kippur war and countless other 'civil wars' in Central America and Africa have been engineered by Kissinger to cull populations as even when it is not the prime aim; mass killings are perceived as a useful by-product of war.

Kissinger is a member of the Club of Rome and in 1974 supervised the production of National Security Study Memo 200 about the implications of population growth. This stated that population growth in the developing world would lead to a desire for self determination of their economies. It continued that the population must therefore be controlled, but this fact must be withheld from the country's leaders. Amongst the countries specifically targeted were Ethiopia, Columbia, India, Nigeria, Mexico and Indonesia.

Indonesia is an horrendous example of conflict creation for the purposes of eugenics and corporate control, while public bodies and the media remain obstinately silent. General Suharto took control of Indonesia in 1965 through a CIA-backed coup and has since been responsible for 500,000 murders in his own country. However, because his administration is subservient to Western corporations, allowing them to exploit the land and the people (e.g. Reebok), this appalling tragedy goes unchallenged in the media. In December 1975 Indonesia invaded the Portuguese colony of East Timor and, in the following years, proceeded to slaughter 200,000 people, a third of the Timorese population. This genocide (eugenics) has been carried out with arms from Britain (British Aerospace's Hawk Jets) and US, approval from the West (Kissinger and Ford were in Indonesia days before the invasion) and complete silence in the mass media. The simple reason is that oil and gas reserves had been discovered off the coast of East Timor which the multinational oil companies could exploit only if controlled by a corporate-friendly culture – like Indonesia.

WHO WE ARE

Until the last couple of hundred years a major tool in the 'programming' of the collective mind has been the belief in dogmatic religion. Religious philosophies generally present a picture of Creation with humankind, even though perhaps 'chosen' by God, to be very much subservient and worthless. People who consider themselves 'free' through the pursuit of their own dogmatic religion are amongst the most enslaved victims of the Illuminati's plan for total take over of mind, body and soul. Fear, guilt and a host of other negative emotions have been instilled into humanity in the name of religion – the Christian guilt due to the doctrine of 'original sin' and fear of the final judgement; Jewish feelings of divine punishment for failing Yahweh; Islamic aggression to convert the masses by the sword; the Hindu caste system in which 'untouchables' have no hope of salvation in this lifetime. Western Catholicism, with its control over all education for centuries and its intolerance of alternatives (usually condemned as heresies with the proponents ex-communicated, exiled or barbarically tortured and killed) successfully kept the masses in cringing subservience to their vengeful, yet supposedly loving, God. The Catholic Church, in turn, has been controlled and bled dry of wealth by an especially sinister organisation which is a combination of elements of Freemasonry and the Mafia, known as P2. Religions are also answerable to the banks.

When scientific developments in the 18th and 19th centuries started disputing the orthodox theological interpretation of 'who we are', people's belief in the church started to wane and they threatened to start thinking for themselves. The Elite consequently hijacked this new science in order to switch the general belief from a judgmental God (which enabled control through fear etc.) to a denial of the existence of God and a belief that this life is all that there is (which enabled control through science and materialism). Darwin's theories on evolution was the first major coup on the mass mindset for the 'survival of the fittest/no God' belief system which has been prevalent in the last century. This theory, which did not originate with Charles Darwin, was essentially the work of the Lunar Society, a revolutionary organisation created to undermine God and overthrow monarchies, which Darwin's family was very involved in. By the end of his life Darwin himself did not believe the argument but the theories had taken hold and have since been taught as scientific fact. Once more our ideas about who and what we are have been programmed into us – beliefs which serve the Elite and their goal of complete control.

Ideas which challenge the now orthodox belief in evolution or seek to publicise the eternal nature of the spirit are marginalised into groups which are subsequently labelled as 'cults' – a word which is instinctively interpreted as 'a dangerous group of slightly insane people'. The stigma has been deliberately attached to the word for this very reason by highly publicised cults and the behaviour attributed to them. For example, the Jonestown massacre in 1978, which research has shown was probably a CIA mind-control experiment, and the Waco 'mass suicide' by burning alive in 1993 when followers of David Koresh were attacked by the FBI and the Bureau of Alcohol, Tobacco and Firearms (BATF) with tanks armed with flame throwers. Coincidentally, the BATF had contacted a local hospital before the raid to enquire about the availability of beds in the burns unit.

Cults which promote a world government and whose belief system incorporates the New World Order are supported by the Elite, e.g. the Moonies, the Church of Scientology and certain strands of the New Age movement. The 'opposite' side is also funded by the same people – the reactionary 'cult buster' groups, like the Cult Awareness Network set up by Dr West, a CIA asset which is heavily involved in Nazi-style mind control experiments.

Education

Conventionally taught and accepted history and science have a fundamental influence on the way that we perceive the world. Therefore, the control of education and the way that these subjects are presented has been of paramount importance to the Elite. This has been one of the main occupations of the Round Table, and in America the task was given to the Rockefeller Foundation by the Carnegie Endowment for International Peace to prevent American life from returning to its pre-World War I state.

The lessons taught in the schools of today are those of confusion (there is no meaning), hierarchical position (envy those above, despise those below), dependency ('success' is measured by the opinion of others and only 'experts' know the truth), obedience (do as others instruct in order to progress) and above all, conformity. A child is simply there to be filled with System-accepted 'facts', regimentally hurried from one lesson to the next to be bombarded with apparently unrelated information with any genuine enthusiasm or interest stifled in the boredom of classroom conformity. A child's intelligence is then measured by his or her meek receptivity to the systematic brainwashing and his or her ability to regurgitate these 'facts' in examinations, whilst the teacher's performance is evaluated by the speed and completeness of the indoctrination. The curriculum is very carefully controlled with standardised textbooks which teachers, whatever their personal feelings on the subject, have to teach in order to retain their jobs. Real questions about the nature of life, the reasons behind the contradictions in accepted historical absurdities, the dreams of self-expression have no part in the strait jacket of System education. People are 'consumers' and cogs in the corporate machine, and those who can accept this role are what the education process call 'successful'. If conformity is the price of 'success', those who seek alternative views and reject the indoctrination are made to experience shame and a sense of failure. We are taught that the Elite system of corporate-led consumerism has been freely created and that it provides the only answer for a meaningful, worthwhile life. Childhood happiness, enthusiasm and excitement for life are suffocated as we are taught to operate within a system which denies the very essences of humanity – love and the ability to question and search for the truth of our current existence.

DEAD MEN TALKING

The Media

Information about and interpretation of current affairs is gained exclusively through the media – newspapers, t.v. and radio. Newspapers are presented as being independent or having a known political leaning and t.v. is supposedly unbiased and independent. This is simply not the case. Information about events come from 'official sources' who can present the view that the Elite want the public to accept. Alternatively, news stories are derived from central news agencies (e.g. Reuters) who give everybody the same story. Newcomers to a media company are expected to toe the conventional line or suddenly their prospects become bleak. Journalists who analyse and think independently are dangerous and are few and far between.

This is not to suggest that every single journalist from the boardroom down to the 'hack' is involved in some massive conspiracy and cover up. Once the framework has been set up (which it deliberately has been over the last few centuries) the system is self-regulatory simply through 'market forces'. Running a newspaper or television station is an expensive business which instantly limits those organisations which can operate one. Such businesses are obviously financially successful in the System, so have an interest in maintaining the status quo. Opinions and stories which challenge the establishment are therefore of no interest to these companies and are viewed as subversive. The media industry is also advertising-based with prices of newspapers kept below the manufacturing costs by advertising income. Multinationals will not support those newspapers/magazines which are viewed as 'anti-business' so such publications are marginalised out of existence simply by market forces. Advertiser-friendly media companies keep their readership in a suitable 'buying' frame of mind by not being controversial, not presenting 'difficult' articles or programmes. The threat of withdrawal of advertising is generally sufficient to ensure the media companies vigilantly filter the stories they present but if one slips through, business organisations often combine forces to pressurise editors into reviewing their content. This is done through letters, law-suits and even parliamentary bills. An example of these so-called 'flak machines' is Accuracy in Media (AIM) a collection of corporate giants, including eight oil companies, whose function is to maintain a corporate-friendly media in the US.

A look at the board members of media companies is revealing about their alleged independence. In America a large number of the directors of NBC, CBS and ABC all have common involvement with Rothschild/Rockefeller/Morgan companies, as well as being members of the Council on Foreign Relations and Trilateral Commission. In Britain, the Daily Telegraph is owned by the Hollinger group who advisors/directors include Henry Kissinger, Lord Carrington, Brzezinski and Lord Rothschild. The current chairman of N.M. Rothschild, Evelyn de Rothschild, is on the board of the Daily Telegraph. A former board member, Andrew Knight (Bil), is now executive chairman of the 'rival' News International, which runs The Times and the Sun, and which is funded by the Oppenheimers and the Rothschilds. Regulatory bodies such as the Press Complaints Commission also have links with the same people e.g. the chairman Lord Wakeham who is a director of N.M. Rothschild.

Most people form their opinions on the basis of newspapers whose political stance mirrors their own. As all media organisations are owned by companies with the same interests and have their content dictated by the advertisers and obtain their stories from the same sources, all 'sides' of public opinion are easily manipulated. This is used to divert attention away from the true agenda:

* Investigators getting near to the truth are branded as anti-Semitic so attention is focused away from their information onto their apparent racism. * 'Expose' books, such as Peter Wright's Spycatcher are publicly opposed by those in government to give credence to their revelations. Their 'exposure' of what are generally innocent people are then believed more readily. * Sensitive information is released when overshadowed by another news story, e.g. identity cards were announced by Michael Howard on the day of the Loyalist cease-fire in Northern Ireland. * Libya has been blamed for the Lockerbie bombing (among other things) to undermine Colonel Gaddafi, when all the evidence points to the CIA and other intelligence agencies. The Libyan leader is, in fact, one of the 'evil tyrants' the media so love to create as a simplistic 'bad guy' at which the public can direct their animosity. He is not exactly a saint but, in the 1980s, Gaddafi was responsible for 14 deaths (mostly Libyans), as compared with the 50,000 corpses at the feet of the regime in El Salvador – an administration installed by the US with a US trained army. * Assassinations are blamed on a lone person with no affiliation to any group. The murder of J.F. Kennedy, for example, was ascribed to Lee Harvey Oswald (who was subsequently murdered himself by a 'lone assassin') but investigations have shown that it could not have been Oswald but it is much more likely that the American President was removed by the intelligence agencies because he did not follow the Elite game plan and was threatening to expose it by 'smashing the CIA into a thousand pieces'.

'Choice'

Public opinion is sold the illusion of choice by maintaining groups in apparent opposition to each other. Again, the majority will believe that they are involved in a real battle for what they genuinely believe to be correct, when in reality the funding and support is derived from the same sources as their opposition. As long as New World Order policies are being promoted it makes no difference to the Elite whether a group is Jewish, anti-Jewish, Left wing, Right wing, Christian, Moslem etc.... it will be used while it serves their purpose.

Another vital tool is instilling a belief that the goals the Elite are striving towards are good and necessary things. This is often achieved by creating a 'problem', which the public react against and call for an official response. The 'solution' which is offered and which is accepted on a wave of public support is the very thing the Elite wanted in the first place. There are countless examples of these but I shall cite just three:

* The 'problem' of violent crime has elicited a wave of public feeling in favour of increased police powers. * 'New age' travellers were suddenly severely harassed by the police and received considerable media attention. When they reacted against their treatment an apparent 'problem' had been created which was met with the 'solution' of the Criminal Justice Bill. This restriction on personal freedom sailed through parliament and the media spotlight was focused away from the travellers to firstly give the impression of 'problem solved' and secondly, they had served their purpose. * The Oklahoma Bomb in April 1995 in which 168 men, women and children were killed was reported as being caused by a fertilizer bomb – despite the absence of any fertilizer at the scene – planted by a 'people's militia' group. In fact, the explosion was caused by a barometric bomb which has a security level on a par with nuclear weapon components. However public opinion had been mobilised against the 'problem' of the 'people's militia' movement and consequently accepted Clinton's 'solutions' of increased FBI powers to infiltrate and attack these groups, the military enforcement of domestic laws, and a media ban on so-called 'anti-government' extremists such as the People's Militia who are fully aware of the workings of America's secret government.

Environmental Movement

A good example of both these methods of manipulation – problem-generating in order to have a solution accepted and control of both sides of the 'debate – is the way that environmental issues have been used in order to justify centralisation of power. Our planet is in environmental crisis and the vast majority of the Green movement is working positively for the good of the Earth, but when environmentalists can aid the New World Order the Elite have no compunction about leaping on the proverbial band wagon.

The Elite's environmental stance is largely co-ordinated by the Club of Rome, launched by the Freemason Aurelio Peccei in 1968. Its purpose is to issue propaganda about the environmental crisis to justify centralisation of power, the suppression of industrial development in the Third World and eugenics. Under its influence the Global 2000 report was produced during Jimmy Carter's Trilateral administration which used untrue 'shock' data to paint a picture of overpopulation and food/resource shortages. The response document called for population control and the restriction of scientific development in the Third World. It is on the back of these documents that the genuine environmental movement is calling for a global solution to a global problem – a view the Elite wholeheartedly endorses. Highly involved in these documents were bankers and politicians who support the IMF and the World Bank which are causing the very devastation of the planet they profess to be concerned about. 'Debt for equity' schemes in which 'environmentally sensitive' land is given by the Third World as payment for debts (which in reality does not even reduce the debt) are the brainchild of David Rockefeller and Baron Rothschild. The same people were behind the Rio Summit in 1992 where the secretary-general was the millionaire oilman Maurice Strong, also a trustee of the Rockefeller Foundation.

All these 'problems' to which centralisation and eugenics are the proffered 'solutions' are caused by the existing policies of the banks, multinational corporations, the World Bank, the IMF etc.. Create the problem, offer the solution...?

The environmental movement has also been used to prohibit the exploitation of nuclear power. (Personally I am not in favour of nuclear power, but I can still see how the issue has been manipulated to serve the Elite.). The oil and petrochemical industries form the backbone of the Elite's income and recruitment. The oil price shocks in the 1970s were manipulated by the 'Seven Sisters' oil cartel and the Bilderberg Group to massively inflate the price of oil. Conventionally, nuclear power forms the only credible alternative to fossil fuels so it had to de discredited. One of the Bilderbergers who agreed to the increase was Robert O. Anderson, owner of Atlantic Richfield Oil Co of the board of Kissinger Associates. He channelled huge sums of money into organisations to oppose nuclear fuel including a grant to establish a group which developed into Friends of the Earth. Research also suggests that the French arm of the House of Rothschild has been seeking to monopolise nuclear power technology and reprocessing technology in time for the predicted exhaustion of oil and gas supplies. The Rothschilds now control 80% of the world's uranium supplies.

The manipulation has also occurred on an international stage. In the 1980s Pakistan, under Ali Bhutto, proposed independent expansion of its nuclear power programme. Kissinger's threats weren't sufficient to stop Bhutto so a Kissinger-inspired coup removed him from power and the world passively looked on as he was hanged.

Mind Manipulation

Mind control experiments, so-called Nazi science, has been on-going for decades using esoteric knowledge about the human psyche. By ridiculing any spiritual interpretation of life and mobilising the forces of conventional science the Elite have convinced the public of the non-existence of psychic, 'higher' levels so it is easy to keep hidden technology which manipulates these levels.

Mass hypnosis is possible by the repetition of a basic theme until it is accepted as fact by the subconscious and then conscious mind. Such messages can be flashed during t.v. programmes or films and are not perceived by the eyes and conscious mind. Alternatively, the mesmerising and sedating effect of television puts the subconscious mind into an ideal state to receive messages sent to the psyche via carrier t.v./radio waves. It is understood by Elite science how, by broadcasting at certain frequencies, non-physical magnetic levels can be imbalanced to cause physical, emotional and mental illness. Technology also exists whereby thoughts can be induced by stimulating brainwaves.

The most sinister and far-reaching mind control programme is Project MK Ultra, run on behalf of the CIA. During Operation Paperclip, Nazi scientists were moved to the US and given prestigious positions at the leading colleges, universities and NASA after World War II to continue their experiments in which thousands of 'lesser human beings' – prisoners, mental patients, victims of paedophilia and incest etc. – have been forced to participate. Experiments have included removing a person's existing personality by electrotherapy and then compartmentalising and programming new ones by psychic driving. This makes the 'subject' obsessed with certain ideas and is undoubtedly used to 'programme' so-called lone assassins. The CIA openly admit to having used this form of subversive technology for use against America's political enemies but flatly denies that it would ever be used on home territory.

Project Monarch

An integral part of MK-Ultra is Project Monarch – perhaps the most damning episode in the history of mind control – whereby the minds of women and children are brutally taken over in order to provide paedophiles, politicians, criminals and practising Satanists with willing sex slaves who could also double as covert operatives by having their personalities and memories switched on and off at will. (See also Further Examples of Manipulation – Satanists)

The details of this horrific plan by the Elite to take over the planet through mass mind-control have come from the ex-CIA mind-controlled slave, Cathy O'Brien, and are described in harrowing detail in her book Trance Formation Of America. After a lifetime in the clutches of the MK-Ultra Project Monarch mind-control program she became what is known as a 'Presidential Model', a sex slave used specifically by the presidents for perverted abuse. Her abusers include the presidents Gerald Ford, Ronald Reagan and George Bush as well as a host of other key US politicians. These fiends would routinely torture and rape her and later her daughter, Kelly, for personal gratification whilst using drugs and electric shock trauma to further compartmentalise her memory of such events in order to hide their actions. Because of her status and entirely programmable mind Cathy was used in many major political/criminal covert operations and was used to pass on Top Secret information in such affairs as the Iran-Contra deals.

Cathy's life began as the victim of multigenerational paedophilic incest. Her first memory in life is being choked by her father's penis in her throat. This initial trauma began to cause her mind to compartmentalise into separate personalities which could deal with traumatic situations – as a mental survival tool – whilst her 'normal' personality was left to deal with everyday events. Her mind dissociated from the memory of abuse whilst developing another personality which belonged to her father and was triggered on the sight of his arousal. This was the beginning of the creation within Cathy's psyche of a phenomenon known as Multiple Personality Disorder (MPD), now known as Dissociative Identity Disorder (DID).

One side-effect of MPD is the creation of a photographic memory. Since her rescue and de-programming in 1988, Cathy has been able to recall in stunning detail every encounter with her adversaries and their sordid plans for world domination. These were freely revealed to Cathy by leading US politicians and criminals over a number of years whilst presuming that their high-tech programming could never be interfered with and it was therefore safe to do so. Another side-effect of the programming is the development of a visual acuity which is 44 times that of the average person.

Subsequent abuse came daily from her father and uncles who had also been victims of paedophile parents. Separate personalities were created for each situation, whilst Cathy was still little more than a toddler.

Her Uncle Bob, a regular paedophilic abuser, often boasted to her that he was a pilot in Air Force Intelligence and worked for the Vatican. It was Bob who first introduced Cathy to child pornographer and head of the local Michigan Mafia, Gerald Ford (of the Warren Commission who investigated the death of JFK, and later became President of the US after Nixon). Ford had begun recruiting 'Multigenerational incest abused children with MPD for its genetic mind-control studies', a Top Secret Defence Intelligence Agency project. By selling Cathy into this programme, her father gained immunity from prosecution having recently been caught selling pornography which involved Cathy and her pet boxer dog, Buster.

Her father was soon enrolled on a two week course at Harvard where he was taught his role in preparing Cathy for the project. He then returned home to enthusiastically announce that the family would be having more children. Cathy now has two sisters and four brothers; each victims of paedophilic abuse.

Preparation for The Project was based upon continual trauma, food and water deprivation, sensory deprivation and included constantly slave driving Cathy into exhaustion just like Cinderella. She was repeatedly prostituted to local Freemasons, police, a Catholic priest, Satanists and relatives in order that she further dissociated and enforced the realisation that there was no place to run and hide. She was also prostituted to Michigan State Senator, Guy VanderJagt (later US Congressman and chairman of the Republican National Congressional Committee which appointed George Bush as president) who gave her a Rosy Cross necklace and told her that he and her Uncle Bob had been to the Vatican where the secrets of other dimensions of existence were kept. On one occasion, both he and Ford brutally raped her in an horrific threesome backstage at a political parade; they then took the stage in front of the crowd which included all of Cathy's schoolmates to present her with a US flag which only moments previously they had inserted into her rectum.

Despite these daily horrors she excelled at her studies; due mainly to her photographic memory. No one had any idea that any of this was going on.

In 1968, VanderJagt introduced Cathy to the Canadian Prime Minister Pierre Trudeau who then abused her and used her for porn involving a French poodle which he had given her as a pet.

Once Cathy reached adolescence and began to develop breasts, VanderJagt found her less attractive and she was 'given' to US Senator and Ku Klux Klan affiliate, Robert C. Byrd who found pleasure in repeatedly torturing her in Sado-Masochistic sex and porn from which she still bears the scars all over her body.

By now Cathy was unable to tell reality from dreams and vice versa. This was reinforced through an advanced form of mind-control known as 'Satanic reversals' whereby every sensory input was controlled and words and sentences perverted to always have sinister double or triple meanings pertaining to abuse. She was further prepared for Project Monarch when she was taken out of school and relocated at Muskegon Catholic Central High School, with other Monarch 'Chosen Ones' as they were referred to.

The final event which literally drove Cathy out of her mind and destroyed her one remaining 'normal' personality happened in 1974 after a parade in Cedar Springs, Michigan when Ford brutally assaulted her and delivered electric shock treatment in order that she would forget the event. Now every compartment of her mind was associated with abuse.

The programme soon began to involve high-tech military bases for further traumatisation and programming. For this they used centres such as the MacDill Airforce Base at Tampa; Fort Campbell in Kentucky; Fort McKlellen at Anniston, Alabama; Redstone Arsenal and Marshall Space Flight Centre in Huntsville, Ala-

DEAD MEN TALKING

bama; the NASA Kennedy Space Centre, Cape Canaveral in Florida and NASA's Goddard Space Flight Centre near Washington D.C..

Cathy was sold and 'married' to her owner, Byrd in a contract which made her father a millionaire overnight. Although 'owned' by Byrd, Cathy was given 'handlers' to keep an eye on and further traumatise her. One such person was Wayne Cox, a Satanist and serial killer his calling card is to remove one hand of his victims which he calls the 'Hands of Glory') who had gained immunity from prosecution through his involvement in Project Monarch. He was introduced to Cathy whilst playing for a country music band at the Grand Old Opry in Nashville, Tennessee. According to Cathy, no one makes it in this town unless they are slaves or CIA operatives. Names of leading slave handlers and CIA operatives include Kris Kristofferson (described by Cathy as a 'Vatican based Project Monarch slave runner'), Boxcar Willie (who has abused Cathy's daughter, Kelly, in three separate mental institutions) and Merle Haggard – whose song 'Freedom Train' is the code-word for this aspect of the mind-control plan. Project Monarch Slaves include the singer Barbara Mandrell and her sisters, who are also owned by Byrd, and Loretta Lynn who's handler is Neo-Nazi paedophile and CIA operative, Ken Riley.

Cox involved Cathy in drug running and cannibalistic Satanism with his mother. He also caused her to conceive six times in order to use the foetuses in these rituals and became the natural father of Cathy's only daughter, Kelly, who was born in 1980. During one drug run with Cox to Tinker Air Force Base in Ouachita National Forrest near Hot Springs, Arkansas, Cathy met, then Governor of Arkansas, Bill Clinton. She was then cued to reveal to him a secret message from Senator Bennett Johnson of Louisiana and then handed over a particularly fine batch of cocaine (Clinton's drug of choice) for his personal use.

In 1980, Cathy was programmed at Fort Campbell, Kentucky by Lt. Colonel Michael Aquino, a confessed neo-Nazi and founder of the Himmler-inspired Temple of Set (Satan), who holds Top Secret clearance in the DIA's Psychological Warfare Division (he was also once charge with ritual and sexual abuse of children at the Presidio Day Care Centre in San Francisco). He used atrocious trauma techniques using NASA technology on both Cathy and Kelly.

Perversely, Lucifarian religions are constitutionally protected in the USA and Britain!

One sex slave training camp is known as the 'Charm School' in Youngstown, Ohio and is operated by the 'Governor', Dick Thornburgh (Governor of Pennsylvania, US Attorney General and secretary for the UN). Here he worked with Congressman Jim Trafficant using high-tech programming techniques.

98

DEAD MEN TALKING

A further insight into the New World Order mentality comes from these passages from Trance Formation of America:

(Byrd) often threatened me that I was considered 'disposable' because after all, "The first Presidential Model, Marilyn Monroe, was killed right in front of the public eye and no one knew what happened".'

Furthermore:

...he loved to hear himself talk and would often drone on and on in his famous long-winded recitations, while I was photographically recording every word he said. He detailed the inner operational structure of the world domination effort, including psychological warfare strategies, and explained how he had and would use his 'expert' knowledge of the Constitution to manipulate it and the so called US Justice System, and more.

...Byrd 'justified' mind-control atrocities as a means of thrusting mankind into accelerated evolution, according to the Neo-Nazi principles to which he adhered. He 'justified' manipulating mankind's religion to bring about the prophesied biblical 'world peace' through the 'only means available' – total mind-control in the New World Order. 'After all,' he proclaimed, 'even the Pope and the Mormon Prophet know this is the only way to peace and they co-operate fully with The Project.' (my highlights added)

...He adhered to the belief that 95% of the (world's) people WANT to be led by the 5%, and claimed that this can be proven because the 95% DO NOT WANT TO KNOW what really goes on in government.' Byrd believed that in order for this world to survive, mankind must take a 'giant step in evolution through creating a 'superior race', Byrd believed in the Nazi and KKK principles of 'annihilation of underprivileged races and cultures' through genocide, to alter genetics and breed 'the more gifted – the blondes of this world'.

Cathy's first position as a 'Presidential Model' was to Ronald Reagan – known to slaves as 'The Wizard of OZ'. One of his favourite pastimes was perverted porn – especially bestiality. He would instruct his personal pornographer, Larry Flynt (owner of Hustler magazine) to make pictures to his own specifications which became known as 'Uncle Ronnie's Bedtime Stories'. Reagan's personal attaché, Philip Habib's favourite pastime was to sodomise Cathy whilst electrocuting her to create the desired rectal spasm. Habib later introduced her to King Fahd of Saudi Arabia whose tastes were frighteningly similar.

Fahd was to fund the Contras via Panamanian Dictator and CIA operative, Manuel Noriega for Reagan and Cathy was used as the messenger in 'Operation Carrier Pidgeon'.

DEAD MEN TALKING

One of the most brutal of all of Cathy's abusers was Dick Cheney (White House Chief of Staff to Ford, member of the CFR and later Secretary of Defence to Reagan – despite having no military background). He would regularly organise an event known as 'A Most Dangerous Game'. This involved releasing Monarch slaves into the woods and then hunting them down with dogs and guns for sport as a means of further traumatising victims as well as for his own perversity.

One operation, organised by Cheney and Ford was 'Operation Shell Game'. This involved Cathy being used as a 'Carrier Pidgeon':

He (Ford) began talking as though I were a machine and he was dictating a message. 'Take this message to Dick Chaney, Pentagon. The Mob has agreed to transfer the $2.3 million (porn profits) to the Bank of Credit and Commerce International. Let's pool our money now and we'll be swimming in it. This operation has been an enterprising success. Let's keep it that way. Cease agreement with Panama. All Mexican channels are implemented (cocaine and heroin). Hail to the chief'.

As a replacement for Cox, Cathy was given a new handler; paedophile, ventriloquist and hypnotist, Alex Houston. (Cox now breeds goats for Satanic rituals and runs a trade in human body parts for Satanists.) In 1982, Houston dealt cocaine to Bill Clinton whilst Cathy was taken to meet his wife, Hilary Clinton. At the sight of Cathy's vagina (which had previously been mutilated without anaesthetic to resemble a demon's head – the head of Baphomet which is worshipped by the Templars and their offshoots) Hilary Clinton became aroused and performed oral sex upon her.

In 1983, George Bush began sodomising and electrocuting Kelly, now merely three and a half years old. Her rectum usually bled for days after. Furthermore, constant threats were made by Bush on Kelly's life in order to keep Cathy in line. He also claimed to be an ET and could activate a holographic image within Cathy's mind in which he would change into a lizard-like alien creature.

Bohemian Grove in California is an exclusive club where all sexual and satanic perversions are catered for – including necrophilia. Attendees are referred to as 'Grovers'. Reagan's Secretary of Education and later Legal Counsel to Clinton, Bill Bennett and his brother Bob assaulted Kelly here in 1988. Bennett has intimate knowledge of Catholic/Jesuit mind-control techniques and is using them to implement 'Education 2000' which is ,'designed to increase children's learning capacity while destroying the ability to think for themselves'. Bennett, like Bush, also claims to be an alien. Another plan known as World Vision is a Jesuit fund raising operation to implement world peace through mind-control.

The Order of the Rose – a Templar derivative – is very prominent among the New World Order brigade. Many slaves have a red rose tattooed on their left wrists. The Canadian Prime Minister, Brian Mulroney is also part of this clique, as is VandrJegt and Madelaine Albright who, according to Bush, '...rose in the UN through me to implement the New World Order'.

Among the Order of the Rose, George Bush is referred to as 'The Rose'.

In 1986, Cathy and Kelly were taken to Mount/Lake Shasta in California under the guise of a music festival run by Merle Haggard. This is the base for a multi-juristictional police force which will be used to enforce the New World Order with an arsenal of black helicopters and an army of mind-controlled military personnel. Here, Bush and Cheney played the 'Most Dangerous Game' with Cathy. As a punishment for being caught, Bush (under the influence of his favourite drug – heroin) sodomised Kelly and burnt Cathy's thighs with a red hot poker.

When Cathy was 29 she became aware that Presidential Models were not allowed to live much beyond the age of 30. Plans were formed and agreed with Reagan that she would meet her end in a Snuff Movie whereby she would be burned alive. At this point Senator Patrick Leahy (Vice Chairman on US Senate Intelligence Committee and close friend of Byrd) 'acquired' her for a time. At his own personal torture lab he abused Cathy which included slowly inserting a wire into her right eye whilst forcing Kelly to watch.

In February 1988, two months after Cathy's thirtieth birthday, both she and Kelly were abducted from Alex Houston by his business partner and former CIA operative Mark Phillips – acknowledged by the US mental health and law enforcement officials as an expert in 'the most secret technology known to man: Trauma-based mind control' which is 'The only form of human control that is absolute'. He managed to smuggle them out of the clutches of their captors to Alaska with the aid of 'insider' assistance in the 'intelligence community' and began an intensive de-programming which has culminated in the recovery of Cathy's sanity as well as the information outlined in Trance Formation Of America.

It was also discovered that Kelly had been 'programmed' by Wayne Cox to die by using a mind-control technique known as 'hypnosleep'. This manifested in chronic and increasingly severe asthma.

According to Phillips the present field of mental health is so backward that:

In the present climate, referring mind-controlled victims to mental health professionals for treatment would be tantamount to subjecting a patient needing delicate surgery to a surgeon who was blind-folded and hand-cuffed.

The subsequent lives of the threesome has been one filled with trauma, death threats and legal battles. Kelly is now effectively a political prisoner in a mental institution because of her suicidal tendencies and is not allowed to have contact with Phillips – one of the few people who could help her to regain her sanity. All requests for legal investigations into the claims made by them to the legal authorities have been prevented 'For reasons of National Security', despite the mass of verifiable evidence which they have been able to uncover This is due to the loopholes created by the National security Act, 1947 and the 1986 Reagan Amendment, which means that the government can censor and/or cover up anything in the interests of National Security.

The extraordinary bravery of Cathy, Kelly and Mark has seen to it that this abuse and its perpetrators will be held accountable for their actions. Through their mass publicity attempts in the face of death at every turn we now have a pretty clear picture of the mentality of the New World Order Elite operatives. It is now up to all of us to see that such sacrifice has not been in vain.

According to my sources in Britain. The British counterpart to Project Monarch is Project Ultra Green and was initiated by a Nazi scientist named Grunenberg.

One US security agency, the National Security Agency, which wields the power behind the CIA and is heavily involved in the Black Ops and Black Arts has a base in England at a place called Menwith Hill which is near Ilkley Moor in North Yorkshire. Here the Elite operate a covert surveillance operation of Britain which includes a mass phone tapping system (try dropping a few of the code names mentioned in this book into your conversations on the phone and you will hear the 'clicks' in the background as their recording machinery is activated by specific 'buzz words') and high-tech satellite surveillance operation which was developed under the cover of Reagan's 'Star Wars' Programme. Interestingly, George Lucas, the writer and director of the Star Wars movies is named by Cathy O'Brien as a NASA/NSA operative.

Fluoride

The apathy of the public towards their manipulation has also been influenced very deliberately by the addition of chemicals to food and water supplies. For example, this happened when sodium fluoride was introduced into our water supply and the majority of our tooth-pastes, supposedly to prevent dental caries in the under twelve-year-olds. What they did not tell the public was that sodium fluoride is a highly toxic by-product of the aluminium manufacturing process and the refining of phosphate rock (see Further Examples of Manipulation – The BSE Case) which was once used as rat poison and also pollutes the atmosphere and water environment due to overuse of the aerosol propellants Chlorofluorocarbons (CFCs). Fluorine is a major component of most of today's major sedative drugs and even new supposedly less addictive drugs such as Prozac (Fluoxetine) and its derivatives. (Prozac also contains benzene which is, according to the World

DEAD MEN TALKING

Health Organisation, 'a known carcinogen with no known safe level'. Prozac is currently the world's most popular anti-depressant despite having documented side-effects such as: suicidal ideation, violent behaviour, nervousness, anxiety, insomnia, anorexia and sexual dysfunction!)

The following statement is extracted from 'Address in Reply to the Government's Speech to Parliament', as recorded in Victorian Hansard of 12 August 1987, by Mr Harley Rivers Dickinson, Liberal Party Member of the Victorian Parliament for South Barwon. Hence the title.

At the end of the Second World War, the United States Government sent Charles Eliot Perkins, a research worker in chemistry, biochemistry, physiology and pathology, to take charge of the vast Farben chemical plants in Germany.

While there he was told by the German chemists of a scheme which had been worked out by them during the war and adopted by the German General Staff.

This was to control the population in any given area through mass medication of drinking water. In this scheme, sodium fluoride occupied a prominent place.

Repeated doses of infinitesimal amounts of fluoride will in time reduce an individual's power to resist domination by slowly poisoning and narcotising a certain area of the brain and will thus make him submissive to the will of those who wish to govern him.

Both the Germans and the Russians added sodium fluoride to the drinking water of prisoners of war to make them stupid and docile.'

After the war, I.G. Farben was dismantled but later emerged in the many guises of the companies with whom they had signed cartel agreements including Procter and Gamble, the company who domesticated the word fluoride with official encouragement in 1958 with the 'Crest' fluoridated toothpaste campaign. Moreover, an adviser to the US Government on hypnotism and psychological behaviour control, Dr. George Estabrooks, later became Chairman, Department of Psychology, Colgate University. Internationally, Colgate was and remains the most ardent producer and advocate for the fluoridation of toothpaste.

Fluoride is active in parts per million and acts as a potentiator for other drugs, i.e. it increases their effect. In 1954, Charles Elliot Perkins, scientist and author stated:

'The real purpose behind water fluoridation is to reduce the resistance of the masses to domination and control and loss of liberty' and, 'I can say this in all earnestness and sincerity as a scientist who has spent nearly twenty years research into the chemistry, bio-chemistry, physiology and pathology of fluorine: any person who drinks artificially fluorinated water for a period of one year or more will never again be the same person, mentally or physically'.

Interestingly, the chemical industry now has a mass market for a once hard to dispose of toxic waste material and the Illuminati have a sedated and more easily controlled population.

A Microchipped Population

In the Elite's misguided judgement the ideal form of control will be via a microchipped population connected to a global computer. Money will be obsolete and all financial transactions will be carried out via a microchip inserted under the skin used in much the same way as a credit or smart card – swipe your wrist over the sensor to pay for your goods. Convenient, easy... and enables the Elite to have complete knowledge about you and your transactions. With no cash alternative if your 'wrist' is refused for some reason you can be prevented from buying anything and effectively ostracised from society. Moves to implement this are already underway and public opinion is being softened up to accept it: in the 1970s Swedish hospital patients were implanted without their knowledge; pets, new-born babies in maternity wards and criminals are being electronically tagged; a need for identity cards is being expressed (to combat crime); supermarkets are experimenting with bar-coded cards to keep a tally of purchases without the need for check-out assistants; the 'pay at the pump' systems recently introduced in some petrol stations; and in 1994 the Intel Corporation was given a five year contract to research into an under the skin microchip for identity/financial transactions.

IBM have already developed an invisible bar coding system of three sets of six numbers which is painless and can be 'installed' on the skin by laser in a fraction of a second without the person being aware of its existence and is currently in use on cattle. Watch out for gradual insistence on personal computerisation and electrical devices which could potentially be used to control us all. Remember, they create problems and then offer solutions.

Dr. Carl W. Sanders is an electronics engineer, inventor, author and consultant with various government organisations as well as IBM and General Electric. He spent thirty two years developing microchip technology for use in medicine which resulted in the chip which he describes as 'the Mark of the Beast'. It is a tiny chip which is recharged by body temperature and whose prime location would, therefore, be in the forehead, just below the hairline, or alternatively on the back of the hand. This chip has been tested as a contraception device in India and as a behaviour modifier in Vietnam veterans, amongst other things. A specific identification chip was developed which contained details of a person's name, picture of their face, security number, finger print, physical description, family history, address, occupation, income tax information and criminal record.

Dr. Sanders admits to attending many 'One World' meetings with Henry Kissinger and people from the CIA where it was discussed, 'How can you control people if you cannot identify them?' and, 'How do you make people aware of the need for something like this chip?' The answer was simple, 'Let's make them aware of lost children etc.' The CIA then came up with the idea of putting pictures of lost children on milk cartons, a procedure which ceased when the microchip became accepted. Bills have been put before Congress in the USA that will allow the government to microchip children at birth, The president of the USA, under the 'Control of Imigration Act of 1986', Section 100, has the authority to deem whatever type of identification is necessary. All of these sinister ploys are merely waiting in the wings to happen, and they have been manipulated into existence with the same problem/solution tactics which have been used for centuries to control the world's population.

Indeed, this interesting passage from the book of Revelation in the Christian Bible does appear to prophesy something similar to the human bar/microchip coding system:

'And he causeth all, both small and great, rich and poor, free and bond, to receive a mark in their right hand or in their foreheads:

And that no man might buy or sell, save he that had the mark, or the name of the beast, or the number of his name. Here is wisdom. Let him that hath understanding count the number of the beast: for it is the number of a man; and his number [is] Six hundred threescore [and]six.'

Revelation 13:16-18

As well as messages from the chip to the computer, messages can also be sent the other way – in much the same way as satellite t.v. receivers can be programmed remotely. As long ago as 1966, a CIA psychologist was talking about brain control through two-way communication between an implanted brain and a computer. Once a chip has been inserted there will be no end to the aspects of our lives which can be controlled – birth control, programmed actions to create more 'problems' demanding 'solutions', etc. A robot society will have been created.

FURTHER EXAMPLES OF MANIPULATION

The abuse of power and exploitation for personal and corporate gain by the visible components of the Elite hierarchy is quite astonishing. In the following cases we have been duped into believing as truth the version of events portrayed by the mass media.

DEAD MEN TALKING

Watergate

In 1972, a Republican surveillance team working for Nixon's re-election committee, subsequently named the 'Plumbers', broke into the Democrat headquarters at the Watergate Buildings in Washington. This was engineered by Kissinger and his protégé George Bush to remove the final pretence of 'democracy' and hand complete control of the US administration to the Elite. As Head of the State Department and the National Security Council, Kissinger effectively ran the Nixon presidency.

The 'Plumbers' were agents working for the White House Special Investigations Unit, created by Nixon (Kissinger) with money from the president of Bush-owned Pennzoil and other business associates of George Bush. At the time the Watergate story broke, Bush had been made chairman of the Republican National Committee yet claimed to have no knowledge of the situation.

After the break-in became public knowledge, Nixon was eventually forced to resign on the release of recordings in which he discussed ways to frustrate the Watergate investigations. The recordings were done by David Young, who worked for the Rockefellers and was appointed by Kissinger, and they were revealed by Butterworth, the White House liaison with the Kissinger-led secret service. In the same recordings, Nixon implicated certain 'Texans' which referred to Bush and his associates, but Nixon was forced out of office before the trial at which this would have been revealed.

Gerald Ford. a 33rd degree freemason and Rockefeller puppet, became president and pardoned Nixon so that the case never came to court. He appointed Nelson Rockefeller to be his vice-president and put him in charge of the Watergate investigations, which, unsurprisingly, discovered nothing of consequence.

Iran-Contra

In 1975, George Bush, who had been a CIA asset since the 1950s, became director of the CIA which, by a series of measures implemented by President Ford (Rockefeller), had increasing power over the US Intelligence services. As his associate deputy director for covert operations Bush named Theodore Shackley who, with Oliver North, had masterminded Operation Phoenix in Vietnam and ran an assassination and drugs operation throughout the 1970s with Donald Gregg and Felix Rodriquez. During the 1979-80 election campaign Shackley became Bush's speech writer (?!) and when Bush became vice-president under Reagan, Gregg, assisted by Rodriquez, was appointed as his main advisor on national security. Oliver North also became an official on the National Security Council. Working out of Bush's office this group co-ordinated the arms-for-drugs racket that has become known as Iran-Contra.

DEAD MEN TALKING

The Sandinista regime in Nicaragua sought to pursue the interests of its own economy and people rather than US corporate interests so the rebel Contras were backed by the CIA. They were supplied with arms in exchange for drugs which were flown on CIA chartered planes into Homestead Airforce Base using a CIA code signal. One trafficker flew weapons to the Contras in return for CIA help in flying cocaine into the US via an airstrip of one of North's CIA associates. Oliver North also co-ordinated the arms-for-hostages deals with Iran. The money was laundered through the Elite's banking headquarters in Switzerland.

One reason for the deals with Iran was to pay back the Khomeini regime for it delaying the release of 51 US hostages to prevent Carter taking the credit. Once he had been replaced by Reagan/Bush the hostages were released as arranged at a meeting in Paris between Iranian officials and Bush, Gregg and John Tower. When the scandal became public Tower led the investigations into the affair which did not prosecute Bush or Reagan and those that were identified as being involved were pardoned by Bush before public trials. Tower was to die in a plane crash just when he was beginning to talk openly about the affair.

The Drugs Trade

The trade in hard drugs is very important to the Elite for a number of reasons: it provides a source of income to finance other covert operations; it creates a 'problem' for which the public demands a 'solution' of increased police powers and the erosion of personal freedom in an effort to stop the supply; and, by addicting large numbers of particularly the younger generation to hard drugs, self-respect and the ability to think independently are diminished.

The background to many engineered conflicts is illuminated by analysis of the drug implications. In Vietnam a Pepsi Cola bottling plant was a drug distribution point with CIA helicopters supplying it with drugs from the fields. Drugs were also smuggled back to the US in the body cavities of carefully labelled corpses.

In 1986, Bo Gritz, America's most decorated war hero was sent by the US government into Burma's infamous 'Golden Triangle' to report on missing US prisoners of war. He discovered a man named Khun Sa who is deemed to be the overlord of heroin in the world, sending an ever-increasing excess of 1000 tons of heroin into the 'free' world per year. He also discovered that the whole rescue mission of the prisoners was being prevented by the CIA because these soldiers knew too many details of the operation between Khun Sa and the CIA to traffic these drugs. Later, he was told by Jerry King, head of Intelligence Support Activity (ISA) in the CIA that

'...we've been ordered to put operation Grand Eagle (the rescue mission) on the shelf as if it never existed. There are still too many beurocrats that don't want to see American prisoners of war come back alive.'

The conflict between the US and Panama was a result of Bush turning against Noriega who was a CIA asset while Bush was director and who had been paid to run drugs. However, having seized power in 1984, despite losing the democratic election and yet still being officially recognised by President Reagan, Noriega incurred US wrath by refusing to bow to their pressure for his country to invade Nicaragua. The US suddenly turned against the Panama administration under the pretext of drugs, corruption and a lack of democracy. In 1988, Noriega was indicted on drug charges all bar one of which pre-dated 1984, to a time when he was still on the CIA payroll. In order to arrest one man the US invaded Panama in 1989, killing 3000 civilians. Allegedly the Drug Enforcement Agency (DEA) paid him $4.7 million to keep quiet about CIA involvement and at his trial no CIA documents were allowed to be examined. A new government was installed by the US, headed by a president and vice-president involved with banks known for drug money laundering and under this new administration drug trafficking from Panama has increased.

Nixon and Reagan and George Bush (despite the latter two being regular heroin users), have led public campaigns against drugs which unsurprisingly have achieved little. In association with the major drug cartels, the CIA has arranged small 'busts' to lend credibility to the campaigns but these are usually to remove insignificant players or larger ones who have outlived their usefulness. In 1981, during the Reagan/Bush administration, the CIA convened a meeting of Columbian dealers to form the Medellin Cartel – an infamous group of 200 dealers. There is also evidence to suggest that the Zapata Oil Corporation is a CIA front and that Zapata Offshore is involved in drug smuggling. Both of these companies were set up and are headed by Bush.

George Bush was succeeded in the White House by Bill Clinton, a Rhodes Scholar, whose drug credentials are on a par with his predecessor. Whilst Governor of Arkansas he created the Arkansas Development Finance Authority (ADFA) which was to finance drug trafficking. All loan applications were handled by the Rose Law Firm, run by Hilary Clinton, and those which were granted were to Clinton's business associates for use in trafficking. For example, one loan was given to Web Hubbel of Park-O-Meter which manufactured retrofit nose cones for drug shipping. The loans were not paid back, but large donations were given to Clinton's election fund. Web Hubbel became acting US attorney general under Clinton, and some think he still fulfils that role behind Janet Reno.

During the Reagan/Bush anti-drug campaign, whilst Clinton governed Arkansas, the United State's biggest drug trafficking operation was set up in Mena Arkansas by a DEA pilot.

DEAD MEN TALKING

Many people speaking out or investigating Bill Clinton have died in mysterious circumstances, for which the official cause of death is given as 'suicide'. Conveniently, in a law introduced into Arkansas by Clinton just prior to the first suspicious deaths no autopsy needs to be performed in cases of deaths attributed to suicide.

Satanism

One of the most sinister elements to the manipulation of society is the abuse of esoteric knowledge by the world's secret societies both for the purposes of political control and for sick personal pleasure.

In the US each year 400,000 children are reported missing, and in the UK this number is 98,000. Not all are recovered.

All over the world children are hijacked into a life of sexual abuse, psychological and physical torture. They are bought and sold by members of paedophile rings, often by their own parents, who act as 'recruiters' and 'handlers' in the lower echelons of the secret society network. They are systematically abused, tortured and murdered in ritualistic ceremonies by people who occupy places throughout the social hierarchy all the way to the top. Eye witness accounts, such as those given by a friend of mine named Patti who was 'recruited' as a child of three, have implicated members of the aristocracy, doctors, lawyers, members of the clergy, high level businessmen, media stars, members of the world's governments (see Who We Are – Mind Manipulation/Project Monarch).

Sophisticated mind control techniques are used to compartmentalise the memories of the abused to prevent them from revealing the awful truth to the public. Patti has displayed many separate personalities whilst recounting her horrific experiences, displaying the classic symptoms of Multiple Personality Disorder. Often victims are too scared to even mention such things to each other, never mind to strangers. They are brought up in the certain knowledge that they can be easily picked up off the streets or from their beds and drugged for use in abuse at any time. They are fully aware also that their abusers are everywhere, including in the medical professions and police. Victims are ceremonially 'married' to the leaders of the cult and are given their own 'dark companion', a sinister thought-form who will be ever present in order to inform on them if they should ever step out of line. They are often forced to take part in the abuse, murder and disposal of other victims in order to ensure a total attack upon the psyche of the individual concerned and the victim is soon convinced that they have become at least as guilty of these crimes as their assailants. Therefore, they are ever paranoid and terrified of revealing the truth to anyone other that those who have themselves been victims.

DEAD MEN TALKING

Methods of abuse are truly horrendous and include: live burials with the uncertainty of being retrieved, physical mutilation, sexual abuse, the enforced killing of family members and animals which have previously been given as pets, the enforced pregnancy for the purpose of subsequent removal of the child for sacrifice, the enforced drinking of blood, eating of faeces and cannibalism upon bodies of sacrificial victims, general sustained humiliation etc.. The list is as long as the imagination of the perpetrators of such atrocities allows it to be.

Many of the Satanic rituals are performed at the altars of out of the way and redundant churches for the purpose of generating terror and negativity within these sacred sites. The energy is then harnessed for personal power and the perpetuation of the Luciferic force upon the Earth (as well as to further traumatise their slaves for mind-control purposes such as Project Ultra Green/MK-Ultra Project Monarch/Freedom Train). In this way the Earth's energy matrix – the collective unconscious, which is continuous with the human psyche, is kept in a negatively imbalanced state – whilst the sickest members of the human race have an obscene outlet for their perverse fantasies..

The British intelligence agencies and the USA's CIA and NSA are well aware of such organised anathemata including the identities of those involved and the code names used for such operations, such as Ultra Green and Project Monarch. Patti herself has given her details to various agencies including England's Scotland Yard. However, this global underbelly is so deeply entrenched in the System that these people are left entirely untouched by the legal system. Many cult-busting and rescue organisations exist, most working in tandem with the police (who are rife with this problem), but are themselves kept a closely guarded secret, supposedly in order to minimise the problem of infiltration. This is yet another way of maintaining overall secrecy via compart-mentalisation within the pyramidal structure in order to preserve the status quo.

Even today, at the age of thirty seven, Patti is regularly picked up off the streets to be drugged, raped, tortured or made to actually perform in Satanic ceremonies in the role of one of her personalities which is a priestess within the cult. All of which further traumatises her and enforces the compartmentalisation of her personalities. Her assailants also have an intimate knowledge of black magic and are able to summon her remotely to various locations under the control of her various personalities in order to abduct her.

One evening, Patti had paid Shona a visit whilst I was at work and spent the entire night flipping from one personality to another. These personalities ranged from the totally meek, 'Nothing', aged three, through variously aged 'Patricias' to the quite nasty and foul-mouthed 'Cathy'. In the early hours she became obsessed with leaving the house to take part in a ritual which she knew was taking place nearby and expressed an overwhelming desire to drink blood. This began at ten past three – the time which Satanists associate with Satan's greatest moment upon Earth – the time of the Crucifixion of Jesus. A little after five, when the ritual would have been completed, Patti began to normalise but revealed to Shona that she had taken a drugs overdose, though not enough to do any serious harm. This was entirely out of character for her as she has spent her life loving and protecting her three children from her 'Family' as she calls them. This did correspond, however, with threats which had been made to her merely a week earlier by five men who had abducted her during a visit to her home town of Darlington, that if she and we did not 'back off' then they would kill her via an injected overdose and make it look like suicide. They had explained to her that this could be prepared easily through a series of manipulated 'suicide attempts' which would give her the appearance of being in a suicidal state.

The extensive information which Patti has revealed of the names, dates and methods of the British paedophile/Satanic ring are now in the hands of many individuals throughout Britain. If any 'accident' should 'mysteriously' befall Patti or anyone involved in this book and its distribution, these names along with a mass of evidence (including prominent members of the aristocracy, active politicians, a former British Prime Minister, eye witnesses, the ring leaders and 'lackeys' etc.) will be made public. Furthermore, I wish it to be known that both Shona and I are in perfect mental and physical health and are looking forward to being present throughout the transformation of the Earth and on into a glorious future.

The BSE Case

In 1986, in Britain, the first recorded case was recognised of Bovine Spongiform Encephalopathy (BSE), a new disease which was affecting the nervous systems of cattle, causing Parkinsonian/ dementia-like symptoms. The official cause was identified by the Ministry for Agriculture Fisheries and Food (MAFF) as cross-contamination of a previously known sheep disease called Scrapie via cattle feeds which contained meat and bone meal from sheep. By 1996, the numbers of cows said to have been infected with BSE had risen to 27,800 despite the ban on meat feeds for cattle in 1989. The increasing incidence of a similar disease in humans called Creutzfeld-Jacob Disease (CJD), in which the brain becomes mushroom-like and full of holes causing sufferers to become gradually more confused until death, has been blamed upon the consumption of infected beef products. Therefore, a mass slaughter of British cattle was initiated in 1996 in order to resolve the problem. BSE has also infected many other animals such as domestic cats, birds of prey and zoo animals given infected meat.

Despite assurances that BSE was confined to very few cases, the number of cases of CJD has increased in England from 27 in 1985, to 42 in 1994, and 55 in

DEAD MEN TALKING

1995.

Significantly, there are three recognised types of CJD (the types 1 and 2 being similar to Alzheimer's Disease with confusion and memory loss as the main symptoms) whereas the cases of CJD since 1985 have been mainly of a new type-3 (which is indicated by additional loss of muscle co-ordination and balance).

This is essentially the story which has been fed to the mass public via the media and has caused a panic among consumers who have begun to avoid British beef products. It even initiated what was described in the press as a 'trade war' with Europe spearheaded by the British Prime Minister John Major in a typical 'white knight' fashion.

The truth of the situation is far more sinister and has implications for everyone, meat eaters and vegetarians alike. The discovery was made by organic farmer, Mark Purdy. That is, BSE and type-3 CJD is caused not by an entirely new form of infection (called a prion by the investigating scientists) but is caused by poisoning by organo-phosphate fertilisers.

Several inconsistencies have been conveniently overlooked by the 'experts' investigating this case:

1. that no organic farmer (those not using chemicals such as pesticides) has had a case of BSE despite using the same meat/bone-meal feeds as everyone else, and 2. that despite virtually the whole of Europe using these same feeds, there have been very few cases of BSE on the continent. So it can hardly be the Scrapie-contaminated feed, can it?

During the Second World War, I.G. Farben (the Nazi chemical company responsible for Zyclon B which was allegedly used to gas the Jews in the Holocaust and who used the inmates of Auschwitz as slave labour and as guinea pigs for testing of chemicals) developed a fluorinated nerve gas known as Sarin which was also used by the Iraquis during the Gulf War. This is an organo-phosphate (OP) compound which is very similar to that used by farmers in low concentrations to spray crops and dip sheep to prevent tick infestation, but it is used in much higher concentrations to treat cattle against warble-fly infestation.

In the 1980s, the MAFF began a war against the warble fly and imposed a mode of treatment upon Britain's farmers. This was that twice a year a preparation of OP concentrate be poured over the backs of all cattle. The OP is fat-soluble and is therefore absorbed by cow through the skin for a systemic effect to occur. Subsequently, an imprecise amount of OP is absorbed and the area most exposed to the compound is the spinal column i.e. directly into the central nervous system. The OP kills the warble fly by attacking the nervous system. The reported cases of BSE have been in the areas of warble fly infestation.

DEAD MEN TALKING

It has been established that, in cases of BSE, the prion protein in the brain becomes corrupted and mutates causing the familiar spongy brain situation. It has also been established that OPs bind to prion protein causing brain cells to mutate in a chain reaction. – as has been established in the case of the OP, Thalamide, a constituent of Thalidomide, which caused massive birth deformities in the late 60s and early 70s. Human brains also contain prion proteins!

Cases of BSE have been significantly higher in Switzerland and Northern Ireland. These countries have one other thing in common with mainland Britain, that is: they also use OPs – predominantly the compound Phosmet – in a strength which is four times that of the rest of Europe.

For several years now, many British farmers using OPs have been developing a severely debilitating condition which is not officially recognised despite the many claims and obvious links to OPs. The symptoms which are displayed in this syndrome are: severe malaise and fatigue, chest pain, Parkinson-like tremors and other nervous disorders. However, organic farmers are not affected by this 'mysterious' syndrome.

Up to more than 25 times the allowed amounts of OPs have been found in conventionally grown carrots in England. The investigations by (MAFF) showed that, in 8% of carrots, the contents were higher than the international Maximum Residue Level (MRL) limit. OPs both attack the brain and weaken the immune system and are undoubtedly a major factor in the 20th Century disease process such as the increasing incidence of recurrent infections and the immuno-suppressive diseases such as AIDS.

The most significant lab tests using this theory have been performed, initiated by Purdey's, research by the Government's Medical Research Council in Britain but have shown to be inconclusive. However, the MRC have admitted that they have not been using actual prion proteins for these tests, but have been experimenting on synthetic prion proteins! Could this be because it was the British Government, through MAFF, in the 1980s who made OPs compulsory and therefore caused BSE? If the truth were accepted then there would be grounds for the recovery of huge sums of money in damages claims both from the government and from the petrochemical producers of the OPs themselves, such as Wellcome and ICI.

The Government has clearly been using the BSE crisis in Britain to achieve a political agenda. Meanwhile, the true cause of CJD is kept well hidden.

THE PHARMACEUTICAL RACKET

In the early half of this century the petrochemical giants organised a coup on the medical research establishments, hospitals and universities. The

DEAD MEN TALKING

Rockefellers did this by sponsoring research and donating monetary gifts to US universities and medical schools where research was drug based and further extended this policy to foreign medical establishments via their International Education Board. Those who were not drug based were refused funding and were soon dissolved in favour of the more lucrative pharmaceutical-based projects.

In 1939 the 'Drug Trust' alliance was formed by the Rockefeller Empire and I.G. Farben. After the war, I.G. Farben was dismantled but later emerged in the many guises of the companies with whom they had signed cartel agreements. These companies include: Imperial Chemical Industries (ICI), Borden, Carnation, General Mills, M.W. Kellogg Co., Nestle, Pet Milk, Squibb and Sons, Bristol Meyers, Whitehall laboratories, Procter and Gamble, Roche, Hoechst and Beyer and Co. (two extant pharmaceutical companies who initially employed convicted war criminals Friedrich Jaehne and Fritz ter Meer as board chairmen). The Rockefeller Empire – in tandem with the Chase Manhattan Bank now owns over half of the USA's pharmaceutical interests and is the largest drug manufacturing combine in the world. Since the war the drug industry has steadily netted an ever increasing profit from sales of drugs to become the second largest manufacturing industry in the world next to the arms industry (also owned by the self same Elite agencies).

Today, health care is a multi-billion pound industry world-wide with ever increasing expenditure by taxpayers into the system which funnels the majority of this staggering profit into the hands of the drug manufacturers who are, as we have seen, headed by the major Elite manipulators of this century. These companies now control the vast majority of health care and set the standards for the practice of medicine in all developed countries. Doctors are no longer free to choose the most reliable and safe forms of therapy available but are at the mercy of their financial reliance on sponsoring (frequently bribing) drug companies. Once out of drug-company sponsored medical school, doctors embark on a career of increasing workloads and have ever increasing amounts of new pharmaceutical products to use and understand. The sheer volume of literature which a GP will receive from drug sales reps has resulted in the present situation whereby GPs are poorly educated about the chemicals which they are giving to their patients and are essentially gleaning most of their post-graduate training from the salesmen of private business. The moral implications of this are staggering.

The number of available drug preparations is now well in excess of 200,000. In 1980, the World Health organisation advised that a mere 240 drugs are necessary in order to provide good health care in the Third World (which should be more than adequate for First World needs considering we are a significantly healthier proportion of the population) whilst in 1981 the United Nations Industrial Development Organisation stated that a mere 26 of these are considered 'indispensables'. Most of the many drugs which are now available are known as 'me-too' drugs, i.e. recombinations and exact reproductions of drugs already available but which are irresistible to other companies who wish to share in their market. For example, the standard analgesics Paracetamol and Aspirin come in a multitude of forms under a variety of different brand names and yet these products can vary in price to a factor of ten or more times for the exact same formula depending on brand type chosen. Often the consumer erroneously presumes that increased price is equivalent to increased quality in this case and are entirely unaware that the drugs they are buying and those which they are rejecting are identical. Doctors are also often guilty of prescribing drugs by trade name and thus netting greater profits for the favoured company whilst cheaper versions are available to the unwary consumer/patient. Usually, before handing in a prescription it pays to consult the attending pharmacist if there is an equivalent and cheaper drug available. This can save some chronic drug users hundreds of pounds per year.

Pharmaceutical companies rely upon ill health in the population to survive and reap their profits. No drug company has a vested interest in curing disease. They do, however, have a massive vested interest in maintaining ill-health, creating disease and manufacturing chemicals which will promote this under the guise of 'therapy' for the symptoms – rarely ever the cause – of disease. Dr John Braithwaite, now a Trade Practices Commissioner, in his expose, Corporate Crime in the Pharmaceutical Industry, states:

'International bribery and corruption, fraud in the testing of drugs, criminal negligence in the unsafe manufacturing of drugs – the pharmaceutical industry has a worse record of law-breaking than any other industry.'

In the US in 1978 1.5 million people were hospitalised because of medication side-effects alone. In 1991 in the US, 72,000 people were killed due to iatrogenic – that is doctor-induced – causes whilst 24,073 died of victims of firearms shootings, which makes doctors nearly three times more lethal than guns! This has serious implications for other countries including Britain because the US are the foremost pioneers in the health care field and what occurs in health care in the US is usually implemented in Britain a decade later.

The drugs industry has managed to sell to the majority of the world the idea that disease is largely an inevitable part of life, especially during the later years. Through its front-line representatives – the medical system – it has effectively reduced the range of choices of health care to which the public has access. Through funding and educational control it has seen to it that natural forms of treatment are largely ignored and grossly under-researched. Those organisations which do reveal the true causes of disease and promote effective forms of disease prevention, such as nutritional medicine, healing and naturopathy are regularly attacked in the mass media and publicly labelled as quacks by pharmaceutically-sponsored de-bunking organisations such as the Campaign Against Health Fraud, now called Healthwatch.

They have also sold to us the idea that natural remedies and cures which have been successfully employed for centuries are 'alternatives' and to be treated with great scepticism and caution. Frequently, we are told of how one or two people have been injured or killed through the misapplication of a herbal remedy by dubious alternative practitioners but are not told at the same time of the thousands who are damaged by the conventional drugs which are handed out like sweets by our doctors.

During their initiation into the Western medical tradition most of our young doctors are repeatedly informed by their superiors that therapies which are alternative to classic western medicine are fraudulent and quackish. They are told that there is no scientific evidence to support any of the claims of psychic healing, crystal therapy, colour therapy and the like and the whole area is dismissed with a superior grin and a wave of the hand. A mountain of study is then hurled at the junior doctors, on top of an already inhumane workload of practical hours, to be spent absorbing the biased views of their forebears. A junior doctor has not even enough time to explore the realms of stress-free relaxation never mind alternative thought and therapies. Much the same methods are used by certain religious organisations to indoctrinate the minds of their followers into a single belief system. The key tactics, to which most doctors will relate, are: maintenance of sleep deprivation so as to minimise resistance to teachings, isolation from the outside world until one is literally eating, breathing and sleeping the set doctrine of the cult, and maintenance of a fear of failure to conform through almost unachievably high level goal setting; often via frequent examinations.

I believe that western medicine is as much a dogmatic cult as popular Christianity or the Moonies. It breeds its young on dogma to the exclusion of free will and reasoned thought in order to perpetuate itself. It is controlled by instilling into its members the fear of failure and it thrives by exploiting the initial motivation of its members, which is love and a desire to help and heal others.

At the apex of the pyramid of medicine lie the controllers; not doctors, but the multinational pharmaceutical companies who exist, not for the benefit of others, but for the desire for money and power. And behind them lies the sinister organisation of global secret societies headed by the Illuminati.

It is through this subtle mind control that the System maintains itself. Veiled in secrecy and fuelled by fear, the monster machine controls every aspect of our lives. The medical system is an integral part, but nevertheless only one aspect, of the overall design which seeks power and neither cares how this power is achieved, nor how many individuals are destroyed in the process.

As an example of the fraud perpetuated by the pharmaceutical companies, the next section will take a close look at the AIDS scandal, which illuminates how these companies have infiltrated every area of the healthcare system are willing to endanger people, allowing them to be killed, for profit via the industry's tool of corruption and front organisation, our own medical system:

What is AIDS?

AIDS is defined as any one of twenty five unrelated diseases plus a positive test for the presence of antibodies to the Human Immuno-deficiency Virus (HIV). It is said to be transferred through intimate sexual contact via the transfer of bodily fluids such as semen and blood. It is also said to be passed on through intravenous means by needle-sharing drug users and infected blood transfusions.

Nearly five hundred scientists world-wide, including eminent doctors such as leading University of California Professor of Molecular Biology, Peter Duesberg, and Australian biophysicist Eleni Papadopoulous-Eleopoulos, Dr Charles Thomas (former Harvard Professor of Biochemistry), Dr Kary Mullis (1993 Nobel Prize-winner for Chemistry), Dr Hank Loman (Professor of Biophysical Chemistry, Free University of Amsterdam), and Dr Steven Lomas (Professor of Preventative Medicine, State University of New York) are now convinced that AIDS is not caused by HIV.

In simple terms, the facts just do not add up. For example, there are many people with AIDS but without HIV and vast numbers of people who are HIV positive are not developing AIDS. The tests for the presence of retrovirus HIV – the Western Blot Test and the ELISA Test – which show up HIV positive status, are so inaccurate that false positive tests can occur due to many diseases such as malnutrition, multiple infections, multiple sclerosis, tuberculosis, leprosy, having once had the 'flu' or measles and the bodies natural response to anal semen.

Once diagnosed as HIV positive, patients are given regular blood tests to monitor their immunological responses, particularly for a drop in T-cell count. T-cells are released in the immune response to disease to attack invading antigens. A significant T-cell drop, in many clinics, is the indicator that active drug therapy should be commenced. However, using T-cell counts as an indicator of disease is entirely useless as the average T-cell count for a healthy person can range from 200 to 2000 over the course of a normal day. Professor Ian Weller, who co-ordinated the British arm of the Concorde AZT trial testing the drug on healthy HIV-positive volunteers, commented:

'The thing we have to remember about CD4 (T-cell) counts is they are very variable. They can vary in an individual over the time of day... lower in the morning and higher in the evening. They can be affected by things that you do such as walking to the clinic, as opposed to riding a bike... the amount of sunshine can affect them. Smoking as well.'

This whole area of inaccurate testing in the area of AIDS and AIDS Related Conditions (ARC) has accounted for many people being incorrectly diagnosed as HIV positive, such as in Africa where there is a supposed epidemic; there is also a massive amount of otherwise unrelated disease there too and it is this factor which is causing the false positives.

Once diagnosed, patients are then initiated onto courses of highly toxic drugs such as AZT, DDI and Septrin, many of the side effects of which are the self same symptoms as those of AIDS.

None of these AIDS defining diseases are new. What is new, however, is the HIV test. All research into this syndrome has been based upon the findings of Robert Gallo, the co-founder and patent holder of the test, which have since been found to be fraudulent. Gallo's partner and co-founder of the HIV theory, Luc Montagnier, declared in 1989:

'HIV is not capable of causing the destruction to the immune system which is seen in people with AIDS'.

One medical doctor who has practised and lectured on medicine world-wide for over thirty five years, Dr. Robert E. Wilner has even publicly demonstrated that HIV does not cause disease by injecting himself with the blood of an HIV positive patient on Spain's most popular television show; yet this never made it to the press outside of Spain! In his book 'Deadly Deception: The Proof That Sex And HIV Absolutely Do Not Cause AIDS', Dr. Wilner cites AZT as one of the major causes of AIDS, he also insists that 'HIV is simply a harmless piece of tissue, not unlike numerous other retroviruses that exist in our body' and that 'AIDS is not transmitted sexually nor is it contagious by any method!'

Dr Duesberg, recognised as one of, if not the foremost retrovirus expert in the world, points out:

'AZT is A Random Killer Of Infected And Non-Infected Cells. AZT cannot discriminate among them. It kills T-cells, B-cells, red cells, it kills all cells. AZT is a chain terminator of DNA synthesis of all cells – no exceptions. It wipes out everything. In the long run it can only lead to death of the organism – and the cemetery. AZT is a certain killer! Who will be responsible for the death of patients (some 200,000 now being treated with AZT and countless thousands who have already died from it in the past decade) that results from AZT therapy – pharmacological homicide?'

DEAD MEN TALKING

And furthermore, that:

'HIV does not cause AIDS... The point that everyone is missing is that all of those original papers, Gallo wrote on HIV have been found fraudulent... The HIV hypothesis was based on those papers.'

It is my opinion that these scientists are correct and that HIV is not the cause of AIDS. AIDS is not a single viral disease but a collection of, in part, unrelated diseases which are caused by disharmonious energies in the fields of the holistic body, brought about by all sorts of reasons. Undoubtedly one of the major causes of death by AIDS-related diseases is the inability of the body to fight off the manifested disease because the body has been weakened by the very drugs given to suppress the disease. Tests have shown that the only effective treatments for AIDS are those which involve the cessation of conventional drugs in favour of unconventional natural therapies such as Essiac, Oxygen/Ozone Therapy and CanCell. However, these natural therapies share a common theme in that they have all been suppressed or withdrawn by governmental agencies and those with vested interests in the pharmaceutical industry.

(To further support the fact that HIV is not transferred sexually, Cathy O'Brien in her book Trance Formation Of America, points out that, despite being prostituted to men in areas supposedly rife with AIDS, none of her political abusers ever wore protection during sex with her.)

Wellcome to Hell

Wellcome (Wellcome Burroughs in the US) began as a pharmaceutical company set up in 1880 by Henry Wellcome and Silas Burroughs. Its links to the Rockefeller Empire were apparent in Henry Wellcome's appointing of John and Allen Dulles of the Sullivan and Cromwell law firm as those responsible for any legal matters relating to the company and his own will. With Henry Wellcome's death in 1936, the Wellcome Trust was set up in conjunction with the company (now the Wellcome Foundation) and this has now become one of the largest funders of medical research in Europe. The Rockefeller connection was also strengthened in the late 50's when Wellcome took over the running of aspects of the Rockefeller funded London University College Hospital Medical School and their joint interests in tropical illness research via the London School of Hygiene and Tropical Medicine.

Over the following decades, Wellcome pursued several aspects of pharmaceutical healthcare with interests in general over-the-counter remedies, antivirals, animal healthcare, genetic engineering and biotechnology. It strengthened its connections within the government, the media, medical academia and the various committees, societies and associations that were continuously being set up to review, regulate and control all aspects of scientific medical research and education. It did this by making donations to many of these organisations, such as the British Association for the Advancement of Science, the Parliamentary Science and Technology Foundation, the Parliamentary Office of Science and Technology, and the British Medical Association's Foundation for AIDS (to which it gave £144,000 between 1988 and 1992), and by placing its own trustees, researchers and 'experts' in prominent positions within them. For example: Sir Alastair Pilkington one time vice president of the Foundation for Science and Technology was a research scientist for Wellcome; Professor C. Gordon Smith, Dean of the London School of Hygiene and Tropical Medicine was a Wellcome trustee; Lord Swann, Director of the BBC in the 1980's was a Wellcome trustee; Sir Alfred Shepperd, a member of the Advisory Council on Science and Technology(ACST) was Chairman of Burroughs Wellcome and the Wellcome Foundation until 1985; Professor Roy Anderson, Head of Pure and Applied Biology at London Imperial College of Science, Technology and medicine and a member of ACST was also a Wellcome trustee.

In the 1980's however, the company went through some major rationalisations. In 1986 the decision was made to sell shares in the Welcome drug company which had previously been owned in its entirety by the Wellcome Trust. In the following six years it also sold off several areas of business including Cooper Animal Healthcare – a joint venture with ICI producing organo-phosphate sheep dip – and its interests in vaccine production. Production of general cough and cold remedies was also reduced to a mere 14% of sales while it began concentrating its funds in the more profitable areas of genetics, biotechnology and anti-virals.

AZT, marketed by Wellcome as Retrovir, had been developed in the 60s as a drug to treat cancer but it had proved to be highly toxic as well as ineffective as it appeared unable to distinguish between cancerous and healthy cells. However, tests in vitro appeared to show some anti-viral properties which was why, after being shelved in the 60s, AZT was re-tested for use in the treatment of AIDS in the 1980s.

Human clinical drug trials, following extensive (though useless) animal testing, usually take place in two parts. Phase I tests for toxicity; Phase II concentrates on the long-term side-effects and efficacy, all of which can take several years. In the case of AZT the Phase II trials in America were halted after 4 months when only 1 of the AZT users as opposed to 19 of the control group had died and the drug was granted a license despite the fact that the patients in the trial were given regular blood transfusions to alleviate the possible side-effects (this should, under usual circumstances, have negated the results of the trial). This licensing of AZT so quickly was unprecedented and made Wellcome's profits double to £1132 million in the space of 4 years! As if this wasn't enough, subsequent licenses for other

DEAD MEN TALKING

AIDS drugs were issued subject to the condition that they would have to be tested against AZT and then only prescribed in conjunction with it.

Incredibly, AZT was licensed in the UK without any clinical trials four weeks before it was licensed in the US. This, perhaps, may have been due to the fact that, of the 25 members of the Medicines Commission who are parliamentary advisers on medicine, 5 had interests in Wellcome; one prominent member being Professor Trevor M. Jones, Director of Research and Development at Wellcome. And of the 21 members of the Committee on the Safety of Medicines who grant the licenses, two had interests in the Welcome Foundation.

Within a short space of time, AZT was licensed in 35 countries around the world and Wellcome were promoting it with media advertising, press releases and all-expenses-paid conferences to which they regularly invited the world's top scientists and physicians, all the while denying any suggestions that it caused harmful side-effects.

Wellcome's influence on the media and the government continued with its donation of £10,000 to the All Party Parliamentary Group on AIDS (APOGA) as, with the Medical Research Council, Wellcome began the trials of AZT on asymptomatic HIV positive patients – the Concorde trials – in October 1988. From that point onwards most of the doctors presenting information and writing for APGOA were also involved in these trials. Not content with promoting their own research in the area of AIDS they also began to attack any alternative treatments or anyone who challenged the HIV=AIDS hypothesis.

Wellcome had also cornered the British market in AIDS testing kits. With the help of Dr. Robin Weiss and Angus Dalgleish from the Institute of Cancer Research, a second generation kit was marketed based on the research by Campaign Against Health Fraud (now Healthwatch) member, Professor Vincent Marks, head of the Biochemistry Department of Surrey University – a department which has received over half a million pounds from Wellcome since 1985. In order to ensure that anyone found to be HIV positive was immediately directed towards 'help' from AZT-promoting doctors, GP's were given very limited access to the testing kits. They had no choice but to send their patients to Wellcome-infiltrated teaching hospitals and STD clinics in London while the promotion and sale of home testing kits was banned in the UK (in 1992), thereby ensuring Wellcome's complete monopoly in all aspects of AIDS treatment and diagnosis.

Education about HIV and AIDS could also not be overlooked and Wellcome donated substantial funds to pay for a £150,000 package for GPs, produced by the British Medical Association.

The Concorde trials themselves, instead of being independent, were almost totally under Wellcome's influence. The initial reason for the trials was to prove that AZT would be effective in preventing the development of ARC and AIDS in otherwise healthy HIV+ patients. Going against all established regulations for the independence of such trials, which in the past had the drug companies supplying the drug and paying the hospitals to do the trials, the Concorde trial was set up jointly between Wellcome, the Medical Research Council (MRC) and the Department of Health. The MRC paid for the treatment and the Department of Health granted the use of six London hospitals, NHS staff and facilities. Anyone with an HIV positive test was encouraged to join the trial without discussion of any alternative treatments whilst being promised up to 3 years of free healthcare despite the fact that the AZT drug was to be administered at 1000mg per day – twice the dose recommended by the US Food and Drug Administration – and the recent reports of serious side-effects such as muscle wasting, anaemia and impotence. Wellcome's crowning glory in this deal, though, was to also insist that the contract gave them complete control over the writing of any reports about the trial. The only report which had to be agreed between all parties was the one for general publication, if indeed any published report was even deemed necessary.

Just to make absolutely sure of obtaining the desired outcome, Wellcome had the help of several 'friends' in the MRC who had just as many, if not more, commitments to industry and business matters than they did to the medical establishment or the government. Lord Jellicoe, Chairman of the MRC's AIDS committee, was a director of the Rockefeller company Morgan Crucible as well as the sugar company Tate and Lyle and was later chairman of Booker Tate confectionery; Sir Donald Acheson worked for the Department of Health but left in 1991 to work in the Rockefeller funded School of Hygiene and Tropical Medicine; Sir Austin Bide was Chief Executive of Glaxo (now in partnership with Wellcome) and had been a director of J. Lyons & Co confectionery in the 70's. Sir David Crouch, MP for Canterbury until 1987, was director of Pfizer Ltd., a pharmaceutical company which was the only manufacturer of a synthesised ingredient of AZT at that time and also ran several public relations companies one of which, Kingsway Rowland, handled Wellcome's AZT account; Dr J. W. G. Smith, director of the Public Health Laboratory Service since 1985 used to be a Senior Lecturer at the School of Hygiene and Tropical Medicine before going to work for Wellcome as head of Bacteriology in 1969; Professor D. A. Warrell was a director of the Wellcome Tropical Research Unit and has also done malaria research funded by Wellcome and the Rockefeller Foundation; Professor C. N. Hales is a specialist in diabetes whose research is often funded by pharmaceutical companies including Wellcome.

With the above as the only 8 members of the MRC Committee on AIDS and their Chairman Lord Jellicoe, it is not surprising that a drug once deemed to be too toxic, which has never been properly tested and whose side-effects, according to the British National Formulary, bear s striking resemblance to the symptoms of AIDS itself, has been allowed to become the AIDS drug of the 90's and has kept the profits rolling in for Wellcome to the tune of an estimated £400 million a year.

'I will give no deadly medicine to any one if asked.'

(from the Hippocratic Oath)

Walter's position as a staff nurse at Newcastle General Hospital's Infectious Disease Unit (ward 25), which is affiliated with the London School of Tropical Medicine, has given me an insight into the world of AIDS treatment which is rarely seen and it only serves to corroborate the research of the aforementioned enlightened scientists, whose numbers are ever increasing. The world of AIDS care and treatment at the NGH has some very sinister elements and I have no reason to suspect that it is isolated to this regional unit alone. Here is an outline of some of the information which Walter has provided:

* According to the code of conduct provided by the United Kingdom Central Council for nursing and midwifery, the nurse's role is to be the patient's advocate and is, therefore, entrusted to provide care in the best interest of the patient and to decline from doing anything which is detrimental to their well being. One of the major areas covered by this is in the administration of drugs; the nurse is responsible for ensuring the correct dosage of drug is given and is responsible also for being aware of the effects and possible side effects of the medication.

However, in the NGH unit, nurses are expected to give all drugs prescribed by the doctor whether or not any information on the effects of the drug are available. Frequently the prescribing doctor is unaware of the true nature of the drugs and thus unable to inform the nursing staff of the effects and side effects of the drugs they are using. Many and varied substances appear and disappear periodically from the drugs cupboard, often named only as a series of numbers or letters. When challenged as to the reason why they have prescribed such unknown entities, the doctors usually reply that their consultant has ordered it to be given. The consultant is usually unavailable for comment.

* The side effects of the drugs have been seen to be potentially harmful. For example, one commonly used drug, Foscarnet, which is given directly into the heart or eyes of a patient, when dropped on a nurse's tights dissolved them on contact. Common side effects of this drug include epilepsy, blindness and dementia. Many patients have entered the unit with minor symptoms such as weight loss and have, in a short space of time, become blind and epileptic through using it. Walter has frequently said to me, 'I'm poisoning people for a living', but if he

refused to give the drugs as prescribed he would lose his job and someone would be found who would administer them. The same is true of the junior doctors who are afraid of the vengeance from above if they were to challenge the status quo. No challenge has yet been made, even after I presented the unit with detailed papers outlining the research which has negated the 'HIV equals AIDS' myth.

* Once diagnosed as HIV positive, many patients are then informed that the only chance they have for extended survival is to use the drugs provided. Obviously the majority of patients, many of whom show very few symptoms, are too afraid not to co-operate with the regime. They then suffer terribly and die a lingering and undignified death.

As a response to many challenges Walter has made to the medical staff to justify their drugs regime, he has been branded cynical and defeatist; as not wishing to give the patients a chance for survival. In reply to this he has asked on many occasions for the doctors to give him even just one example of anyone whom they have cured of AIDS or significantly improved the quality of life. Not one of them has been able to give such an example.

Even if we were extending people lives, in doing so we also inflict upon them such diseases as makes for little or no quality of life. What is the point of an extra year of life if that year is spent as a living vegetable? If we do have a prognosis of death, then surely it is better to live that remaining life to the full with our eventual demise being as gentle and as dignified as possible.

* On one occasion, the unit exceeded its drugs budget and feared a crisis in care. At this point Wellcome stepped in and offered its services for free on the condition that they would supply the drugs as long as all research notes were given directly to them in return. It appears that the only figures who were aware of anything like the full picture were the consultants in charge and the research nurse appointed by the company, none of whom were willing to reveal anything of the results of these apparently blind drugs trials.

In effect, this means that the patients on this unit are being treated by the pharmaceutical scientists as human guinea pigs, in order to test the various drugs supplied. How are we to know that these drugs are genuinely safe for the purpose of therapy? Might they simply be poisons or ineffectual chemicals thrown onto the research pot in a vain attempt to happen across some element of cure? Are they even actively seeking a cure, knowing what we do of their motivation?

Some of the drugs which have been identified and are in regular use have long since been discontinued in other areas of medicine because they are ineffective and/or dangerous. For example, A.Z.T. was once considered too toxic to be given to terminally ill cancer patients!

DEAD MEN TALKING

Interestingly, the official patient leaflet, 'HIV and AZT, the choices', as supplied to AIDS departments by Wellcome, gives merely three examples of side effects of the drug, i.e. anaemia, which they say effects up to 40% of users; headaches in 1-10% of users; and sickness in 25% of users which: 'almost always disappear after a few weeks of treatment'. The leaflet also states:

Most people do not suffer side effects when they take AZT early. If they do occur, there are ways of coping with them. They may be reversed, if necessary by stopping treatment.

If you thought that you may be facing death through an incurable disease would you stop taking the drug that has been hyped as giving an extension of lifespan, I wonder?

Septrin is a combination of two antibiotics and has been shown to be far less effective and far more liable to dramatic side effects than either of the components when used individually (interestingly, it is also nearly three times more expensive than the more effective and less harmful constituent ingredient Trimethorprim).

Even Thalidomide is now being used on Ward 25 for its anti-emetic properties.

* Many patients diagnosed as terminally ill have drawn up living wills in which they often request a cessation of active treatment in the end stages of disease. These are frequently ignored by the doctors who continue to pump toxins into dying patients and claim to be simply following orders from above. The point of which escapes myself and Walter and quite often the doctors themselves.

* When a patient dies, relatives are officially informed that their loved ones are deemed as dangerous waste and must, therefore, be sealed and cremated for hygiene reasons. No mention is made of autopsy or further experimentation and yet Walter has witnessed conversations amongst doctors regarding autopsy findings on such people who were supposed to have gone to cremation unmolested. Is this further pharmaceutical research?

* One evening, in the absence of an available doctor from the unit, Walter had to call upon a consultant from another area to advise upon a matter. Whilst this covering doctor was attending to the issue Walter made known his concerns about the dangerous amounts of drugs a patient was prescribed. This consultant agreed with Walter that it was excessive and dangerous and complied with his request to discontinue the majority of the drugs. He also admitted to Walter that there was definitely something extraordinary and far reaching going on in this area which was beyond his jurisdiction. Furthermore, if he had his way, the majority of the drugs given on the unit would never have been prescribed in the first

place. However, 'see no evil, hear no evil, speak no evil' seemed to be the order of the day and that was the end of the matter.

All of this information is deeply disturbing. As more and more evidence mounts against the HIV theory, it seems that the only way to survive AIDS is to steer clear of the medical profession and its terrible drugs. If it is true of this one syndrome then how true is it of other areas of disease? Just how manipulated are we by these companies? And how much wheeling and dealing is going on behind the scenes between consultants and pharmaceutical companies which directly effects our well-being?

AIDS is a huge money spinner providing millions of pounds of profit per day in drugs sales and its offshoot market of condom sales (Wellcome also has links with the London Rubber Company). It has instilled a fear in the heart of our society of free sexual expression and has given rise to much bigotry from the poorly educated who see AIDS as a judgement from God or a punishment for active homosexuality. It has created a huge charity industry, netting millions of pounds from the world population to fund further research to rid the world of this affliction. And how much misery and negativity has it generated? Further research means more experiments on both animals and humans. And the figures for economic growth just rise and rise.

Truth – A Cure For All Disease

As another example of the medical conspiracy; would it shock you to find out that there are, in use today, several medically proven cures for cancer? One such cure is Essiac and has been in use since at least 1922; it has no known adverse side effects. It is made from four common herbs and elevates the immune system. In 1937 it came within three votes of being legalised as a cancer treatment in Canada and was passed on to the British Cancer Campaign by its founder, Rene Caisse, via the Prince of Wales. And yet today, it is still only available through selected, virtually underground, outlets world-wide. I have many dozens of case studies which testify to the efficacy of this treatment (see Appendix IV).

Furthermore, in the 1930s a man named Royal Raymond Rife developed a very high powered microscope, almost seven times more powerful than those in use at the time, which could detect organisms which cause diseases such as infections and cancers. He did this by illuminating these organisms at their own specific frequency of light and could, therefore, examine them and their effects whilst they remained alive as opposed to killing them first using dye stains or high powered electron microscopy as was the norm. He then discovered that, by altering the frequency of their environment microbes could mutate and change their size and shape to resemble viruses and bacteria alike, thereby enabling the same microbe to cause many diverse diseases. For example, the same germs which cause pus – streptococci – could also become the germs which cause pneumonia – pneumococci – in response to an alteration in their environment. Rife also discovered that by bombarding these organisms with higher frequencies of light, he could destroy them. He demonstrated that it was possible to create and destroy cancers at will and succeeded in curing otherwise terminal patients of this disease, as well as others such as polio and typhus, in almost 100% of cases.

Today, it is conventionally accepted that single specific germs are responsible for single specific forms of infection. This theory was advanced by the French scientist Pasteur but was disputed by his rival Bechamp who was in favour of the mutation theory known as pleomorphism. We are rarely informed in text books that, according to his co-worker, Dr Duclaux, Pasteur himself changed his mind and revoked his 'germ theory' in favour of one closer to that of pleomorphism. However, over 100 years later, Pasteur's original germ theory is still the standard working model for the understanding of the action of microbes in the body.

Many types of bacteria exist in a symbiotic relationship with our bodies all of the time and only become symptomatic once the physical body begins to deteriorate due to an unhealthy lifestyle. Bacteria are then free to scavenge the 'soil' produced in the disease process, i.e. when the tissues degenerate to a similar frequency as the microbes, releasing dead organic matter similar to viruses upon which these microbes feed (remember Wilner's definition of the HIV retrovirus?). They then excrete this dead matter as waste products via the bloodstream, faeces or other exudates such as mucous. The extent to which the bacteria can multiply is limited to the amount of soil upon which they have to feed and could not be capable of invading the body to the extent to which science would have us believe unless there was already an adequate food supply. Furthermore, as has been demonstrated in Rife's vibratory work, it is possible for these microbes to mutate into other forms and even to cancer-causing agents according to their environmental conditions, defined by the degree of concentration of waste products and the vibratory rate. The subsequent systemic and metabolic reaction to these toxic excreted waste products, such as sore throat and high temperature (the body's natural way of eradicating the bacteria), are generally the symptoms of diseases which are given priority in day to day general medical practice, whereupon drugs are usually given to suppress them. In giving antibiotics we often succeed in killing the very microbes which are removing the diseased body's dead matter during the natural healing process. In doing so we also open up our bodies to other forms of disease such as fungal infections which are usually kept at bay by the natural presence of bacteria.

Another effective cure for AIDS and cancer has been successfully employed in clinical practise all over the world for at least fifty years and is a cure for virtually all germ diseases. This is Oxygen/Ozone therapy. The principle behind it is simplicity itself and is the reason why the pharmaceutical companies and drug agencies are so afraid of it that they have conspired to suppress it also. It is conventionally accepted that the majority of germs are anaerobic, which means that they survive without oxygen. Therefore, if one floods the bloodstream with oxygen, these organisms cannot survive. Oxygen is one of the fundamental and most necessary elements to human survival. It exists as air, water and most of our food sources such as carbohydrates. The human race has evolved in levels of oxygen far higher than exist in today's polluted and tree-depleted world and we are all running on less than is desirable for optimum health; especially the city-dwellers. Foods and food supplements which release high levels of oxygen such as in the form of Hydrogen Peroxide are beneficial to our well-being. Indeed, Hydrogen Peroxide itself, when taken in dilute form or applied directly to wounds is one of the most effective antiseptics and healing compounds there is.

I believe disease is the result of disharmonious energy fields which can be caused by both physical and non-physical disharmony. Thus, dis-ease can be eradicated by oxygen therapy because it boosts the immune system by raising our vibratory rate, thereby making our bodies healthy. It is a simple fact that disease cannot exist in a healthy body.

According to the testimonies of international MD's assembled at the May 1983 Sixth World Ozone (a concentrated form of Oxygen Therapy) Conference in Washington, D.C.:

Ozone eliminates... viruses and bacteria from blood, human and stored... Medical ozone is successfully used on AIDS, Herpes, Hepatitis, Mononucleosis, Cirrhosis of the liver, Gangrene, Cardiovascular Disease, Arteriosclerosis, High Cholesterol, Cancerous Tumours, Lymphomas, Leukaemia... Highly effective on Rheumatoid and other Arthritis, Allergies of all types... Improves Multiple Sclerosis, ameliorate Alzheimer's Disease, Senility and Parkinson's... Effective on Proctitis, Colitis, Prostate, Candidiasis, Trichomoniasis, Cystitis; Externally, ozone is effective in treating Acne, burns, leg ulcers, open sores and wounds, Eczema and fungus.

In 1976, the US FDA hindered the progress of this form of therapy by stating: Ozone is a toxic gas with no known medical uses.

And yet, one doctor using ozone in his work with colonic cancer patients, Dr Hans Neiper, from Hanover, despite refusing to divulge the names of his cancer patients, stated in 1987:

'President Reagan is a very nice man.' And, 'You wouldn't believe how many FDA officials or relatives or acquaintances of FDA officials come to see me in Hanover. You wouldn't believe this, or directors of the American Medical Association (AMA), or American Cancer Association, or the residents of orthodox cancer institutes. That's the fact.'

Oxygen/Ozone therapy researcher and ambassador, Ed McCabe states:

Let's compare medical ozone therapy with prescription drugs. In 1978 the FDA reported 1.5 million were hospitalised in the USA due to the side-effects of medication. On the other hand, medical ozone has been legally used in clinics world-wide on a daily basis since the forties, and in Germany 644 ozone therapists were surveyed, and they reported 384,775 patients had received 5,579,238 ozone treatments. The side-effect rate was only 0.0007% during 5.5 million dosages! Yet, each year approximately 140,000 people in the US die from prescription drug usage.

To this day researchers maintain that the exact causes of and cures for cancer are unknown whilst many others who claim that they do know are frequently the victims of a conspiracy of suppression by governmental agencies and corporate business interests.

It is vital that we understand the true nature of disease if we are to be effective in its eradication. It is imperative that we use the total sum of our knowledge to combat disease and work together as a multi-disciplinarian society, not in isolated, self-interested units. We must open our eyes to the realities and seek the best of conventional and unconventional medicine. We must concentrate on why we are ill and not simply seek to eradicate symptoms of disorders which we often see as inevitable. Disease is not our natural state, it is not inevitable. It is an outward physical display of disharmony whose cause is far more significant than its symptoms. The responsibility for health lies with all of us, not only with doctors or governments.

How many millions flock to the doctor and expect some treatment for a symptom, caring not for the cause but seeking only the relief of discomfort? And who is to blame them? They are victims of the pharmaceutical conspiracy too. According to these scientists, and medical practitioners who find employment within the System, there is little evidence to give credence to any form of medicine other than their own. Or so they and we are told.

They seem deaf to the testimonies of the healers and the healed who stand before them as living proof of the power of mind over matter, homeopathy and herbalism etc. It is healthy to be sceptical but there is a danger of sceptic thought becoming septic thought if it fails to reason with an open mind and allow for progress. Any doctor who fails to open their mind to the information such as is presented in this book is missing the opportunity to fulfil their true role as healers of the sick. There is without doubt a conspiracy of wilful ignorance amongst the cult of western medicine, as even scientifically verified proof of the healing power of channelled energy has been ignored by the majority of practitioners.

One smoke-screen which is constantly employed by the major drug companies is the regular promise that they are 'currently working on a new form of treatment which could soon revolutionise the treatment of...'. Such stories are picked up by the press and t.v science programmes with great fervour. They are nearly always described in terms of 'miracle cure' and point out that adequate funding is necessary for the fulfilment of the prophecy in another 2 or 3 years time. However, when 2 or 3 years time finally arrives we have all conveniently forgotten about the promised miracle drug whilst anxiously awaiting the fulfilment of yet further promises of drugs which are 'hoped' will one day prove to be the end of yet another terrible disease.

And this is the industry which denigrates the field of natural health for taking advantage of the sick and for so cruelly promising fake cures and providing false hope! The obvious lesson here is that to disguise your own sins you must accuse your enemies of them and to always do it before your enemy has a chance to formulate their defence. Mud usually sticks to the one it first lands upon. This a political trick which has been used to devastating effect by the key manipulators of this century in all areas and has been used to shift public opinion in favour of some of the greatest atrocities ever committed.

The Elite via chemo-pharmaceutical companies and food and water production services penetrate all areas of health care and use it to promote and execute their policies of population control, mind control and 'divide and rule', whilst making vast sums of money into the bargain.

Vivisection – far more than an animal rights issue!

This section is intended to be read in order that the sinister implications of animal experiments upon the whole of mankind are thoroughly understood. I am aware, from personal experience of street campaigning for animal rights issues, that many people who care passionately about animals find it simply too distressing to see or read any form of evidence to this effect. Consequently, I have chosen not to give practical details about individual animal experiments in the coming discourse

Instead I will focus upon the scientific fraud perpetrated by vivisectors and how their warped ethos that vivisection is a valuable scientific tool has corrupted the progress of medicine and upset the delicate balance of the minds of millions world-wide. I seek to show how vivisection is an integral part of the manipulation of society (the vivisectors themselves being amongst the most completely manipulated of all) by the very same consciousness and indeed the very same people

DEAD MEN TALKING

I have already discussed.

Nothing is worse than vivisection! No other single factor causes more pain, distress and death to humans and animals.

Nor is there any less scientific or ethical method of research currently being employed in industry or educational establishments anywhere in the world.

Unless you have read the books and seen the video footage which I and thousands of other anti-vivisection campaigners have been required to endure, nothing in your imagination can paint for you anything like the true picture of the hell of animal experiments. In fact, if you can conjure up the most heinous spectacle of abuse within your mind, be assured that this is precisely what is being done today, but probably much worse, around the world in schools, universities and research labs owned by private companies – and then some. It is being done with our money, and in order to provide huge mega-wealthy pharmaceutical companies with staggering profit and as an excuse to provide jobs for vivisectors. It is also perpetuated to ensure that mankind never becomes learned about the true nature, cause and cure of disease.

Two thousand animals per minute die as a result of gruesome experiments; that is 250 million per year; approximately 3.5 million per year in Great Britain alone. Over 75% of these experiments are done without anaesthetics, and when they are, they are often inadequately applied. Most experiments are done with public money. 0.2% of the animals used are for the testing of cosmetics. In Britain there are merely 19 Home Office inspectors to cover 20,000 licensed vivisectors.

The practise of animal experimentation has been the mainstay of medical and biological research since the early 1800s even though it has brought about not one major breakthrough in medical science. And yet, every medical student, in order to pass his or her exam and advance in their chosen career must quote the results of animal experiments.

How can respect for life, compassion and empathy be taught to and nurtured in our doctors through a practise which necessitates the ignorance of pain, suffering, anxiety terror and death, as is the case with the training process of US doctors who regularly dissect live animals as part of their training? The answer is simple: It can't.

The animal experimenters are the cornerstone of the highly corrupt and manipulative pharmaceutical industry. These are a pseudo-scientific fraternity who earn vast amounts of money for their employers by performing unbelievably barbaric experiments which can be used to (falsely) substantiate claims that their drugs are safe for human use. Dr. James D. Gallagher, Director of Research of Lederle Laboratories in the Journal of the American Medical Association, March

DEAD MEN TALKING

'Animal studies are done for legal reasons and not for scientific reasons. The predictive value for such studies for man is meaningless – which means our research may be meaningless.'

There is no British or European law which states that new drugs, chemicals or cosmetics must be tested on animals. However, animal testing ensures that vivisectors get the results they want in order to sell their dangerous chemicals to an unwary public. In numerous legal trials of drug companies who have caused fatalities and injuries, the most effective defence which has been used time and again is that: 'All of the usual and required testing had been done to establish the safety of the drug in question'. A standpoint which most legal authorities are not qualified to dispute. Indeed, the 'experts' upon whom they call for advice in such matters are invariably members of other drug companies or drug sponsored agencies and therefore the animal testing fraternity.

Animal experiments have been cited in many court battles over drugs damages claims and have been used both to defend the idea that such disasters were unforeseen because adequate testing had been employed, but have also been successfully used, as in the Thalidomide case in December 1970, to admonish the drug company (in this case Chemie Grunenthal) who testified that animal tests could never be conclusive for humans.

The very idea that a test or operation done on an animal will show results which are directly translatable to humans is plainly ridiculous. As has been stated by some of the greatest and most influential physicians in medical history: the anatomy, physiology and psychology of animals is entirely different to our own in many ways, and this difference is further exaggerated in the case of animals bred for and/or housed in laboratories. This can be plainly illustrated in many ways; here are just a few:

* The LD 50 (Lethal Dose 50%) test, which is the standard toxicity technique used to establish how much of a chemical toxin is required to kill half of a number of animals. These animals are specifically bred to be exactly identical in every way, i.e. genetically and physically they are the same size and weight. And yet, an equivalent dose of a toxin, in equal quantity and strength will succeed in killing merely half of the batch whilst leaving half to suffer varying degrees of disablement. These results are then haphazardly translated to give the figure for safe and fatal levels for humans. There are 12 different methods which determine statistically the safety of chemicals for humans from animal experiments. These may disagree by up to a factor of four. * It is accepted that animal tests are successful in identifying cancer-causing agents in only 37% of cases. This means, in effect, that the results of the tests are more times wrong than right and are signifi-

cantly statistically worse than tossing a coin. * As stated by Hans Ruesch in The Naked Empress or the Great Medical Fraud:

'Two grams of scopolamine kill a human being, but dogs and cats can stand hundred times higher dosages. A single Aminata phalloides mushroom can wipe out a whole human family, but is health food for the rabbit, one of the favourite laboratory animals. A porcupine can eat one lump without discomfort as much opium as a human addict smokes in two weeks, and wash it down with as much prussic acid to poison a regiment of soldiers. The sheep can swallow enormous quantities of arsenic, once the murderer's favourite poison. Morphine, which calms and anaesthetises man, causes maniacal excitement in cats and mice. On the other hand our sweet almond can kill foxes, our common parsley is poisonous to parrots, and our revered penicillin strikes another favourite laboratory animal dead – the guinea pig.'

It is fortunate for many that penicillin was never tested on guinea pigs at the outset where it would have immediately been discarded as dangerous. And if you want to prove that vitamin C is useless, withhold it from the diet of dogs – which produce vitamin C in the gut. Moreover, the whole discipline of surgery and post surgical recovery was hindered for hundreds of years after the Greek Galen (Second Century AD) showed through animal experimentation that the principle laid down by Hippocrates (Fifth century BC) was incorrect – that hygiene and a good diet (as well as establishing the simple fact that nature heals) was essential to good health and medicine. Galen maintained this standpoint, which seems bizarre by today's standards, because animals did not readily succumb to infections following childbirth and surgical procedures. Galen's animal experiments caused a rejection of Hippocratic values and a reduction in surgical asepsis. This destructive attitude was supported by the Catholic Church and was only substantially reversed in the 1800s following the discovery of the germ and how cleanliness and sterilisation could prevent bacterial infection.

The following is a list of drugs which were passed as safe for human consumption on the back of animal tests and the damage which they subsequently caused:

* Eraldin (for heart disease) – Corneal damage including blindness. * Paracetamol (painkiller) – 1,500 people had to be hospitalised in Great Britain in 1971. * Orabilex – caused kidney damages with fatal outcome. * MEL/29 (antihypertensive) – caused cataracts. * Methaqualone (hypnotic) – caused severe psychic disturbances leading to at least 366 deaths, mainly through murder or suicide. * Thalidomide (tranquilliser) – caused 10,000 malformed children. * Isoproterenol (asthma) – caused 3,500 deaths in the sixties. * Stilboestrol (prostate cancer) – caused cancer in young women. * Trilergan (anti-allergic) – caused vi-

ral hepatitis. * Flamamil (rheumatism) – caused loss of consciousness. * Phenformin (diabetes) – caused 1,000 deaths annually until withdrawn. * Atromid S (cholesterol) – caused deaths from cancer, liver, gallbladder and intestinal disease. * Valium (tranquilliser) – addictive in moderate doses. * Preludin & Maxiton (diet pills) – caused serious damage to the heart and the nervous system. * Nembutal (insomnia) – caused insomnia. * Pronap & Plaxin (tranquilliser) – killed many babies. * Phenacetin (painkiller) – caused severe damages to kidneys and red blood corpuscles. * Amydopyrine (painkiller) – caused blood disease. * Marzine (nausea) – damaged children. * Reserpine (anti-hypertensive) – increased risks of cancer of the brain, pancreas, uterus, ovaries, skin and women's breasts. * Methotrexate (leukaemia) – caused intestinal haemorrhage, severe anaemia and rumours. * Urethane (leukaemia) – caused cancer of liver, lungs and bone marrow. * Mitotane (leukaemia) – caused kidney damage. * Cyclophosphamide (cancer) – caused liver and lung damage. * Isoniazid (tuberculosis) – caused liver destruction. * Kanamycin (tuberculosis) – caused deafness and kidney destruction. * Chloromycetin (typhoid) – caused leukaemia, cardiovascular collapse and death. * Phenolphthalein (laxative) – caused kidney damage, delirium and death. * Clioquinol (diarrhoea) – caused blindness, paralysis and death. * DES (prevent miscarriage) – caused birth defects and cancer. * Debendox (nausea) – caused birth defects. * Accutane (acne) – caused deafness and kidney destruction.

(Taken from Vivisection: Science or Sham by Dr. Roy Kupsinel, and Naked Empress by Hans Ruesch)

Vivisectors often claim credit for many advances in medicine which have been brought about by non-vivisection methods. Frequently, they will quote animal experiments which show the same results without also disclosing the pioneering previous non-animal discovery. One example of this is the case of vaccinations. Whilst it is certainly true that many diseases which have decimated mankind for centuries, such as polio, smallpox, whooping cough, tuberculosis, diphtheria and tetanus have seen a dramatic decline over the last century or so, it is not because of the introduction of vaccinations. Figures show that such diseases were long in decline before the introduction of vaccinations and that the rate of fall was severely impeded once they were introduced. Advances in hygiene, sanitation, nutrition and wealth status are the obvious reasons for the improvement of the world's health overall. Vaccinations are responsible for causing many of the diseases they are supposed to cure as well as compromising the immune systems of the vulnerable, especially babies who are statistically more likely to suffer Sudden Infant Death Syndrome within weeks of having their initial standard vaccinations.

The vivisectionists are master manipulators. They invest huge amounts of money in massive PR organisations such as the Research Defence Society in the

DEAD MEN TALKING

UK. Furthermore, they have infiltrated many areas of the Anti-Vivisection (AV) movement and have created much confusion in the minds of the public as to the truth behind this barbaric trade in misery. An example of this was highlighted in possibly the greatest expose of vivisection industry ever written, The Slaughter of the Innocent by Hans Ruesch:

> An interesting case was the Animal Protection league of Basel. Its president, Dr Rudolph Schenkel, professor of ethology, criticised the revival of anti-vivisectionist feeling in Switzerland. Thereafter, the establishment press could write that 'even the animal defenders disapprove of the antivivisectionists' views.' A closer look at Schenkel revealed that:

> 1. His league had received a donation of 200,000 Swiss francs (about $100,000) from Hoffman-La Roche, 'for its animal shelter' – with no questions asked. 2. His own wife was experimenting on animals in the endocrinology department of Ceiba-Geigy.

> When my CIVIS organisation brought about these facts, Schenkel dropped all pretence of being an animal protectionist: at the next convention of Swiss animal protection groups (SPCAs), he argued that 'since laboratory animals are a product of human enterprise, we can do with them as we please.' (My highlight added.)

(This infiltration tactic is not solely within the realms of the AV movement but is widespread throughout the animal rights movement. This is exemplified at present by the large scale enrolment of blood-sports practitioners [fox and stag hunters etc.] with the RSPCA whereby they are steadily creating a significant policy influencing force by taking advantage of the apathy of many members who do not turn out to vote upon Society matters. The RSPCA also has financial investments in companies that support vivisection.)

The smoke-screen perpetuated by vivisectors that it is preferable to test drugs on animals than on humans, and the emotive stance that 'it's your child or an animal', is probably the most effective way that they ensure public support for their industry. What they always fail to say is that all drugs are tested on humans immediately after the animal trials and often without the patient's knowledge or consent. Those that are informed of the trial are usually reassured to know that 'animal studies have shown the drug to be safe'.

AV supporters are simply people who have come to realise the truth about this situation and have committed themselves to being a part of the process of change and reformation to abolish this massive and system of cruel fraud, both for the sake of the animals and humans. However, they are usually portrayed in the media as extremists; an inevitable side-effect of a necessary evil. Ordinary people who are deemed responsible enough to bear and raise children, minister to the sick, save lives, handle the nation's wealth, run for political seats etc., once they have made an AV stance, are immediately demoted to, at best 'irrational' and 'oversensitive', or, at worst, 'people-hating terrorists' with no right to express an opinion about such matters. Once branded as such they are given about as much regard as are the animals in the laboratory cages and are made largely impotent on the political scene because MPs do not consider it a wise career move or vote winner to consort with anyone considered to be extremist.

In the case of vivisection, the public is all too willing to accept that it is a necessary part of modern progress and not really cruel at all. One reason for this is because the alternative, i.e. the truth, is almost too great a burden to accept. Such a stance is often taken in defence of one's own sanity as a mental survival technique in order that one does not go mad with the anger, sorrow, frustration and terrible empathy which the idea of vivisection evokes in us. Therefore, the vivisectors have yet another advantage over the masses in the battle to keep them convinced of the verity of their cause, whilst the AV organisations have to face a perpetual uphill struggle against the tide of wealth, mind control, tradition and human apathy which is forever on the side of the manipulators.

As George Bernard Shaw once stated, 'Whoever doesn't hesitate to vivisect will hardly hesitate to lie about it'.

By creating a 'healthcare' (more accurately termed 'ill-healthcare') system which relies upon the misleading results of animal experiments, the manipulators of this century have ensured that, within the system, the true causes and cures for disease will never be revealed. This in turn creates a self-perpetuating industry for the multinationals who, by creating disease via their drugs, can be assured of massive funding in order to discover a) the reason for the drug error, which is guaranteed to involve further animal studies, and b) further drugs to treat the results of the initial drug error. In the, by now, all too familiar pattern: the manipulators perpetuate the problem of a state of global ill health and therefore the need for the solution which is offered in the form of more and more pharmaceutical involvement.

For the sake of your selves, your children and the animals: WAKE UP PEOPLE! Take back your power over your own health and stop supporting these barbaric and sick individuals. Only you can do this. The time to do this is now.

In 1975, a man called Dannion Brinkley was struck by lightning and had a near death experience which he recounts in his book 'Saved by the Light'. During the twenty-eight minutes while he was officially dead he was led by a spirit being through the dark tunnel to a crystal city. He was visited by thirteen beings who are described as light beings similar to classic ETs and angels.

DEAD MEN TALKING

He recalls a total of 117 events showed to him on a screen which pertained to predicted events on Earth between 1975 and 2000. At the time of the release of his book in 1994, 95 of these events had occurred, including Ronald Reagan's presidency, the Gulf War, the Chenobyl disaster and the fall of the Soviet Union. Events which have not yet occurred include American bankruptcy, the development of chemical and biological weaponry to be used against France and mass destruction due to World War III.

One of the final visions he was shown was computer chip technology slowly infiltrating every aspect of our day to day lives. Ultimately the controller/owner of this technology would become corrupt a see the potential for world supremacy. Eventually a computer chip would be inserted under the skin of every member of the Earth's population containing total information of everyone's medical history, social status and credit rating which could be read by a scanner and fed to a mainframe. Governments would use these chips to control the population and could also dissolve the chips to release a lethal virus in order to avoid the costs of an elderly population. Those who refused chips would be outcasts from society, unemployable and untouchable by the System's benefits.

Dannion was informed by the Beings that if mankind did not deter from the projected future then these things would come to pass. If, however, action was taken now then it could all be avoided. They informed him that those who have decided to come to Earth are seen as adventurers and are the heroes and heroines who have come to co-create with God where no other spiritual beings have had the courage so to do. The parting message was that the answer lies in 'treating others the way they themselves want to be treated'.

Dannion Brinkley's experience is not unique by any means. Every day people are becoming aware of our angelic hosts and are being given messages of guidance and hope for the future. I have seen such a being of light myself during astral projection and I know they exist all around us, within the higher vibrationary atmosphere of the Earth. We are being given our final warnings and opportunities to do all we can to emerge from the despair of the old dark order into the new future of light. The only way to achieve this is to recognise the pitfalls of the Luciferic influence and live our spiritual ideals in deed as well as in thought.

Firstly, we have to be aware of the clues to the methods employed by the Brotherhood in their ultimate goal of centralised world control. The tools they use to fight their ultimate wars are ourselves. They program our thoughts, our very conception of who we are, what is right and wrong and we, in turn, give them what they wish in the belief that this is the right, or the only way to live long and prosper. We build the prisons in which to house ourselves and hand the keys to our gaolers who are the Brotherhood elite. The crazy part about all of this is that we do it willingly and because they ask us to.

In order to facilitate the Transformation we must resist the urge to identify those who would seek to control us as hopelessly 'evil'. We must recognise the System for what it is and seek to change it in a loving, positive and balanced way. Even at the highest levels of the Brotherhood elite, the most misguided of the Illuminati, are not immune from the effects of the global reawakening. It is those who are most imbalanced towards negativity who have the greatest positive potential. If just one of these elite Luciferic controlled minds is returned to its natural balanced state then virtually the entire process could be reversed over night. This is a potential, and any potential is possible. It all depends on how much energy we channel into that potential to make it a reality.

Furthermore, it is essential that we take what we are being fed through the media and education with a pinch of salt for not all of it will be truth. Events are engineered on a global scale and then a version of it is transmitted to us in order to perpetuate certain states such as fear and apathy within the mass population. So much of little consequence to us is thrown our way to divert us from free thought and we are bombarded with sex, violence, sport and graphic horror. We are often more concerned with who is being transferred from which football team to another, or what the royal family had for tea than the fact that the planet is being destroyed around us and our neighbours are dying of cold, starvation and despair for the want of a little kindness and love. These are very effective diversionary tactics and manipulative devices.

We must begin look at the world through new eyes if we are to really make a difference and take back the right to autonomy and free will which is ours by Divine law. This is a long term plot against humanity, a war of stealth and attrition; a war which the majority of us are not even aware exists because of its scale and slowly cumulative nature. By viewing all of these things on a large scale and by linking patterns and events which we are traditionally encouraged to see as separate, we can piece together the real agendas behind the Illuminati smoke screens. Nothing in the universe is truly separate from anything else. If we analyse just who it is in the world who benefit from the negativity and manipulation, we see that it is the same people over and over again. They represent a consciousness which is like a black hole and is sucking in our vitality with every passing day. This is the direction of the energy flow and its polarity is towards negativity. Wherever we see this trend and recognise it we can begin to work to reverse the polarity back towards the balance point. This relies on our ability to recognise Truth and be prepared to act on our knowledge. It takes you and me, and it takes love.

These methods which they use to persuade us to imprison ourselves are very basic, yet awesomely effective. They engineer situations within our society up to the point where the public are so outraged that they insist on action from those in power. The powers that be (Brotherhood pawns) offer, as a solution, the very thing it wanted to impose in the first place. The public accept the proffered solution so the Brotherhood's desires are implemented with public support. For example, in order to give the police greater powers of arrest, detention and search-at-will to serve the Brotherhood, they manipulate society into creating more crime and despondency. The people cry out for a solution and the politicians come up with more government legislation to counteract the problem. What better way to gain greater control over a population than persuade its people that, for an improvement in their quality of life, they need a larger network of agencies such as MI5, CIA, FBI and the police, and with greater powers than ever before? We must always be on the alert for the hidden agendas behind legislation and economics before we subscribe to the suggested solution. Remember, these people kill or cause people to be killed for profit, pleasure and power. No one is inexpendable and most of the executors of these hidden agendas are entirely unaware or wilfully ignorant of what they are really being used for.

Where we see terrorism, where we see wars, legislation against minorities to restrict their freedom, anywhere we see more powers given to the establishment and less to the free people we must ask ourselves the true reasons behind these actions.

It has been shown how the bankers financed and helped to manipulate into existence the major wars of this century; how the same banks that were backing Hitler and the Nazi war machine during WWII were also behind the Allies. At the end of the war, with the world in chaos and the people's morale depleted, these same banks and their pawns, the politicians, were able to reassemble the world's economy right on target for the New World Order. The future world army was initiated under the guise of a Peacekeeping force we now know as the United Nations. And the people were so grateful to these powers for ridding the world of such an evil menace that they entirely surrendered themselves, once again, to the policies and propaganda of the people who had created the war in the first place. And so, the process continues to this day.

We must challenge automatic thought patterns and habitual life styles which are the weapons employed against us. We must constantly question and never betray ourselves to the power of thought-forms of the masses. The world is full of fashion victims, not only in the sense of clothing but in life-styles and thought patterns too. These fashions have been provided by, fed, watered and nurtured by the Brotherhood in order to feed their lust for money and power.

Every penny we spend gets back to their banks in the end. Everything we work for and achieve will be theirs if we allow it. Moves are under way now to replace money entirely with credit. Credit cards, debit cards and smart cards are now being developed at such a runaway rate that soon we will all be rated as credit. Technology exists now to use chips in cards both for access to personal details and to transmit messages into the psyche of the carrier to control behaviour. More and more opportunities are being sought to use this micro-technology: as tags for criminals, as pet identi-chips, as surgical implants and as locators for potentially missing children and babies. It is a small step to the 'under-the-skin' control chip.

Efforts are under way to centralise world government powers. Plans for a federal Europe under a single European government have been under way for years now. Step by step, power is taken away from the masses and delivered into the hands of the few.

Watch out for calls for larger armies and greater powers. Have you noticed how the U.N. 'peacekeeping' forces are always too late and in too little numbers to actually be effective? Watch out for a call for a centralised world army on order to provide greater 'peacekeeping' potential, it would really be a double bluff to give more power to the Brotherhood elite.

Watch out too for those situations which the ruling classes and governments vehemently oppose and be careful not to support something just because those whom you oppose are against it. This is one of the oldest, but most effective tricks in the book and it has duped millions time and time again. Don't allow the further decline or the consequences may be disastrous. Always be true to yourself first and foremost and see beneath the veil of deceit.

The coming Transformation to a unified multidimensional Christ consciousness will affect everyone, the Brotherhood included. We can only be controlled if we allow ourselves to be so. Nothing is impossible. We are the vehicles for the Divine Consciousness, we are the creative hands of God. It is up to all of us, and that includes the Brotherhood, to re-evaluate our position, for we cannot escape ourselves and the karma we create.

As Mark Phillips once explained to Cathy O'Brien:

Good always prevails through positive application, whereas the bad guys are hindered and slowed in their criminal endeavours through having to cover-up their negative actions with lies to support lies. This inevitably allows the truth to emerge.

MIND CONTROL

THE SECRET HISTORY

The Secret History of Mind Control

CKLN-FM Mind Control Series

CKLN 88.1 FM

Ryerson Polytechnical University Toronto

Ontario International Connection Mind Control Series Producer/Interviewer: Wayne Morris

Wayne Morris:

Good morning and welcome to International Connection. We are in show #33 in our series on Mind Control, and today we are going to hear a presentation, The Secret History of Mind Control, given by Walter Bowart at the Ritual Trauma Child Abuse and Mind Control Conference in Atlanta in October, 1997. Walter Bowart is an investigative journalist and author of one of the original books about mind control in the late seventies entitled, Operational Mind Control. And now, Walter Bowart:

Introduction by Sylvia Gillotte:

I guess Walter almost needs no introduction because he was really probably the first person to publicly write about mind control and its origins and so forth. His book, Operation Mind Control, is available at his table at the back. Most recently Walter was involved as a consultant in the making of the movie, Conspiracy Theory, and some of you may have seen him actually interviewed for an HBO special promoting the movie. It was the first time I ever got to see what Walter looked like so I could recognize him when he came. He has the Freedom of Thought Foundation, which he will tell you about. He is going to share his information with you, so welcome Walter.

DEAD MEN TALKING

Walter Bowart:

I would like to thank some people. I was going to save it until the end but I want to get it right up front since a couple of them are here. I would like to thank Mike Coyle for what he contributed to this. What you are going to see is a series of out-takes, some are from videos, and a lot of them are still ... it's a very rough presentation of what's going to be a documentary. I would like to thank Mike Coyle who is retired from the field. He had the Mindnet Journal which was on the internet, and he did a terrific job of research. He is finding that a lot of the critical things that we are going to talk about as we get toward the end of this show, are actually removed from journals ... pages torn out of academic research journals and things. Somebody doesn't want this information out.

I am going to cover things going back ... Sylvia asked me to do the history of mind control but I'm going to go farther afield ... probably than most of you had heard about. It is so far beyond any technology you are talking about, like electromagnetic spectrum stuff ... we are into post-quantum physics here, and now we are working with physicists.

I would also like to thank Blanche Chavoustie who is here for the long years of friendship and the documentation and research that she has helped us with and Cheryl Welsh, who I think is not here, who also contributed boxes and boxes of research, and Doreen Pratt who is hospitalized and not able to travel ... she is blind, legally blind, and you will see some of her work in this presentation. And I would like to thank all the members of the Freedom of Thought Foundation for their assistance, and friendship and guidance over the 20 years that we have been doing this.

The big key to the thing is that only the small secrets need to be kept. You can find just about anything the government is doing by going into scientific journals and doing research. But the big secrets are kept by public incredulity and your study and your experience is in an area which is not secret. All this has been known for a long time, but people don't want to believe it and there is a great deal of denial.

[Slide] With the evolution of man came the evolution of science, and here's an example of an early treatment by the foremost practitioners of "mental health science". This is an etching from 1745. It shows a ward in Bethlehem Hospital in London. It was pronounced Bethlem, and it became Bedlam, the famous synonym for the nuthouse.

[Slide] A patient of Bethlem, William Norris, was confined there for 12 years, bound by chains a foot long and to an iron rod at the head of his bed. He died in 1815. Another patient at Bethlem, who we do not have a picture of was James Tilley

Matthews. He was incarcerated there for 35 years and escaped only by death, and it is a very interesting story. In the late 1700's he had gone to France as a spy for the British Admiralty, posing as an import-export agent. He travelled in the highest circles of French society. Things went wrong for him when he fell into the hands of Franz Anton Mesmer, the father of hypnotism. Mesmer used to play parlour games by having aristocrats stand in tubs of water while he played DC current over their heads, to what purpose we don't know.

[Slide] This may be one of the first perpetrators of mind control ... one of the founders of our country ... Benjamin Franklin. He was the US ambassador to France at the time, and if you remember, he was the discoverer of electricity which was DC electricity. He discovered it when he flew a kite on a wire during an electrical storm, and it was a shocking experience. Franklin may have used that later for the effects we now know DC current gives. It will induce amnesia easily. Franklin was asked by the French government to look into the activities of Mesmer and his claims of miraculous cures with electricity. They hit it off real well, but it's not surprising. They were both the brothers of the same secret society ... the Masons. Franklin filed a lengthy report favourable to Mesmer to the French government. Another brother Mason who frequently visited them in Paris was Adam Weishaupt, the founder of the Illumaniti. These coincidences bring a lot of questions to your mind about what were these guys really doing over there, and what did they find out?

Mesmer happened to be, believe it or not, the godfather of Amadeus Mozart. In fact he raised Mozart, and of course Mozart was this incredible genius musician and his biography will show you more than one obvious example of someone who behaves as if he were suffering from Dissociative Identity Disorder. You can conclude that maybe Mesmer played around to enhance the musical abilities of Mozart at the cost of other parts of his personality.

[slide] We are back to James Tilley Matthews and after a few years of influence by Franklin and Mesmer, he beat a path as soon as he could back to England, reported to the Admiralty the French had developed a devastating instrument of war, an "airloom" which could weave thoughts into a man's mind.

[slide] At the top it says "Illustrations of Madness", that's the name of the book written by John Haslam, the apothecary (in modern terms, the resident medical officer) to Bethlem Hospital toward the end of Matthews' stay. In the first decade of the 19th century Haslam wrote this whole volume called "Illustrations of Madness" just singly on the Matthews case. It was published in 1810. It was the first book length case study of a single patient in British psychiatric history. According to Roy Porter who repackaged Haslam's 1810 book "Illustrations of Madness" in 1988 ... that's the only way you are going to find it. There are rare vol-

umes, you have to pay at least $40 for a used copy.

Because of the book, Matthews' fate became a cause celebre everywhere - in Britain and the United States. It was used against Bethlem Hospital in general, and Haslam in particular, ironically, when the institution came under scathing scrutiny by a House of Commons committee investigating madhouses in 1815. A few years before the madhouse era, there were only a few people declared insane, but by the late 1700's and the early 1800's, there were hundreds of thousands of people now in these madhouses, so-called. While Matthews is interesting to us for other reasons, he was the cause celebre that created social reform in the madhouse business.

According to Porter, the significance of his case was way back about two hundred years ago, he was describing experiences that modern victims of mind control are now describing, even using some of the same terms. Today Matthews would be diagnosed as having "delusional disorder", and I think delusional disorder is a misdiagnosis for a whole lot of things. Maybe he would be diagnosed as suffering from schizophrenia or paranoid schizophrenia, which we now know is an extremely rare disease. When I wrote "Operation Mind Control" back in 1978, there were only 25 MPD cases diagnosed, now there are hundreds of thousands. Most of the people I was writing about were called schizophrenic by the doctors ... and they weren't. Of course, they were D.I.D.

A Dr. George Birkeck of London examined Haslem in those days, and testified before the King's Bench that after paying James Tilley Matthews six visits at Bethlem and having attempted "by every mode of examination which he could devise" to discover the real state of his mind, he said Matthews was not insane. Matthews was talking about sudden death squeezing, lobster cracking. He was admitted on January 28, 1797 to Bethlem after he had been behaving oddly for quite a while, about a year, and among his strange behaviour was writing a letter to his benefactor, Lord Liverpool, who was in the Admiralty and was part of this intelligence scam that he was involved in, "I pronounce your Lordship to be in every sense of the word a most diabolical traitor after a long life of political and real iniquity during which your Lordship, by flattering and deceiving and more than anyone contributing to deceive your King who believing your hypocritical professions, has to be the detriment of many of the country's friends, loaded you with honours and emollients. You have made yourself a principal in schemes of treasons founded upon the most extensive intrigues which have not not only long since laid this country at the feet of its most bitter enemies who have assassinated France, to reap further advantages from those who by such wickedness might in such general assassinating scandal mount the throne ..." and so forth, written in the grand prose of that day. And that will get you locked up, even today that would get you locked up ...

DEAD MEN TALKING

But he is talking about thought-making. Haslam, the doctor who treated him, said, "In this situation he continued for many years, sometimes an automaton, moved by the agencies of persons hereafter to be introduced to the notice of the reader." And of course he talked about spies, thugs and assassins who were putting voices in his head and controlling him. Matthews insisted that in some apartment near London Wall there is a "gang of villains, profoundly skilled in pneumatic chemistry who assail him by means of an airloom." Of a variety of tortures he described so colourfully, were "fluid locking, cutting soul from sense, stone making, thigh talking, kiting involving magnetic impregnations ... sudden death squeezing, lobster cracking caused by pressure from the 'magnetic atmosphere surrounding the persons assailed', apoplexy working with a nutmeg grater, lengthening the brain, thought-making while one of these villains is sucking at the brain of the person assailed to distract his existing sentiments, another of the gang will force into his mind a train of ideas very different from the real subject of his thoughts in which is squeezed upon as the desired information by the person sucking." "Laughter-making, poking, pushing up the quicksilver, bladder filling, tying down, bomb bursting, gas plucking (the extraction of magnetic fluid from a person assailed), foot curving, lethargy-making, spark exploding, knee nailing, burning out, eye screwing, sight stopping, roof stringing, vital tearing, fibre ripping brain sayings ..." and other descriptions of physical and psychological tortures caused by some invisible means which Matthews put into the high tech terms of his day.

Now, this is very similar to what people are describing today. This is the way he drew a layout of the way he was assailed and interrogated by these 17th Century assassins and he said that a pneumatic machine [slide] this is a sketch he made of it ... was used, this was the high technology that was doing all this. If you are interested in this, try to find the book, you may have to do a search for it. But the EM targeted victims of today are not sounding much different than that. This guy is pretty colourful and of course the language is very arcane.

Matthews ... he was the first. It was 200 years ago. He is the first single case ever chronicled in the psychiatric literature that we know of. This is nothing new. Could it be that Franklin and those other guys came up with something that they really did use, because that's what Matthews claims. Today we have the category, and I don't like the term but it is used, "Wavies" — those are people who are targets of electromagnetic waves of some kind, or I prefer the term "EM targeted individuals". Some of these people claim to be alien abductees or government mind control victims, or satanic abused people. There is nothing in Matthews' description that these groups of people haven't also described experiencing.

Then you have to ask, doing what I did for 20 years, hearing all these stories, you are gathering probably the largest data base ... using a 27 page questionnaire, I am looking for mind control victims and of course our questionnaire is on mind control - but it kind of gives you an indication of everything else, including the alien abduction scenario which is very peculiar, very unusual. We have the largest data base ... and after you hear this, you say, "could it be that these delusions, if they are delusions - do we as a species lack such imagination as to keep coming up with the same thing over and over for 200 years?" Can't we go beyond this? Shouldn't madness be really 'out there'? But something is happening here. There is a pattern to this, and you hear people who don't know each other, have had no contact with this thing at all, who never read a book on it, saying the same thing. I sit down with some survivors who have experienced trauma abuse and trauma based programming and compare notes, it will be the same. And it runs true.

This is later. This is now the early 19th century [slide] — we've got the Lavery Electric Phrenometer - it was the high tech of its day, intended to accurately measure the bumps on your head and so predict the nature, type and behaviour of individuals who would hold still for it. And it was taken very seriously for a while, until somebody said, "hey, there's no data base for this, you know?"

[slide] Early 20th century - "Mental Poisoning", it was a popular book written by a psychologist in the early days when people were hearing voices, mental poisoning. And then we got more scientific - this is an obsolete version of Colin Ross's book - he made a contribution to the field by doing that research. But here we go in the 1920's or 30's - everybody was hearing voices, everybody, and all you had to do was turn on a radio. There was no need for implanted electrodes to control your behaviour.

[slide] Here's a Nazi rally in pre-war Germany. Students of Marshall McLuhan will tell you how radio created Nazism, the blitzkreig, and mass obedience like nothing before it. As one psychoscientist put it, "the stentorian voices of the mass media are more universally powerful than the indiscriminate persuasions of any mind altering drug." Most of the survivors in this room probably don't watch a lot of television, right? Does anybody want to confess? Okay. (Never owned one? Yes.)

[slide] Now this is the guy - Freedom of Thought Foundation is going to have an award - and all of you will have a chance to vote on who is going to get the first one - it's very expensive to make those little statues but nobody will pick it up so we can just peel off the brass plate every year and use the same one. We have a few candidates. Jolyon West is a candidate, Martin Orne is a candidate, there are two or three others. But they will all be on the ballot. I have been working on this brain which is about this big, and it's gold, and it's fried black and it's broken off and it's got two electrodes on it and it sits on kind of like a beer can - kind of a nice looking thing.

DEAD MEN TALKING

It's called the Mengele Award after Josef Mengele, this guy here. That's Joe, and he was one of the mind control men, you know, from the ubermentsch ... there's nothing like opening a skull and letting your bare fingers run through someone's brain or freezing human beings to near the point of death and then finding out through trial and error that the easiest way to defrost someone is to put them close to another naked human body. And these are just a few of the brutal experiments, though some of that was valuable for hypothermia ... all of the records of what Joe Mengele did in Nazi concentration camps, and all of the records of his research are now on file at the National Archives. We should probably get them all - I think some of them are still classified. But these are the people he is working on - these are his subjects. Of course Mengele was fascinated by genetics. I haven't really addressed genetics and most survivors realize that it is multigenerational, most sons and daughters of Masons realize that is part of the Masonic belief is that if you program or if you train or educate or whatever the word is, a person over two or three generations the knowledge begins to be true ...

We are heading that way and these twins were a part of Mengele's studies and he did a number of things. Twins appear to be telepathic. With NLP you can understand how that works, and our workshops demonstrate what looks like telepathy by mirroring and matching. If you can sit with somebody and match their breathing pattern and establish this incredible rapport, you will experience, if you are sitting there in a state - imagining sitting there on a mountaintop and the wind is blowing or whatever - you will pick up the wind and you will pick up all the sensory experience that they are having. You might not put it together in the right way, you might say "I am driving in my convertible and the wind is in my hair" or something, but twins are known to be - and you can't match any better than twins - they suffered great atrocities at the hand of Mengele and they are here and they have been interviewed, and that's the last picture that was taken of Dr. Josef Mengele who was said to have been in Arizona in 1960, there is a persistent rumour. But of course they say he wasn't, he was in Argentina and he died down there and yet they are not sure that those are his bones ...

It is also one of the persistent rumours that he was brought over in Project Paperclip. We know he worked on a farm in Germany for a few years before the end of WWII. There is the question of the Green programming, and the two proteges he had that were sent to Harvard and all that, and I am sure you have heard of this and more, but there is no proof of it. I keep harping on this - we won't find any documentation or proof until we repeal the National Security Act. As you begin to research in this thing, and I have been smashing my head against the NSA for 20 years. They do whatever they want. Colonel Fletcher Prouty is a friend of mine. He said "they are over there now", he lives nearby, you can look out the window. "See the lights are on. They are xeroxing forged documents." The National Ar-

147

chives are locked up as far as this stuff goes. Anything that is useful, anything that is about mind control, and we'll get back to that ...

There are so many doctors - I guess Colin Ross is writing a book about it - he's following up on some of our research that we did 25 years ago. He's gotten the papers of Dr. Estabrooks and Estabrooks knew Milton Erickson, who I think was a great guy myself, but he did work for the government, and they all knew each other and Ewen Cameron comes in, it was a Who's Who of everybody who worked in the psychiatric mental health profession of that particular generation, my father's generation.

Sociologists as well, it's been going on for fifty years. Guys like Robert J. Lifton who is thought of very highly, worked with Dr. John Mack, the alien guy, the UFO guy. They had a partnership - they worked in a little company that was funded by the CIA MKULTRA project. And in national mental health, all the universities were used - you know the story - and Operation Mind Control gives you a big list on all this stuff. I mean, it's just scratching the surface.

And I hear some of you gasp at some of this stuff. Have you read Lifton's book, "The Nazi Doctors"? That's a pretty interesting study of how - it takes up the obedience to authority kind of thing, how people can be made to do things they wouldn't ordinarily do. Lest you gasp repeatedly throughout this presentation, let me generalize. Virtually every psychologist, psychiatrist, sociologist, cyberneticist, and so on of that generation previous to mine, were funded either wittingly or unwittingly by the CIA. The CIA through a number of cutout organizations co-opted the entire mental health profession and put it to work on mind control. It's a hard thing finding people that aren't part of the game, you know, part of the bad guys.

A few years after the end of WWII, about the CIA was being founded, and one of their first concerns in 1947 - the Soviets engineered a show trial against Roman Catholic Cardinal Minzente who appeared before a kangaroo court in a trance and confessed to everything he was accused of which a few years later he couldn't remember. The CIA looked into this and they said 'oh they've got something we don't have, and we need this". We'd better look into this. It was a fledgling agency in those days. We're celebrating its 50th anniversary and I got a big kick out of George Bush standing up next to Richard Helms, who went to jail and was convicted of lying to Congress, he was the Director of the CIA, and Nixon was singing this man's praises, saying what a great patriot he was. If you are a patriot, you lie to everybody, you lie to your country. That's how far our morals and ethics have fallen.

[slide] These are some of the things you find on the internet too, you find a lot of very good stuff, very succinct. And that talks about Harris Isabell in 1955,

part of MKULTRA Bluebird, the hospital in Lexington, Kentucky and things ... of course Nelson Rockefeller wanted to become president one day and he was standing at the bedside of lady liberty when she gave birth to her bastard child, the freak of nature, part of the invisible Cold War, information - they christened the baby "Information Warfare", they called it. The father nicknamed it "Brainwashing".

Brainwash. A previous speaker used the term. It is very non-specific, and the term "mind control" isn't much better. But "brainwash" was coined by a CIA propaganda specialist, Ed Hunter, and he advised Allen Dulles who gave a speech at the UN and that's how the term "brainwashing" got started. Dulles' brother was John Foster Dulles. He was the Secretary of State, and Allen called himself the "Secretary of State for Unfriendly Governments". He was the Director of the CIA. They talked about the insidious Fu Manchu Communists in Korea and China who had brainwashed our clean-minded American boys and made them confess to crimes that they did not commit. According to Dulles the Chinese had a way of making strong-minded Americans hallucinate that a US Marine wing had flown a mission over North Korean held territory, dropping germ bombs. Colonel Charles Schwabel here took most of the heat. He was one of the men who allowed himself to be filmed to the US use of germ weapons. The cries of "brainwashing" could not drown out the later revelations that the Marine Air wing had indeed dropped germ bombs on the insidious yellow peoples fighting against the U.S. Later it was revealed that the secret labs at Edgewood Arsenal had developed a race-specific encephalitis germ which infected only oriental people.

... Fu Manchu. Which turned out to be nothing more than isolation, deprivation, alienation ... what this guy was talking about. Very standard stuff. Nothing romantic about it. Just the same old take a person, put their hand in a vise, close the vise, say "talk". They'll talk at some point. That's what brainwashing was. It's like our prison and educational systems. Simple things. The Chinese didn't use drugs or anything sophisticated. But they did get these people to confess readily. So guess what happened? Those of us who served in the military service - we all were the beneficiaries of that - The Code of Conduct. You gave your name, rank and serial number and nothing else. But you wait a certain time and then you can tell them anything because the only thing you have to worry about is tactical information which gets obsolete very fast.

I talked to Laird Gunderson and guys that were in Vietnam and they really stood up to torture. It's an interesting thing to see those men come back in the fifties, standing at a strange angle, behaving like these automatons -it's very interesting - just what isolation, deprivation, alienation can do to somebody. I suffer from it myself, being a writer, sitting in front of that computer so many hours. I catch myself in the mirror, staggering around. So the result was The Code of Conduct.

Out of this came the best psychological study ever done - on 3000 men who were POW's in Korea. They studied them all with a finetooth comb. Most interesting, they had three categories: the guys that collaborated outright with the enemy, the guys who resisted the enemy to the death, and the guys that just went along with the enemy. The ones who just went along with the enemy were the same guys that just went along with our military, they were draftees. The guys that collaborated with the enemy outright were the people in our own military who were known as gung-ho. The people that resisted the enemy were the people that resisted our own military and they wanted us all to resist the enemy the same way that those guys did. They studed the "resisters" and they found there was a spectrum of on one hand, there were the criminals, and then at the other end, there were the ones who were highly creative. They began to study more and they saw that criminality is nothing more than misplaced creativity. We have an actual industry in this country of misplaced creativity.

Slide - Brainwashing in Red China. Edward Hunter, the man who coined the term "brainwashing" wrote several books about it. Then came the fictional version of that story by Richard Condon, The Manchurian Candidate. That caught everybody's attention. I knew Richard when he was alive. He was a PR flack who dropped out. He was sixty, and this was his first novel and it was a big hit. It was the story of a guy who was captured - Laurence Harvey played the assassin in the movie. He was programmed. They captured him behind enemy lines, take him up to Manchuria, programmed him, then he came back. He did assassinate the candidate for president who happened to be a guy he didn't like anyway, it was his stepfather, so ... the Queen of Diamonds over the phone triggered the assassination. I asked Condon over the phone - now that he can't defend himself - some guys are writing that Condon knew all about this. He loved my book back in 1974 - I think he saw a rough draft and he wrote great things about it. He said he just read Pavlov and Salter, and invented the rest because it was a pretty basic premise. Frank Sinatra was in the film, he was one of the progrmamed POW's, and he bought a large piece of the film. It's an interesting movie to watch. When Kennedy was assassinated, he pulled the film out of circulation and it remained out of circulation for probably 15 years which I thought was interesting. Maybe he knew something about the assassination of Kennedy that we don't know.

Slide - These are some of the 1940 stills that I found of soldiers under hypnosis being marched around ... demonstrating before others. In 1978 I went all over the world with these slides. It was shocking to people. They didn't know you could be made to do something against your will and without your knowledge. They didn't know you could do mind over matter kinds of things with your body, control blisters, what have you. I learned from Anthony Robbins when I saw 200 people walk over a bed of coals as long as this room - they were trying to do the Guinness Book of Records. It was a mesquite fire, the hottest kind of fire because of the oil which stuck to their feet. 60% got burns, but 40% didn't. Now you explain that to me ... Andy Wile, the new age healer, he's an MD - he wouldn't walk in it. He knew what a hot fire was. We know you can control blisters.

Cathy O'Brien tells an interesting story about being burned between her breasts with nitrous oxide while in a hypnotic state, and having a baphomet appear - a demonic star, goat like figure which was used by Knights Templar and has a whole history - apparently Noriega was very superstitious and she had a message, she claims, from high ranking government (George Bush) to give to Noriega. To get his attention, her handler gave her that cue phrase and that baphomet appears - it would only come out in that state. Things like that can be done, and have been repeated in laboratory experiments. But in 1940 they weren't doing that. I just threw this in as a filler, because what we are talking about is how to divide your mind.

If Daddy hasn't already done it - I don't know what this guy said - he said it happens at an early age - it's got to be emotional - true. But he didn't say it's got to happen before you can speak. Real DID has to happen before you can talk. So that's a very early age, probably a year, if not before. All of us that have had - that know a lot of MPD stories - realize that there are personalities and different identities anchored to various body parts. I have a great video of the most wonderful little lady - she's on our website - Patty - and I have never seen anybody react like this little lady. She herself is the schoolhouse, and she is full of children, trying to burst out. It's almost like her eyeballs move sideways, and one comes out and says "hey, what about me?" - and she can't control this when she gets started. I was trying to do an interview with her, and I said "let me anchor your executive personality". She is a volunteer for certain police things, she has her take-charge personalities, very competent. I wanted to anchor her in that, so I said "let me touch your knee and every time you go off in another personality I will touch your knee and that's your executive, all right?" So I thought I had anchored it pretty good. Well in the middle of the interview here is this little kid again, so I touched her knee, and she says "what do you think you're doing? you're just touching my knee with your finger ... they used a cattle prod". Then she looked at the camera. My girlfriend was the camera operator, Pat - both of them were Pat - they got along great. But she had this great big old studio video camera. And she says, "you know, we did that before, but there was never a woman running the camera ... we were making blue money". I didn't know what blue money was, which is child porn as it turns out.

Slide - The doctor on the right is B.F.Skinner, and this is his daughter, Debbie Skinner. He was at Harvard, he was respectable, this was the apex of respectable scientific research. He used to work with pigeons, chimpanzees -but this is his daughter, Debbie, and the box they said kept Debbie from being disturbed. She would awaken in her sleep and they would carry on with their regular lifestyle and Debbie was protected from traffic outside, it was air conditioned and everything - Debbie looks pretty happy there. Remember that the beginning of - you've heard a lot about Pavlov. And the Russians have always been big fans of the dark side of our science. They love cybernetics. I'll get to Norbert Weiner in a little while.

They loved a guy named J.B. Watson who was the founder of behaviorism. He had an illegitimate child, Little Albert, which I was surprised to learn this was his child, with the nurse who worked for him. Watson finally got defrocked and he went to work for Madison Avenue. He is the father of mind control in advertising. The most interesting thing about Watson ... here's this little baby, Albert, crawling along the floor, and they want to condition Albert and they had a white bunny rabbit and they let the bunny rabbit out of the cage. As soon as the bunny rabbit would emerge Little Albert would say "whoo woo" and go running for the bunny rabbit, he would get to a certain proximity of the bunny rabbit and Daddy would drop this big steel bar, clanging behind Little Albert, make him jump and cry naturally. Watson did this repeatedly until Little Albert was afraid of anything white, anything that moved that way, anything furry, all of his life.

This boy, the son of the founder of behaviorism, and Debby Skinner, the daughter of one of the leading proponents of behaviorism and if you understand behaviorism, you know it works ... it is a science, and it is uncanny. Both of these young people committed suicide in their twenties. What does that say about their parents and their heritage, this kind of approach to the study of human psychology, I guess it's called. So, that's Debby and the box. Skinner was the apex of science, American intellectual establishment, Harvard University.

Slide - This is the nadir of American intellectual establishment — this is William Jennings Bryant III in L.A. - he is the founder and director of the American Institute of Hypnosis. Anybody heard of him? Yeah. He can run three hypnotic subjects at a time with that panel ... program three people. I was trying to get an interview with him, he kept dodging me as has Martin Orne -once I got him on the golf course and almost succeeded but he ran away. Bryant died on the stage in Las Vegas of a heart attack - according to his widow, within hours of his passing - it was like magic - the signal was sent - the CIA showed up at his office and at his private home - and removed every scrap of paper from his library. There is reason to believe that he was, as is alleged, the programmer of perhaps Sirhan Sirhan, the assassin of Robert Kennedy and maybe one of the programmers of Candy Jones who was the number one pin-up girl during WWII. Slide - Candy Jones. Betty Grable was number one, and she was number two, something like that. She wrote her own book called The Control of Candy Jones - some people would now try to deny that was true ... but indeed it runs true. She was programmed to commit suicide at a certain time by jumping off a cliff. She married a guy - I think the only reason she married him was because he started loosening her programming. His name was Long John Neville, he was a talk-show host in New York, and he was an amateur hypnotist. He started working with her - you can reintegrate just like that (snaps fingers) unless you are continuously restimulated, the natural tendency is to pull it all together again and reintegrate. Suddenly she remembered, "gee whiz, I went on all these trips in southeast Asia", she remembered having her hand in a box with scorpions stinging her and all kinds of other things. Being basically a pigeon, a courier for the cryptocracy ... ran out of three letter words ... secret government. Whatever he did shook loose the thing - she didn't jump off the cliff.

Another - somebody should write a book about Marilyn Monroe. She was an abused child. You know how it goes. Daddy is a pedophile, and Daddy is making movies of abusing the kids in the neighbourhood, and he ships them through the mail and the postal inspector finds this and says "ah we're going to arrest these guys" and they give it to some federal branch of law enforcement because it's a federal crime and then somehow it gets bumped over to the department of defence and the department of defence guys - who are probably CIA or NSA or whatever - they show up and say "ah you're going to jail for a 25 years - otherwise you work for us." Then they say "now we'll show you how to program them." So the whole family ends up and the children of those children end up working for Uncle Cryptocracy for the rest of their lives. You will hear that story over and over. I hope you hear Brice Taylor's presentation, that's a story about this. The reason I know she is real is because I met her when she was with the guy that she can't see anymore ... but I know who it was. A movie star who was a handler. That was years before I met her again in a mind control context. But I think she has totally sanitized her book so that she doesn't name any names. But it should. Operation Mind Control names the names because I got permission to use an earlier version and I changed her name of course so you will have to put two and two together if you want the real story.

[Slide] It says "How to Hypnotize" - this was in a comic book in the 40's or 50's. It was a big thing. Everybody was hypnotizing everybody. Little did they know, just accidentally you can really send somebody on a spin and really have some problems. I hope you don't think I meant to use the word "spin" deliberately. [Slide] That's Cathy O'Brien. I am sure many of you know her or heard her story. It's written in the book "Trance Formations in America". She brought the term "Presidential Model" to the fore, and she presents a kind of National Enquirer version of the MKULTRA story, naming names, sexual preferences, perversions, dimensions and identifying marks of the genitalia of the high government officials. That's probably her main defence. She says "okay". Remember Michael Jackson? They had him drop his drawers because some kids had identified him. Well, she says that about some of the major presidents and secretaries of defence and what-have-you which I think is a great thing to do.

[Slide] She calls it Monarch mind control there - that's the picture. It gives the name of her shrink there, and I called up her shrink and said "can you put me in touch with this lady?" and she called me and I used her pseudonym in the book. She then sent me a blow-up of the picture that she didn't even know was there, because it was on her passport, she had given it to the reporter, the reporter spilled coffee on it, but they had a negative of the picture. The reporter blew the picture up and sent it back to her and she was surprised to find these two images on it. One is the famous butterfly connoting that she was a sexual slave, programmed, and the rose is the assassin program. We find in Operation Mind Control there is a pin for evening wear - the butterfly pin or the rose pin. Some on a lower level, they would actually tattoo the women in certain places. Some of the cattle prods 200,000 volts DC will give you melonin, and give you a nice little mole. Some of them are burned with moles in a certain shape on the face, and you meet many survivors that have had every mole taken off their body just for that reason, because they knew this was identifying. Any of the perpetrators that know the programming can access the person, depending on what pin they are wearing or what they know about the programming.

The history of mind control is the history of male chauvinist secret organizations at work preying upon women. But there are some other things. Women are uniquely susceptible to trauma and especially sexual trauma. The reactions - the difference between men and women in the MPD thing - this mind control falls into MPD - it's just a naturally occurring phenomena which would probably happen in nature. If you go up to a victim at car crash, and they are in the state of what we call "shock" - and give them your card and say "you'll send me a thousand bucks tomorrow, come over here and sit down, are you okay?" change the subject - probably that person will give you a thousand bucks the next day because they are in a state of shock. If you give an embedded command in a positive framework - it's just the way people are - we are all that way. Nothing special about it. So that state is used to traumatize small children - naturally occurring state - is accessed by the government. My cousin - he's the reason I got into this - he was traumatized and we didn't know it. He had a drunken father who used to beat him and his mother up, that wasn't a big deal, it was no big deal - but when he joined the service it showed up on the tests - there it was. This was a person with a high tendency to dissociate - we can use him. He was trained as a courier, to carry secret messages locked behind post-hypnotic amnesia blocks. And today he is still having trouble. He can't sleep very well, so many years later, and he has had

DEAD MEN TALKING

13 years of therapy, he was in hypnosis. It's pretty well in there. He remembers the atrocities he had to witness at interrogations, which ended with decapitation and things like that, really hideous stuff, military stuff, which really hit him.

That little lady was used in ... she was a bomber by the time she was age 3. She was like a set up person who would hang out with the assassin and distract somebody while the guy bumped him. Just a little innocent kid coming into a place like this. Oh a little package, you know. Puts it down, later the place blows up, that kind of thing. She has pretty much recovered, doing really well, I am happy to say.

The best literature on mind control and survivors is self-published literature. The publishing companies won't touch this stuff any more. The only reason I got Operation Mind Control published in 1978 was that my agent was an agent. He belonged to Naval Intelligence. He is now one of the biggest agents in New York, and he paid me a whopping advance because they wanted to control it, and then, man they printed a million copies and ate it, and paid me full royalties and you never found it again. In two weeks it was gone. Now they are paying $650 a copy - if you've got a used copy of Operation Mind Control, sell it. Of course now you can get one for free by becoming a member of of the Freedom of Thought Foundation.

[slide] This was one of the early things of the male chauvinist society - it was called The Battle for Men's Minds, a book by William Sargent. Here is Dr. Sidney Gottlieb of the CIA. He was the guy who gave 147 different drugs to people. John Marks in The Search for the Manchurian Candidate or the Church Committee Reports cover him pretty well. He is a scientist, a doctor. And of course we know about Timothy Leary who is a psychologist, he is the producer of the flower generation, the psychedelic sixties and the slogan "turn on, tune in, drop out" - he worked with Henry Luce and the CIA to turn on the generation known as the Baby Boomers. When I asked Leary if he was witting or unwitting when he got his LSD from the CIA, he said, "Who you would work for - the Yankees or the Dodgers? You want me to work for the KGB?"

[slide] This is a blank slide in memory of Dr. Frank Olson who flew, jumped, or otherwise exited from the 16th floor of the Pennsylvania Hotel in New York City back in the 1950's, and Olson's family was paid $750,000 wrongful death - the federal courts claim act keeps you from suing the government for wrongful death - but it turned out, after the autopsy - the family exhumed the body of Olson - his skull was fractured before he was thrown out the window. He was killed before he was thrown out the window. They probably just laced him with LSD. He was an Edgewood Arsenal chemist and he had qualms about dosing people agains their will and without their knowledge at Edgewood. So they killed him and threw him

out the window and made it look like a suicide. Now the family is suing under a different law, and maybe they will get some real money out of this - the culprits should be prosecuted, but we can't prosecute anybody until we - what are we going to do? Repeal the National Security Act and then give everybody amnesty? Man, there's a lot of criminals, a lot of murderers.

[slide] This is Harold Blauer I used to make a joke, on his ass before the government put him there forever. He was a tennis pro. He was given an overdose of a mescaline derivative by the CIA. Every minute of his death is chronicled in cold blood descriptions in their classified files. You can find it verbatim in Operation Mind Control. Like Olson's family Blauer's family received a quarter of a million dollars from Uncle Sam, but they are suing again because he was a private citizen. He didn't sign up.

Now you get the idea right? If you sign up for the government, you're going to give your life for the country. The National Security Act suspends all your civil rights, you get it? After you've given your life for the country, since they didn't need you to survive, they're going to use anything you've got - your body parts, your mind, your soul, anything. That's the way the game is played. Most of the victims of mind control are government related. May 2nd or 3rd generation. Our files contain very detailed debriefings, drawings, sketches of high ranking CIA officials' daughters. Now why would they do this to this person who is now a very competent secretary, and who has been harassed and tortured since she was a small child by some incredible technology that is more advanced ... since she is not one of the DID kind. This is really incredible.

But of course Walter Reed is a place where they program people and ... this story. I just got this recently from Blanche I think, "Sing a Song to Jenny", it's the true account of a secret US raid into China. In 1978 I am in San Francisco doing a talk show for KPIX TV - normally they bus in women's clubs and there I was, the bus broke down, and I am left with nothing but the phone lines which was fortuitous because a Commander in the Navy called and said, "I was on the Black Pajama team working behind ... and they sent us to Walter Reed and now we all have cardboard memories." And this is the story of one guy, not the same guy I think that I talked to, but this is probably the same story of mind control soldiers operating behind enemy lines.

The CIA documents ... to create an involuntary assassin. That was in the seventies, and that was published. That's one of the English editions of Operation Mind Control. That one is worth $650 on the used book market. This is The Mind Manipulators by Alan Scheflin, it came out a year later. Journey Into Madness, Gordon Thomas ... he is Irish and to me, kind of thinks like an Irishman, 'why mess up a good story with the truth?' so he takes wild flights of probably untruth ... but

DEAD MEN TALKING

he does cover Ewen Cameron's experiments in Canada very well, and it's good for that. Of course, as a result of Ewen Cameron's experiments, they paid off pretty heavy to the families up there. These people weren't in our government, and Cameron was working under the payroll of the CIA for a long time, doing the experiments for the CIA. Cameron was at the same time the President of the American Psychiatric Association and he was the head shrink for the Nuremburg Trial. You can see the connection with psychiatry ... that's probably why psychiatry stopped dead in the water, probably why it doesn't work, what they are trying to do. And of course, it was useless. We just spent fifty years and how many millions and billions of dollars, and we didn't come up with anything.

David Ferrie was a hypnotist, he was a pilot for the CIA and he was probably the guy who was an on the scene handler for Lee Harvey Oswald, who was probably just a patsy. He said he was a patsy. They ran a CSE on his statement and it appeared to be true, and believe it or not, stress free. So he looks like just a patsy. But David Ferrie had false eyebrows, a wig ... strange dude.

This is another victim of mind control, he was programmed. He was a White Russian. George de Mohrenschildt is his name and he was a friend of Lee Harvey Oswald and Marina Oswald. A friend of mine, Eddie Epstein, was interviewing him for Time Magazine and they took a break for lunch and Oswald got a phone call, and simply said "I understand". Then he took a gun and killed himself. Bang. Just like the Manchurian Candidate. His family believes that's what happened.

This is Luis Enjarocasetio (sp) an attempted assassin of Ferdinand Marcos in the Phillipines. He was arrested by the Phillipine National Bureau of Investigation, the equivalent of the FBI. They called in, unlike in the USA where nobody believes this could happen, those guys called in a hypnotist and began to deprogram this guy. They found four different identities when he was in custody. He had 40 hypnotic sessions from April 3 to June 25, 1967. He displayed four distinct personalities. He was put into a trance and given an empty pistol. In the first personality he would follow whoever was talking with the pistol, pulling the trigger over and over. In the second personality he would aim only at the picture of Marcos and pull the trigger over and over. In the third personality he would end up falling off the table to the floor and remain motionless. The report said, in the last state, a "pathetic sight takes place - the subject turns the pistol to his own temple and squeezes the trigger as many times as his name is repeated."

Notice his clothes. He's got this little sweater kind of thing, notice his haircut, general look. When Sirhan was arrested, the same kind of thing. The interesting thing is that they both had diaries, they both left underlinings. They both repeated things and kind of chanted their program. They both predicted before the crime that they were going to do this.

DEAD MEN TALKING

Sirhan is arrowed. The other guy is Spanish, some kind of Hispanic background. They look enough alike to be brothers. Castile believed that a guy that sounds like Allen Dulles was his father. You find this in the programming. These sadistic jokes are played. Sirhan as you know was programmed to kill Robert Kennedy, and did apparently, shot at him, was in the room anyway. When in custody, he was visited by Dr. Bernard Diamond, shown here, who was hired by the defence, and Diamond is an expert in hypnosis and defence. He thought immediately that Sirhan had been programmed by the way he responded to hypnotic command. At one point he put him in deep trance, and he found that he couldn't speak, but he could write answers. Here's the way it went. He showed him a page of his diary and asked, "is this crazy writing?" "Yes, Yes, Yes," Sirhan wrote. "Are you crazy?" Diamond asked. "No, No, No," Sirhan wrote. "Well, why are you writing crazy?" Diamond asked. "Practice, Practice, Practice," Sirhan wrote. "Practice for what?" Diamond asked. "Mind control, Mind control, Mind control," is what Sirhan wrote.

Here's a guy who did a lot of our work, funded by the CIA through the National Institute of Mental Health. The CIA gave the money to NIMH who gave the money to Harvard University who gave the money to Jose Delgado, famous neurologist who back in the 50's and 60's did a lot of amazing work. He went before Congress I think in 1962 or 1963, and it's in the Congressional Record, and he called for a "Psychocivilized Society" in which everybody would have an electrode implanted in their brain and it would be for the benefit of us all. I know a little kid, he's 15 years old, he's a cyberpunk, and he can't wait to have that because he wants to know the baseball scores. He says "why do I have to remember all this?"

There's a stimoceiver transmitter and receiver in the brain of the bull at the right place and the bull didn't even really attack. That's a puny bull if you ask me, and Delgado looks like a real chicken and he's backing up. He has the cape but he doesn't have the sword and he has the radio transmitter and then the bull gets to a certain point and he pushes a button, and the thing goes into reverse. I mean it was unbelievable, and you can get that. I have seen it even on educational television shows ... A&E did this, it was called "The Bad Trip to Edgewood." That's the headquarters at Edgewood Arsenal, Fort Detrick, Maryland. They started out with monkeys of course. They tried everything ... they started out with gas and injections and that led to human experimentation.

See that mouse and the cat ... that's a famous thing from the sixties. Here's a cat on LSD. This cat is afraid of these mice, and it keeps leaping away. It's unbelievable to see that, and it's a famous experiment. They used a lot of LSD. Of course they cornered the market. I think they went to Sandoz Labs and bought every existing dose of LSD.

DEAD MEN TALKING

This guy, Bill Jordan, is a medical "volunteer" and he was a Lt-Colonel —he was probably the highest ranking volunteer. They thought they were going to get gas or something, tear gas — they gave him 100x the normal dose of LSD and these guys now 40 years later are still walking around having flashbacks, epileptic seizures. They gave huge doses — 7000 men were given LSD in these huge doses between 1955 and 1975.

This guy is Col. James Ketchum who was the Army psychiatrist who ran it. Ketchum revealed to Bill Kurtis, who was the A&E anchorman, that they had tested BZ which puts the test subject into a 3 day stupor and is followed by memory loss. They were interested in anything to induce amnesia. One of the test subjects did try to sue the government and he got to the Supreme Court and was turned down because of the Federal Torts Claims Act. But the dissenting opinion of the judges compared the Edgewood experiments to the Nazi experiments of WWII. This is on record. Col. Ketchum didn't take it all that seriously. He said "Most of the volunteers thought of it as an interesting adventure. Many volunteered to do it again." While these injections were going on, other things were being done.

In Lexington, Kentucky (Lexington is a federal "drug rehabilitation" - I don't think there is such a thing as rehabilitation in the prison system these days - there is no concept of it. But in those days they still called it a drug rehabilitation project). They would give them rewards of heroin if they would take LSD and other things. Here's a guy in such a stupor, he can't sit down. This guy starts out early on playing solitaire, pretty soon the cards are all over the table, and he is just a mess. This guy I think is counting spiders on the wall that he thinks are there. This guy is breathing some gas that they measure and then they filled the whole room with BZ or psychotoxic gas then they would put the guy in this suit and see if the suit protected him. Of course they started out with animals. This fellow says it made him violent. It changed his personality and he hasn't had a relationship with his family for 30 years because of it.

Of course that's what they wanted to do. BZ and some of these other drugs were known to produce a violent reaction. One of the things they experimented with was PCP, angel dust, which is now "an underground recreational illegal drug". This is a group of soldiers walking through a cloud of BZ and it brings to mind some eerie scenes from a movie I would recommend that you rent from the video store, called "Jacob's Ladder". This is a movie that is really about the Buddhist afterlife, the guy is already dead. He was part of the Army BZ experiments and he is reliving his life which did take place in Vietnam. It looks very much like this, they reproduced in the movie the whole feeling of this kind of monstrous experimentation.

Of course, here is Richard Helms, and here he is lying to the President's

DEAD MEN TALKING

Commission on the assassination of President Kennedy which was one of his first big lies that was documented. Then he went on to lie to Congress and that's when he got sentenced to some time for that. Here's something from Defence Intelligence Agency Report Task #T72-01-14: "Parapsychology can be harnessed to create conditions where one can alter and manipulate the minds of others." This is from Hans Ulrich Dresch, he's a PhD who works in an alcohol rehabilitation program today, and he was a victim of mind control. He was actually an American citizen, but he was born over there of military parents and raised there. He was used in some kind of mind control experiments. Since he is a psychologist, he talks about all those things -MPD, hypnosis, drugs, and all the other stuff. This can be found on the internet and it's probably 40-50 pages long.

This is Alan Frey's early research when he was with G.E. and it's the "Human Auditory System Response to Elctromagnetic Energy" - in other words, "we are going to put voices in your head" by remote control from a distance. And that was in the 60's, and Ross Adey is another guy who did the research - he was at University of California, Riverside, and he did a lot of research on modulating microwaves so you would hear a voice from a distance. There's a guy in New Mexico who is in Operation Mind Control who will sell you a microwave you can keep in a paper bag. It's about the size of a radar gun. You can buy them now over the counter. Q. is that kind of mind control technology used to discredit the individual, or is it actually used for programming. I would say both. I would say the number one thing is programming because if you take all the technology - drugs, hypnosis - all this electronic stuff - if you take it away the human mind is still the human mind and it works the same way. Basically you can explain that by understanding the subconscious. A lot of it happens over a long period of time. I don't know about 20 years, but I know about 10 years.

Here's another one. Spontaneous regression. This was way before the New Age thing of regression, past life regression. The military and the government were researching this thing. This guy Schneck - this was from State University of New York College of Medicine - a CIA project funded it - and they knew damn well what a powerful regression was. Even if it is just a metaphor.

The father of all this stuff - the greatest mind about hypnosis - and a guy who also worked for the government - was Milton Erickson. When I interviewed him he talked very slowly - you could go into trance just listening to him in a warm room. But I liked him a lot, and of course he is the main model for what is now known as neurolinguistic programming. He had polio so he could not interact with people and he watched how they communicated, and out of that came this beautiful science which is used in computers. "The use of hypnosis in intelligence and related military situations" by Seymour Fischer (sp) 1958 - a declassified CIA document. "The use of hypnosis in warfare" by Alec McQuart, unclassified, it's in the open literature. "Experimenting with the possible antisocial uses of hypnosis" by Milton Erickson. He said there is no problem to it, all you have to do basically is to manipulate context and get an individual to do something against their will and without their knowledge. It was done in a laboratory in a government study where a soldier was made to attack his commanding officer. All they had to say was "this is WWII - this guy is a Japanese guy - it is kill or be killed". They didn't know he had a knife in his boot but luckily they had two armed guards standing there.

This is "Assassination in Hypnosis: political influence" by Joseph Berndt in 1968, after the Kennedy assassination. "Rewriting the Soul" by Ian Hacking, Canadian. He's a sociologist so parts of it aren't correct but it's really interesting to read this different point of view, and he tells some anecdotes about Colin Ross that are pretty good. Elaine Pagel's a friend of mine who did the Nag Hammadi texts and anybody who has had satanic ritual abuse should probably read this book and understand the origin of satan and understand how deeply rooted it is in our society, in Judeao Christian Aristotelian philosphy. This is Mikey's paper, "Mind War". You know Mikey? Yeah, Michael Aquino. This is his very own handwriting. It is the headquarters of the Imperial Storm Trooper Force Office of the Chief of Staff, Mind War Center, Hub 4, and it's the final version of an article going to the military review, "Parameters", which is a war course journal psyops community - the head of which is near my home town in Arizona. He was just then a Major, and he talks about John Alexander's military review and psyops and stuff, and what gave me the creeps is #11 - he cites Operation Mind Control as a source. That gave me a chill. Here he is when he was reviewed for a possible adverse - they are going to throw him out of the Army for molesting children at the Presidio - and of course they couldn't prove he did it, but they couldn't prove he didn't do it - they did a weird thing which they can only do in military law. They didn't acquit him, but they didn't convict him. They just said "we are going to gather more evidence" and of course they are still gathering evidence.

So here he is, a satanist, and high ranking guy - he retired from the military. People raised a stink about it, but the Pentagon says no problem, there's a guy buried in Arlington from the Civil War who is a satanist. This is freedom of religion.

And of course, cybernetics, Norbert Weiner, "Control and Communication in the animal and the machine". The father of cyberpunk. And of course the Russians were of course very good at this and they know what obedience to authority means. Let me tell you a little bit about this guy. He's a member of the KGB, head guy, Vladimir Zukov, a KGB parapsychologist. He's an adept at telepathic hypnosis, a psychic who was especially trained to use a variety of instruments to affect other people's minds at a distance, if you can believe it.

DEAD MEN TALKING

This is part of the history. We are coming to the end. The only success story of that kind of psychotronic warfare is this chess match between Karpov and Korchnoy and Karpov was the darling 27 year old chess champion and Korchnoy was the former chess champion that had defected to the West, so they wanted to make sure Korchnoy lost. Korchnoy, after the thing was over, says he tried to get this guy removed and he complained and complained. He said "he forced me to make bluffs I didn't want to make, he forced me not to play strong. It was Zukov and the powers of mind control that led to my loss." And it was a prestigious international victory for Karpov and Soviety parapsychology.

Here's a photo of Dr. Karl Nakaliev at work in a laboratory on a crystal ball - it's a psychotronic device which allegedly focused the mind in what is called biocomm-unication. The Soviets took it seriously and developed it to a reliable degree and of course our controlled remote viewing is the same kind of thing where we put something that has been generalized and non-specific and unscientific and we disciplined it.

Here are psychotronic devices - the mind concentrates and spins that little wheel. It's from a movie and it's available from A&E. Uri Geller did that for the Stanford Research Institute and Ingo Swann. These are psychotronic devices - they are really interesting. They are not a dental tool, not a sculpture tool, not a kitchen tool - they are used like magic wands to focus energy and direct the mind. This guy is the leading Soviet parapsychologist - when he would do stuff like that, they were measuring his brainwaves so they could duplicate his results. Now we did similar things. One of the most interesting studies the USA did was to measure the brainwaves of people with Multiple Personalities, put them into different personalities, and measure their brainwaves. Each personality had a different brainwave pattern. They then recorded these patterns and sent them to another shrink on the west coast. They then sent the subject to that shrink and told the shrink to play these signals back. I don't know if they played them auditorally — I think so. They stimulated the personalities by playing back the brain wave signals.

This is a psychotronic factory where they are making psychotronic weapons in the Soviet Union and the parabolic mirror looks like ... you can become your own CNN. You know they were seriously doing this - it's not just those of you who have experienced some of this stuff. But these are for you who want to tinker and build your own - take a look at this one. Non lethal weapons, being sold, being promoted in this country for law enforcement and it is the most dangerous step we can take. That kind of psychotronic weaponry or any of the other nonlethal weaponry, especially since the military people and the law enforcement people will be the first targets of it. The term nonlethal is a misnomer because they are lethal.

162

DEAD MEN TALKING

You know this guy - Dr. Becker. Most of the stuff he talks about is obsolete but it's a must read if you are a serious student of this stuff. Here's a picture of the transponder. Everyone is claiming about having implants. Most of the people who claim they have them are claiming they are from extraterrestrial sources. These are terrestrial implants.

This is a 1960's technology. They have different sizes - small, medium, large. They have some for goats, pigs, dogs. You can buy them from your veterinary store. This is a small one. That's the tip of a guy's finger. That is the electronic technology.

This is all obsolete. Nanotechnology is where it's at. Talk about implants - they don't have to do that stuff. If you want to transplant a transponder in somebody it's going to be the size of a molecule and it's going to be run on an energy source that will last more than a human's lifetime. You will be dead, your body will be decayed and that thing will still be sending off the signals. Nanotechnology is where it presently is at ...

They were talking about putting them in teenagers with the idea of tracking them.

This is Dr. Gwen Deans' comparison between thought reform on the left which is Lifton stuff, ritualized abuse in the middle, and abduction on the right. This is one of her earlier things. There is a bigger one I've got in the slides and we are going skip it ... but this gives you the essence of the thing. First, trivial demands are enforced - the middle one says "must learn cult rules". What you are seeing in the phenomena, the experiences of these individuals who talk about government mind control, or thought reform, or ritualized abuse or abductions is the same thing. Hundreds of reports.

Back to the shrinks. Sidney - Francis Crick, Nobel Prize. Says he found the human soul - the guy's an idiot. But this is the problem with our science. This guy won the Nobel Prize, discovered DNA, but he has no right to talk about the human soul. It's a theological question.

Microwave harassment and mind control experimentation by Julianne McKinney. She was involved in the harassment program which is now defunct. Cheryl Welsh and other folks ... that's Ed Light who runs the Mind Control Forum. These people were on CNN, got a hatchet job when they came out, and of course they didn't find any signals ... they came out with all this instrumentation to measure the environment and they found all kinds of pollution in the environment but this is the normal pollution, and of course it had nothing to do with what they were saying. The scientist said we could find nothing - no reason why these people should be complaining - like Ed is complaining here of the sounds, the hurt, the

163

pain, perhaps voices in his head. Try to tell somebody you are hearing voices in your head. Every time you are making love to your husband there's the voice telling you how to do it, how you are doing it wrong - at the most intimate times in your life there's a voice talking to you. When you are sleeping there are voices talking to you, lights shining at you, 24 hrs a day, year after year. You go to a doctor. He looks it up in his manual - and he says "delusional" or "you're a paranoid schizophrenic". There are only four basic things -hearing voices is only in there four times basically. And then they give you a drug and suppress the symptoms. What does that do?

You know about the radiation experiments. A lot of the mind control victims were used in the radiation experiments. Many of them have Graves disease, lost their thyroids and because mind control victims don't talk or they can be stopped from talking. So they were used in that. At the end of the President's thing on radiation, "Trance on Trial" Alan Scheflin's book -they don't believe in hypnosis, you can't be made to do something against your will in the courts of law. They just don't recognize anybody who has ever had hypnosis. They are discredited as witnesses. It's like a bunch of simpletons.

Multiple personality disorder and criminal responsibility. Very important document written by a UCLA law professor - Ellen Saks. You need that. You need to read that. It's a long thing.

Q. DSM IV has a new options book and there is a category called "Spiritual Problems" - it's the first time that the DSM committee acknowledged that there is something called a spiritual problem. They are defining it in four sentences unfortunately. The proposal was 11 pages. It was a miracle that they accepted it. What they are saying is when there are actual spiritual experiences that are going on right now and are not in alignment with our previous religious experience. I would advise somebody if they are going to go see somebody in the medical field, to refer to that.

This is Robert Moodie and his brother, they look like twins. This man is on death row right now. I am his only link to the outside world. He is diagnosed MPD, DID. I worked with him before he could even get that diagnosis because the aliens' voices in his mind told him to do "choo-choo train" on the test so he would do true, true, false - true, true, false -choo-choo train - and they couldn't get any proof. Psychiatrist got up in court and said he is malingering. But a couple of them said you'd better rule out DID, this, that and the other thing. The judge just said "I'm not going to rule it out." They put him in the nut house for six months and they couldn't do anything with him. He came back and he still wasn't competent to stand trial. He was insane at the time of the crime. And the whole thing about DID and the law has to be re-examined and re-structured.

DEAD MEN TALKING

Here's a guy - I began to work with him. There's Mary, there's Bob. See if you can see some of the changes in him. You can do it in the film, you can really see it. That's the killer personality. His name was XE. He was programmed in a Marine Corps - killed two women in Arizona. He is sentenced to die after his four appeals are exhausted. Anybody want to write to him ... This is Dr. Joyce Vesper who thanks to Colin Ross, we finally found a doctor in Arizona - she is the Arizona Director of the ISSD and she came forward, gave him a five hours of tests, looked at 200 hours of sample videotapes we had taken of this guy. He turned into a little kid. When the Miranda warnings were read to Moodie, he was a nine year old, he didn't know his name. The reason they caught him is he turned himself in to this Sheriff's department saying "run my fingerprints, I don't know who I am". He had a picture of a little girl in his pocket. That was his daughter. He didn't know who she was. He was in amnestic fugue. It's not justice - it's got to change. You can get hit on the head, something else can happen to you, and suddenly you are on death row. It's not the way you treat people.

This is a novel by Michael Youssef, "The Voice" and it's about the voice of satan in a christian preacher of some kind.

Dr. Sheldon Deal looked at - Patrick Flanagan created a thing called the neurophone which proves that somebody can be deaf, their cochleas taken out and they can still hear with this thing. Nick Begitch will tell you more about this thing. There are some incredible therapeutic effects with this thing - that's what Dr. Deal did a study - hearing people can hear a conscious sound and then this thing kind of plays it to your bones, I guess, to the other part of your ear. Begitch will explain it to you. I have known this guy for 30 years. He's a naturopath, holistic healing, used to Mr. Arizona and stuff. Wonderful guy, serious researcher.

Voices in the head - a famous Philip K. Dick novel about VALIS - Vast Active Living System. This is Jack Sarfatiks' physics group talking about VALIS and conscious computer spacecraft from the future, time travel, and all that kind of thing, which is coming up fairly prominently in quantum physics. Of course there is something now called post-quantum physics and there are sub-atomic particles called beables - and you had better familiarize yourself with that.

In the 1950's it began - the new science - and the University of Arizona was going to be the first university in America with a chair for this new science, called Cognitive Science, the study of consciousness. This year in April there's a conference discussing this - psychologists, psychiatrists, neurologists, linguists, cyberneticists, theologists, philosophers - all getting together to talk on that topic. Heavy on the computer thing, artificial intelligence is very important. But it all started in the fifties.

J.B. Ryan, Duke University, 1950's - CIA project in extrasensory perception.

DEAD MEN TALKING

They are the guys who used the Zener cards that you saw in Ghostbusters. Very important studies. Denied by the CIA. They said "we spent so much money and nothing happened". Don't believe it.

Now they admit - remote viewers even - that's pretty far out. Astral projections, out of body experiences - now it's called controlled remote viewing. I like this book a lot - Dave Morehouse - seems like an honest guy - talking about his experience in the remote viewing thing. The CIA finally admitted it, but here it is in 1975 in a press release telling you all about it. So it's been known that far back - but 1996 they admitted to it.

Here's John Mack, thanks to Blanche, a little thing about John Mack at Harvard, talking about UFO's - working with Lifton. And there's John Shirley, talking about hypnosis. There was a serious study about alien aspects done at MIT and one of the papers in here talks about - they found out that the so-called abductee community was highly dissociative. So the same thing you find in ritual abuse, you find in mind control, you find in alien abductees. And of course, for the first time now, people are beginning to say "yeah I do remember there was a government guy standing around with those little grey things". And of course how many survivors have been asked not to talk about their "alien experiences"? About three years ago I asked that question, and just about everyone I could identify as a survivor raised their hand. They have been told not to talk about it, because it discredits their credibility. They are already telling pretty fantastic tales, you know. There is nobody talking about the Lori Lingenfelter story, or even Cathy O'Brien doesn't talk a lot about her NASA training - but Lingenfelter says that she was trained to be a hostage "witness" - a specially hypnotically trained witness on some kind of an alien ship in a swap deal you know. Incredible stories, but it's worth checking out.

Here is Dr. Dean who did the comparison accounts with ritual maltreatments and ritual abduction, and this is the appendix E in Operation Mind Control. It is just amazing to me to find everybody talking about the same thing in slightly different variations.

Of course on the fiftieth anniversary of the so-called Roswell thing comes out and says yeah I was the guy who placed all the high technology into the R&D stream of the defence developers. He talks about the skin of the craft, the propulsion system, night vision goggles. One thing he doesn't talk about and admits they were there - mind control devices on the ship allegedly, but he doesn't talk about it. His movement away from that, his sudden avoidance of that subject, is to me what gives credibility to this account. You wouldn't talk about it if you were using it the way it apparently was being used. They had a headband that blew the graph, and stuff, he says.

DEAD MEN TALKING

If you read the report from Iron Mountain, you realize how to motivate an economy without war can be a very difficult problem, so there is the Green movement, the ecology movement. Space exploratiion - a bottomless pit. You can sink a lot of money into that but the best motivator is to pose an outside threat of alien invasion. How are they doing? Only 55% don't believe in UFO's in a CNN poll in 1997. Are there visitors from space? 60% don't believe it. They are not doing so well in planting that idea.

This is an implant ... I don't know if you can see it ... it comes from UFO community. It is quite a bit different than the one we showed before, that is actually in production.

You have to read about physics so you might as well start with Tim Allen, it's a pretty good book on basic quantum physics.

Michael Persinger, a neuroscientist in Laurentian University in Sudbury, Ontario is blindfolding people and putting an automobile with selanoids and playing magnetic waves over their temporal lobes, and 80% of the women he claims have temporal lobe epileptic experiences automatically, frequently from time to time throughout their lives. This guy was funded by the NSA ... (Q. he is funded by the US Navy ...). Well you know what he's doing? He is saying that UFO's are electrical phenomena from earthquakes and he's demonstrating, beyond question, that your consciousness can be altered and controlled at a distance, without breaking your skin. It is very transparent though, in the research papers and in his conclusions, his conclusions don't match his arguments. It is pretty obvious. But what he is demonstrating is that a person can be influenced by magnetic waves from a distance, remotely. That's amazing, that he is standing out there doing that ... I don't believe a word the guy says.

The physics of immortality - a must read - Frank Tepler. He says you can find God in the codes and stuff like that. And this is a wonderful thing -hard to find - out of print - Elizabeth Rauscher, she worked with Andreja Puharich, for a while. She has done a lot of government contracts. Electromagentic Phenomena in Complex Geometries and Non-Linear Phenomena, Non-Hurtzian Waves and Magnetics Monopoles. The whole layout of the questions that you've got for "can it be?" Yes it can be and it has been, and it is being.

Then there is Rupert Sheldrake - if you talk to physicists they will say don't pay attention to him - he is only a biologist. Physicists say we make the machines for the doctors, and we only put two buttons on them, one is "off" and the other is "on" ... that's all they can handle. They don't consider doctors scientists ... But this is a very interesting idea, if you know about morphogenic fields. These guys are a hoot, and they are on the internet - Jack Zarfatti, Paul and Fred Allen Wolf - all of them write books and stuff. They are talking about supraluminals, faster than light travel. The answers to your questions about "what's happening to me?" including Carl Preberim, he's a neurologist - he talks about DID/MPD on a subatomic level - and that's the only way to address the question. It reads just like NLP, what he's talking about - the way the tunnelling occurs - and it's pretty amazing. So physics is where it's gotta go ... I don't have time - but if you want some real understanding of the mechanics of what is going on and what you are going to face in the future - because this new technology -once you've been targeted as a guinea pig - it's not going to stop until you stop it, or we stop it. PQM means post quantum mechanics.

That's the answer right there - the microtubule - when I first saw it, it was drawn by Dr. Stewart Amiroff in his scribbling way - it was black and white and it looked like yin and yang - and I said, "wow, it's an on and off switch" 1 is 1, 1 is 0. In the cytoskeleton of the DNA which is that structure of your DNA, it's made up of things that look like pomegranate pods represented by the red and the blue. 1 is a +1 and 1 is a 0, just like a computer. They are programmable by a signal but there's a back way, a feedback phenomenon that is occurring. We don't know what the signal is yet, they haven't decided what that is, the signal of consciousness ... but this is where they are at. In this kind of thinking lies the answer to some of the things that people are thinking. Whether or not it is just a metaphorical paradigm shift that we are experiencing and anthropomorphizing and living out ... or in fact ... as I believe ... somebody understands how to use that or they are dabbling with it. Microtubules in the cytoskeleton of DNA.

New World Vistas and the Space Powers - some of you already know about this ... 13 volumes published by the Air Force. They predict that within the next 50 years, and if they are saying this that means they have already done it ... we are going to have a been there, done that learning technology. Did you ever see the movie, Brain Storm? Rent it, see it. That's what they are talking about. They have probably already got it. Whereas you wear a helmet, record your experience on some kind of medium, play it back to the other guy, the other guy has the taste, touch, smell, sound, sight of the other person as it is happening.

So that's the answer to me. That's what we have to do.

DEAD MEN TALKING

High-Tech Slavery

Mind Control Slavery and the New World Order by Uri Dowbenko

New Improved Entertainment Corp.

PO Box 43

Pray, Montana 59065, USA

High-tech slavery is alive and well on planet Earth. Ever since World War II when the United States Government's Project Paperclip sponsored the resettlement of about 2,000 high-level Nazis in the United States, the technology of mind-control programming has advanced rapidly.

"The Germans under the Nazi government began to do serious scientific research into trauma-based mind control," write Fritz Springmeier and Cisco Wheeler in their book, The Illuminati Formula used to create an Undetectable Total Mind Controlled Slave. "Under the auspices of the Kaiser Wilhelm Medical Institute in Berlin, Josef Mengele conducted mind-control research on thousands of twins and thousands of other hapless victims."

Mengele, known as "the Angel of Death", was one of the approximately 900 military scientists and medical researchers secretly exfiltrated into the United States, where he continued his 'research' and trained others in the black arts of mind control. This work in behaviour manipulation was later incorporated into the CIA's projects Bluebird and Artichoke which, in 1953, became the notorious MKULTRA. The CIA claims that these programs were discontinued, but there is no credible evidence that "The Search for the Manchurian Candidate" (the title of the definitive book by John Marks) ever ceased.

In fact, Captain John McCarthy, US Army Special Forces (Ret.), who ran CIA assassination teams out of Saigon during the Vietnam War, told his friend, LAPD whistleblower Mike Ruppert, that "MKULTRA is a CIA acronym that officially stands for 'Manufacturing Killers Utilizing Lethal Tradecraft Requiring Assassinations'".

DEAD MEN TALKING

Thus the CIA's official obsession with producing programmed killers through the MKULTRA contained more than 149 sub-programs in fields ranging from biology, pharmacology, psychology to laser physics and ESP.

More recently, new evidence points to the continuous use of so-called trauma-based programming techniques to accomplish the same goal. This includes the deliberate induction of Multiple Personality Disorder (MPD) in involuntary human subjects - in essence, human guinea pigs.

MPD has been reclassified by the American Psychiatric Association as Dissociative Identity Disorder (DID). The psychiatrists' bible, the Diagnostic and Statistical Manual (DSM-IV, p. 487), characterises it by:

A. The presence of two or more distinct personality states;

B. At least two of these identities or personality states recurrently take control of the person's behaviour;

C. Inability to recall important personal information that is too extensive to be explained by ordinary forgetfulness;

D. The disturbance is not due to the direct physiological effects of a substance or a general medical condition.

No matter what name is assigned to the problem, however, to create this condition by conscious intent is an atrocity so depraved that trauma-based mind-control programming remains the de facto Secret Holocaust of the 20th century. Known as the Monarch Project, it has been verified and corroborated by numerous survivors like Cathy O'Brien, author of TranceFormation of America, Brice Taylor, author of Starshine, and K. Sullivan, author of MK. No paper trail has been found which leads from the CIA's MKULTRA program to the Monarch Project - a catchword for mind control which involves US military, CIA, NASA and other government agencies.

The Franklin Cover-up, attorney John W. DeCamp's groundbreaking book about high-level pedophilia, also describes the sordid details of Monarch. "Drugs are not the deepest level of government-sponsored evil," he writes. "I think the lowest level of Hell is reserved for those who conjured up and carried out the 'Monarch Project'. 'Monarch' refers to young people in America who were victims of mind-control experiments run either by US government agencies such as CIA or military intelligence agencies."

DeCamp's client, Monarch abuse survivor Paul Bonacci, has a story which parallels the victimology of O'Brien, Taylor and Sullivan - an extensive cross-corroboration of perpetrators and their methodology. It's simply "the production of a horde of children in whom the soul is crushed, who would spy, whore, kill and commit suicide", in the words of investigative reporter Anton Chaitkin, quoted by DeCamp in his book.

Recovering Monarch victims speak of ongoing trauma through "ritual abuse", also known as "satanic ritual abuse" because of the identifiable iconography of a belief structure associated with Satanism or Luciferianism. By using drugs, hypnosis, torture and electroshock, the Monarch criminal perpetrators have produced new and succeeding generations of victims.

This is not science fiction, but science fact. MPD involves the creation of personality "alters": alternative personalities or personality fragments which can be used for specific tasks - usually for illegal activities like delivering drugs or other black-market activities (mules), messages (couriers) or killings (assassins). These alters, or soul fragments, are segregated and compartmentalised within the victim's mind by the repeated use of stun guns, drugs and hypnosis, which isolates the memories of their experiences.

An alter can be accessed by anyone who knows the "codes" or "triggers". These triggers, which induce an altered or trance state in a programmed victim, can be anything including telephone tones, nursery rhymes, dialogue from certain movies or hand signals.

According to Springmeier and Wheeler, whose 468-page book has become a reference in the field, "...the basis for the success of the Monarch mind-control programming is that different personalities or personality parts called 'alters' can be created who do not know each other, but who can take the body at different times. The amnesia walls that are built by traumas form a protective shield of secrecy that prevents the abusers from being found out and prevents the front personalities who hold the body much of the time to know how their system of alters is being used."

The mind-control programming, however, has not worked according to plan. In fact, the perpetrators, in their arrogance and hubris, never dreamed that their methods could fail. The retrieval of survivors' photographic-like memories of actual abuse incidents, including images, sounds and smells, constitutes a major exposure of human rights abuses. These victims bear witness to the secret atrocities of the so-called New World Order.

MORE ON ILLUMINATI MIND CONTROL

According to John Coleman, author of Conspirators Hierarchy: The Committee of 300: "...the Illuminati is very much alive and well in America... Since the Illuminati is also known as Satanism, it must follow that the CIA was controlled by a Satanist while Dulles had charge of it. The same holds true for George Bush [a member of the Order of Skull and Bones].

DEAD MEN TALKING

"Given the ghastly mind-control experiments constantly being conducted by the CIA, and its past connections to fiendish monsters like Dr Campbell and Dr Sidney Gottlieb, it does not take much to conclude that the CIA follows satanic roads," Coleman concludes in his monograph, "Illuminati in America".

With regards to "the brainwashing capabilities of the Tavistock Institute as well as US Department of Defense projects like the Advanced Research Project Agency", Coleman writes that "...the bottom line of the projects is mind control as predicted by the book, The Technotronic Era, by Zbigniew Brzezinski. The project goes by the name 'Monarch Program' and it is a vast project involving not only the CIA but the Army, Air Force and Navy with all of their skills and vast resources."

SULLIVAN'S TRAVELS

The horrific torture and sexual abuse of children, also called "satanic ritual abuse", has been a key component in the creation of mind-controlled slaves.

Mind-control survivor K. Sullivan has written an astounding book called MK, a fictionalised account of her life, which describes the world of multiple personalities. To her credit, Sullivan has been able to reconstruct from her memories the actual mechanics and methodology of going from one alter state to another. A programmed assassin and sex slave, Sullivan says she was abused and raped by Robert Maxwell, Henry Kissinger, George Bush and Billy Graham, among others. One of her controllers was deceased CIA operative James Jesus Angleton, who has been widely regarded as a KGB and Mossad asset.

In a recent interview, Sullivan spoke about her background as a "family-generational slave" to the elite and about her stepfather, now deceased, who was initially her primary programmer. His cover was a church-going, upstanding citizen, a professional mechanical and systems engineer with a curious interest in robotics.

"There were a number of people who trained, conditioned, then broke my will, broke my psyche and programmed me in different altered states," she said in a recent interview. "My father was the one who did me the most. He did it through terror. He did it through torture. He was a very brilliant man, and he seemed to enjoy doing it to me and other children."

Confirming that her father was "horribly abused as a child", Sullivan added: "I know that for certain. His father was a Welsh Druid who had been sold as a child to a ship captain who brought him over to the US. At least that's the mentality in my family, for slavery of children to be okay. I heard this from older family members. They've never denied it. But my grandfather was a covert Druid as well. I'm sure he brought the religion over with him. One of the things he would do is go to the graveyard near his house and dig up bodies, then take them into the basement and take them apart and have fun with them. And he also did rituals out in the woods sometimes at night. He would sacrifice babies. And I was exposed to that. So I'm sure my father was, too, which left him no other alternative but to become like his father."

And how is this behaviour related to Satanism or is it just generational child abuse?

"I think it's both," she answered slowly. "And what it boils down to is these people are doing illegal activities. Criminals tend to find criminals. They tend to gravitate toward each other. It's amazing how they can find each other out. My grandfather developed connections to the Mafia in our area. I understand it was the Colombo family. I don't know what he did exactly, but I do have one memory of riding in a cement truck where he and other drivers with cement trucks were using the cement from the trucks to bury several bodies. So I guess they just did whatever needed to be done. That was in New York and Pennsylvania. My father was an assassin as well as other things, and these people really enjoy killing people. He killed people more for favours than for hire. He got to have as many kids as he wanted to raise."

Her father also had CIA and NASA connections. "The CIA work seems to be rather covert. He worked for Western Electric and later on for AT&T," Sullivan said. "I found out, since then, that Western Electric has had very strong CIA ties. I have been able to go through some of his papers since his death in 1990, and I have found on his desk calendar for that year that he had several contacts with NASA. Since then I have remembered that there were several facilities that he took me to that were NASA facilities. The NASA connections seem to be directly connected to the Paperclip connection. The Nazis were brought into the country and then were integrated into the NASA structure after the war.

"My father, because of his Celtic background, had very low self-esteem," continued Sullivan. "Being exposed to some of these Nazi war criminals seemed to mean a whole lot to him because he had a mother that was German. Between the Celtic background and a German mother, these men built up his self-esteem as far as being Aryan. He very much identified with them, and I think, from what I understand, he got a lot of his training especially from one man I knew as Dr Schwartz. He had slightly wavy black hair and very dark eyes. He was slim. I can't say his height because I was just a child. He had a definite German accent. People called him Herr Doctor or Dr Schwartz, one of the two. Sometimes he was called Dr Black. He was a pedophile for sure and he was a very cold man. He liked to make kids think that they would feel safe with him, but he would do something that would upset the children and then they would be afraid of him after that."

DEAD MEN TALKING

MULTI-MODE PROGRAMMING

Sullivan said that she was used to sexually service both males and females in the Beta mode, and to do assassination, bodyguarding and intrusions in hostage situations in the Delta mode.

And what is Alpha, Beta, Delta and Theta programming?

"Alpha was the basis for all the other programs," she continued. "It seems to be where a lot of information was stored in my memory, in my mind, that was used by programmers to develop the other programs. It's where some of my more generic alter states were also stored. Beta was the sexual servicing part of me. They also sometimes called the alter state 'Barbie'. It was supposed to be named after Klaus Barbie." Like Barbie doll?

Survivors Cathy O'Brien and Brice Taylor were also subjected to Beta, or sex-slave, programming. They, like actress Marilyn Monroe, were called "presidential models", mind-controlled slaves for the use of high-level politicians.

According to Springmeier's book, "...in 1981, the New World Order made training films for their novice programmers. Monarch slave Cathy O'Brien was used to make the film How To Divide a Personality and How To Create a Sex Slave. Two Huntsville porn photographers were used to help NASA create these training films."

Sullivan recalled: "I was used both as a child and as an adult in those alter states, and I had more than one. In those alter states I would not resist. I had no anger. I was an absolute sexual slave and I would do whatever I was told to do."

Delta programming is military-assassin programming that has trickled into popular consciousness through movies like La Femme Nikita, its American remake, Point of No Return, and The Long Kiss Goodnight.

Regarding the Delta programming, Sullivan said: "...it was when I was used to do hits, kills, and also bodyguarding and hostage extraction. I had a great number of alter personalities that had specialised training and had different modes to do different things."

Why was the training kept separate for different alters?

"Part of it was so I wouldn't recall too much at any one time - if I did start to remember," she said. "And also because they hand-pick each part out for a certain type of situation. If you had a part coming out that was very loyal to people that that part was bodyguarding, you don't want that part going off and killing somebody. And you don't want a part that's specifically programmed to kill coming out and feeling sorry for the target. So you have to keep the emotions and the motives separate as well. And so that's why they had to have different parts."

Sullivan's description of Theta programming seems to correlate with the development and use of so-called extrasensory powers and extraphysical abilities.

"Theta was where they used - I don't like the word 'psychic' because I think it's been so misused - thought energy," she said. "I just knew it as magnetic-type energy from the individual to do a number of different things that they were experimenting with, including long-distance mind connection with other people - even in other countries. I guess you would call it 'remote viewing' - where I could see what a person was doing in another state in a room or something like that.

"It was both actual programming and experimentation. Because what they did -they kept it encapsulated in several parts of me, several altered states. It was a lot of training, a lot of experimentation."

Theta programming also implies the use of thought energy to kill someone at a distance.

"A lot of times I ran across other victims with Theta programming," Sullivan said in a recent CKLN radio interview. "One of the movie and book themes they used extensively was Dune, by Frank Herbert. It won't be too hard to figure because what they taught us was that we could cause things to happen to other people. It was to build up rage inside. It would come out in a form of pure energy that would hit them... They had talked about people imploding internally in their digestive organs. I don't know because I can't see what goes on inside another body, but I do know that it does work."

The calculated admixture of doing good and evil seems to be a hallmark of the Illuminati methodology. It's as if they recognise, at a spiritual level, that all the horrible karma they create can be balanced by generous philanthropic gestures; for example, giving a billion dollars to the United Nations, or other feats of extraordinary compassion.

"Also, they tried to use me for hands-on healing because I had a grandmother who was a healer from Sweden," said Sullivan. "So they were trying - that was me and several other survivors I talked to since - to use them in that mode also. And hands-on healing means that you would focus electromagnetic energy into the other person's body."

BRICE TAYLOR'S ORDEAL

Another book, Brice Taylor's Starshine: One Woman's Valiant Escape from Mind Control, corroborates Cathy O'Brien's and K. Sullivan's experiences. Even though it's a fictionalised account, the book clearly indicates that major crimes have been - and are being - committed by the major players of the world's power elites.

Brice Taylor was also a "presidential model", and in a recent interview she went into intimate details of her many experiences with politicians promoting the New World Order.

"What it [being a presidential model] means," she explained, "is that your program is to have sex with presidents; and I did overhear this, that different politicians were encouraged to use CIA escorts for sex, so they wouldn't be in a vulnerable position if they ever disclosed any national security secrets to anyone on the outside, or for blackmail."

And how would she characterise this so-called New World Order?

"It is an attempt to bring in a One World Government in which elite families have things the way they want. Their belief was that the planet was overpopulated and that something had to be done: psychological and biological warfare. They considered mind control as a tool, their ace in the hole, something really different that would act as an invisible weapon."

ADVENTURES WITH HENRY K. AND THE COUNCIL

In her recovery, Brice Taylor also had memories of being used by Henry Kissinger as a mind-controlled courier.

"If you program someone to have a perfect photographic memory and total recall, then you have the capacity to be able to deal with many different tasks and assignments simultaneously," she explains. "Henry Kissinger created a 'mindfile' inside of my head. I would be sent around to all these leaders to keep their data - on some of their projects or whatever their agenda was - sorted. When they'd meet people, I would be programmed by either Kissinger or Nelson Rockefeller. This was in the mid-1960s."

But who's running the 'show'?

"I think there's this other layer that I call 'the Council' in my book," Taylor explained. "I know that this is a group of men that stand head and shoulders above even Kissinger and the Rockefellers. They have been genetically engineered in a way that they have [she hesitated, searching for the right words] different leadership abilities and that they are actually the ones running the plan."

They refer to themselves as "the Council"?

"Yes. When I was telling other people within the intelligence community about it that were involved in it, they said they call themselves the Council. The CIA has all these mind-control operatives that are working for the Government.

DEAD MEN TALKING

Then there's the Council, which also understands about the mind-control project. But the Council is not CIA controlled. They could take someone like myself and be able to debrief me to find out what my agenda was."

MORE BAD MEMORIES

And how did Ms Taylor first figure out she was suffering from MPD and that she was a programmed multiple?

"It started in 1985," said Taylor. "I had a very serious car accident in which my head went through the windshield. I began to have memory flashes like a memory bleed-through from one alter to another. I think what occurred was I began having access to both sides of my brain. Before, with all the sophisticated programming, half my brain was shut away from me. Now the neuron pathways had opened up because of the accident. I know of other women who have also had memories come back."

So a blow to the brain had broken up the programming?

"Exactly," she said. "What happened is my memories began coming back. I was in school, working on my Master's degree in psychology, when a flood of memories came back. I have a closet full of journals. I wrote down everything I was remembering. Once I got to a certain level, I had a lot of therapeutic support because, every time I'd start remembering, I'd want to hurt myself or kill myself. I lost control of my body in a car on the freeway in the fast lane one time as I was trying to really understand how programming worked. I was trying to understand from inside; a part of me was trying to explain programming to me, and I was on the freeway in the fast lane and I could not move my body. It was terrifying. These are the kinds of things I had to constantly fight.

"When I deprogrammed I literally spent two years in my bedroom, drinking coffee, just writing everything down," she said. "They programmed me with perfect photographic memory. When memories came back, like the ones with Kissinger, I not only could hear his words and his voice, I could smell his cigar. I could smell his farts. I mean, I could hear and see as I remembered everything in my mind."

THE SATANIC RITUAL MURDER CONNECTION

Missing children, sexual abuse of children and pedophilia around the world all point to the involvement of an organised network of high-level criminals who covertly control the legal system. Former FBI agent and private investigator Ted Gunderson agrees. He claims that "there's a considerable overlap from various groups and organisations, but one of the driving forces is the satanic cult movement today".

DEAD MEN TALKING

In his video, Satanism and the CIA's International Trafficking of Children, Gunderson refers to the notorious black magician Aleister Crowley. "The Satanists have used his writings as a guide," he says, referring to Crowley's Magick in Theory and Practice.

In Chapter XII, "Of the Bloody Sacrifice" (p. 94), Crowley writes: "It would be unwise to condemn as irrational the practice of those savages who tear the heart and liver from an adversary and devour them while yet warm. In any case it was the theory of the ancient Magicians that any living being is a storehouse of energy, varying in quantity according to the size and health of the animal, and in quality according to its mental and moral character. At the death of the animal this energy is liberated suddenly.

"The animal should therefore be killed within the Circle [the satanic circle] or the Triangle, as the case may be, so that its energy cannot escape. An animal should be selected whose nature accords with that of the ceremony - thus by sacrificing a female lamb one would not obtain any appreciate quantity of the fierce energy useful to the Magician who was invoking Mars. In such a case a ram would be more suitable. And this ram should be virgin - the whole potential of its original total energy should not have been diminished in any way. For the highest spiritual working one must accordingly choose that victim which contains that greatest and purest force. A male child of perfect innocence and high intelligence is the most satisfactory and suitable victim."

"We're talking about human sacrifice here," says Gunderson.

More recently the 'tradition' of human sacrifice has been promoted by the late Anton LaVey, founder of the Church of Satan, who wrote in the Satanic Bible (p. 88) that "the only time a Satanist would perform a human sacrifice would be if he were to serve a twofold purpose; that being to release the magickian's [sic] wrath in throwing a curse and, more importantly, to dispose of a totally obnoxious and deserving person".

Note the casual reference to murdering someone because he or she 'displeased' the Satanist/black magician. Ding dong, LaVey is dead, but his crimes live on. He's been named by several of his victim-slaves as a mind-control perpetrator. The late 'perp' himself wrote in the Satanic Bible (p. 90) that "the ideal sacrifice may be emotionally insecure, but nonetheless can in the machinations of his insecurity cause severe damage to your tranquility or sound reputation".

The Satanists, after all, follow Crowley's injunction: "Do what thou wilt. That is the the law." In other words, Satanists as gods themselves will decide what to do - bypassing God's laws as well as the laws of men. It sounds like the modus operandi of the Illuminati.

DEAD MEN TALKING

Gunderson makes this further comment in his video: "In my estimation, there are over three million practising Satanists in America today. How did I come up with these figures? I have informants. For instance, in the South Bay area of Los Angeles with a population of 200,000, he told me there are 3,000 practising Satanists. That is where the well-known McMartin Preschool case took place. I have an informant in Lincoln, Nebraska. In Iowa City, Iowa, a town of 150,000 - 1,500 Satanists. It averages to about 1.5 per cent of the population."

Gunderson asserts that "...50,000 to 60,000 individuals are sacrificed every year. There are about eight satanic holidays."

The sick joke of it all? The FBI keeps a count of stolen or missing cars, but has yet to keep a tab on missing children in America.

CRYPTO-SATANIST IN THE FBI?

You shouldn't be surprised to know that FBI Supervisory Special Agent Kenneth V. Lanning, of the Behavioral Science Unit of the National Center for the Analysis of Violent Crime, denies the existence of satanic ritual abuse in his 1992 Investigator's Guide to Allegations of Ritual Child Abuse. Lanning's intellectual posturing and specious reasoning should be studied as a prime example of serpentine logic. His semantics are brilliant, as he claims that "the words 'satanic', 'occult' and 'ritual' are often used interchangeably" and "it is difficult to define Satanism precisely". Then he frames the discussion of Satanism in non-judgemental terms, that "it is important to realize that for some people any religious belief system other than their own is satanic".

As Pilate asked "What is truth?", Lanning asks "What is Satanism?" He writes that at "...law enforcement training conferences, it is witchcraft, santeria, paganism and the occult that are most often referred to as forms of Satanism. It may be a matter of definition, but these things are not necessarily the same as traditional Satanism." He almost trips over himself declaiming the impossibility of knowing the definition. Then he dismisses satanic ritual abuse as a simple psychological problem: "Obsessive Compulsive Disorder".

Of course, if he had taken the time to interview true believers, he would know that it's an actual belief system based on the ritual performance of torture and murder in loyalty to Satan and as an exchange for future rewards from the forces of darkness.

Lanning's denial, ignoring the evidence of mind-control atrocities and ritual abuse, is astonishing. Is Lanning a crypto-Satanist? He's publicly denied it, but he didn't have to bother. His "freedom of religion" is protected by the US Constitution.

DEAD MEN TALKING

FATAL JUSTICE REVISITED

Private investigator Ted L. Gunderson was dragged kicking and screaming into the netherworld of Satanism, child kidnapping, drug smuggling and other corruption.

Before he retired in 1979, Gunderson was the FBI Special Agent in Charge (SAC) in Los Angeles. He headed the FBI office, where he had 800 people under him and a yearly budget of over US$24 million. Since then, Gunderson's role as a private investigator and security consultant has led him to expose CIA drug dealing, child kidnapping and trafficking, mind control, and satanic murder-for-hire groups. He has also investigated many high-profile cases like the Dr Jeffrey McDonald case, the McMartin Preschool case, Nebraska's Franklin Cover-up case, the Oklahoma City Bombing case, the Inslaw/Octopus case, and many other real-life criminal conspiracies.

"Shortly after my retirement, I was asked to investigate the Jeffrey R. McDonald case as a private investigator," said Gunderson in a recent interview. "He's a doctor who was convicted of murdering his wife and two children at Fort Bragg, North Carolina on February 17, 1970. I put in about 2,000 hours on the case. He had been convicted and sentenced to three consecutive life sentences. Much to my surprise, the evidence that I read, the information I developed...I've established beyond any question of a doubt that this man is absolutely innocent."

Jerry Allen Potter, author of Fatal Justice, a powerful point-by-point refutation of Joe McGinnis's cover-up book, Fatal Vision, agrees. His book exposes McGinnis's best-seller as pure fiction.

Gunderson continued: "I obtained a signed confession from Helena Stokely, the girl in the floppy hat, for those who are familiar with the case. She said Dr McDonald did not commit these crimes. They were committed, she said '...by my satanic cult group. It was my initiation into the cult that night,' she said."

After a while, Gunderson realised that the McDonald case was a classic case of US Government crime and cover-up.

"She gave me detailed information about movements within the house. She told me she attempted to ride a rocking horse in the child's bedroom that night, but she couldn't ride it because the spring was broken. The only way she could have known that was to have been there that night.

"I submitted an 1100-plus page report in March 1981 to Judge William Webster, who was then the head of the FBI, with a personal letter to him and to the US Department of Justice. Much to my surprise, my 19 witnesses including Helena Stokely started calling me and telling me, 'Hey Ted, they're trying to get me to recant.' And I'm telling myself, 'That isn't the responsibility of the FBI. The FBI is supposed to gather information, not destroy it.' And that was my first clue that we had a serious problem in that case and in the other cases I handled. I noticed in each instance that evidence was destroyed, lost, stolen; that there were strong indications of corruption.

"So I asked myself, 'What's going on here?' And over the years I started gathering materials. Up until about two years ago, I kept saying, 'There's a loose-knit network operating in this country, involving drugs, pedophilia, prostitution, corruption, etc. From my research, I'm convinced it's much more serious. It's much more than a loose-knit network. It is a conspiracy. And you know how the media goes after you when you use that 'c'-word. And I'm going to prove it to you. By the way, this conspiracy involves pornography, drugs, pedophilia and organised child kidnapping.

"My 'missing children' lecture documents that the Finders, an organisation in Washington, DC, is a CIA front," said Gunderson. "It's a covert operation involved in international trafficking of children."

He was referring to a US Customs Service report which states that the Finders case is to be closed because it is "an internal CIA matter".

Gunderson added: "These people - the satanic movement in the world - have set up preschools for the purpose of getting their hands on our children. The parents drop them off at nine in the morning and pick them up at night."

Far-fetched? Think again. In The Law Is For All, Aleister Crowley writes: "Moreover, the Beast 666 [Crowley's reference to himself] adviseth that all children shall be accustomed from infancy to witness every type of sexual act, as also the process of birth, lest falsehood fog and mystery stupefy their minds whose error else might thwart and misdirect the growth of their subconscious system of self-symbolism."

SPIRITUAL WARFARE AND SATANIC IMPERIALISM

Sexual abuse of children and horrific mind control technology may be tenets of 'faith' for the Satanist believer as well as the programmer. Or they may be symptomatic of a larger struggle on a cosmic scale. When you peer in the face of Absolute Evil, you cannot remain complacent.

Therapist Dr M. Scott Peck, author of The People of the Lie, writes: "...at one point I defined evil as 'the exercise of political power that is the imposition of one's will upon others by overt or covert coercion in order to avoid...spiritual growth'".

Psychologist Erich Fromm, author of The Heart of Man, defines this struggle

DEAD MEN TALKING

between Good and Evil as biophilia (the love of life) vs necrophilia (the love of death). "The necrophilous person is driven by the desire to transform the organic into the inorganic, to approach life mechanically as if all living persons were things," he writes. "The necrophilous person can relate to an object - a flower or a person - only if he possesses it; hence a threat to his possession is a threat to himself... He loves control and in the act of controlling he kills life... 'Law and order' for them are idols..."

In the end, it may be that spiritual warfare - or the clash of the absolutes - is the real reason why ritual abuse and high-tech mind control have been exposed. Satanic imperialism continues unabated, and the battle for planet Earth moves to the next stage.

References:

* Coleman, John, "Illuminati in America", World in Review (2533 N. Carson St, Carson City, NV 89706), USA, monograph, 1992

* Constantine, Alex, Virtual Government: CIA Mind Control Operations in America, Feral House (2532 Lincoln Blvd #359, Venice, CA 90291), USA, 1997 (USD$14.95)

* DeCamp, John, The Franklin Cover-up: Child Abuse, Satanism and Murder in Nebraska, AWT, Inc. (PO Box 85461, Lincoln, NE 68501), USA, 1996, 2ed (USD$13.00)

* Gunderson, Ted, "McMartin Scientific Report" (1993); Corruption: The Satanic Drug Cult Network and Missing Children, vols. 1&endash;4; Satanism & the CIA's International Trafficking in Children (video, USD$20.00), Ted Gunderson, PO Box 18000-259, Las Vegas, NV 89109, USA

* Marks, John, The Search for the Manchurian Candidate: The CIA and Mind Control, McGraw-Hill, 1980

* Mind Control Foundation website, www.mk.net/~mcf

* Mind Control series, CKLN-FM, website, www.mk.net/~mcf/ckln

* O'Brien, Cathy (with Mark Phillips), TranceFormation of America: The True Life Story of a CIA Slave, Reality Marketing (PO Box 27740, Las Vegas, NV 89126) USA, 1995 (USD$20.00)

* Potter, Jerry Allen and Fred Bost, Fatal Justice: Reinvestigating the McDonald Murders, W. W. Norton Co., New York, London, 1997

* Springmeier, Fritz, Bloodlines of the Illuminati, Ambassador House (PO Box 1153, Westminster, CO 80030), USA, 1999 2ed (USD$20.00)

* Springmeier, Fritz and Cisco Wheeler, Illuminati Formula used to create an Undetectable Total Mind Controlled Slave, Fritz and Cisco (916 Linn Ave, Oregon City, OR 97045), USA, 1996 (USD$59.00)

* Stratford, Lauren, Satan's Underground, Pelican Publishing (PO Box 3110, Gretna, LA 70054), USA, 1998 (USD$10.95)

* Sullivan, K., MK, K. Sullivan (PO Box 1328, Soddy Daisy, TN 37384), USA, 1998 (USD$18.00)

* Taylor, Brice, Starshine: One Woman's Valiant Escape from Mind Control, 1995 (USD$20.00); Revivification: A Gentle, Alternative Memory Retrieval Process for Trauma Victims (1998, USD$7.50), Brice Taylor Trust, PO Box 655, Landrum, SC 29356, USA

About the Author:

Uri Dowbenko is CEO of New Improved Entertainment Corp. He can be reached by e-mail at: u.dowbenko@mailcity.com

DEAD MEN TALKING

The Current Situation

Mind Control: The Current Situation

By Harry V. Martin and David Caul

Copyright © FreeAmerica and Harry V. Martin, 1995 Copyright © Napa Sentinel, 1991

In July of 1991, two inmates died at the Vacaville Medical Facility. According to prison officials at the time, the two may have died as a result of medical treatment, that treatment was the use of mind control or behavior modification drugs. A deeper study into the deaths of the two inmates has unraveled a mind-boggling tale of horror that has been part of California penal history for a long time, and one that caused national outcries years ago.

In August of 1991, the Sentinel presented a graphic portrait of some of the mind control experiments that have been allowed to continue in the United States. On November 1974 a U.S. Senate Sub-committee on Constitutional Rights investigated federally-funded behavior modification programs, with emphasis on federal involvement in, and the possible threat to individual constitutional rights of behavior modification, especially involving inmates in prisons and mental institutions.

The Senate committee was appalled after reviewing documents from the following sources:

The Neuro-Research Foundation's study entitled "The Medical Epidemiology of Criminals."

The Center for the Study and Reduction of Violence at UCLA.

The Closed Adolescent Treatment Center.

Senate Investigations of the History of US Mind Control (Based on Testimony before the Senate Sub-Commmittee on Constitutional Rights)

A national uproar was created by various articles in 1974, which prompted

184

the Senate investigation. But after all these years, the news that two inmates at Vacaville may have died from these same experiments indicates that though a nation was shocked in 1974, little was done to end the experimentations. In 1977, a Senate subcommittee on Health and Scientific Research, chaired by Senator Ted Kennedy, focussed on the CIA's testing of LSD on unwitting citizens. Only a mere handful of people within the CIA knew about the scope and details of the program.

To understand the full scope of the problem, it is important to study its origins. The Kennedy subcommittee learned about the CIA Operation MK.-Ultra through the testimony of Dr. Sidney Gottlieb. The purpose of the program, according to his testimony, was to "investigate whether and how it was possible to modify an individual's behavior by covert means".

Claiming the protection of the National Security Act, Dr. Gottlieb was unwilling to tell the Senate subcommittee what had been learned or gained by these experiments.

He did state, however, that the program was initially engendered by a concern that the Soviets and other enemies of the United States would get ahead of the U.S. in this field.

MK-ULTRA Past and Present

(From testimony and files obtained under Freedom Of Information Act)

Through the Freedom of Information Act, researchers are now able to obtain documents detailing the M.K.-Ultra program and other CIA behavior modification projects in a special reading room located on the bottom floor of the Hyatt Regency in Rosslyn, VA.

The most daring phase of the M.K.-Ultra program involved slipping unwitting American citizens LSD in real life situations. The idea for the series of experiments originated in November 1941, when William Donovan, founder and director of the Office of Strategic Services (OSS), the forerunner of the CIA during World War Two. At that time the intelligence agency invested $5000 for the "truth drug" program. Experiments with scopolamine and morphine proved both unfruitful and very dangerous. The program tested scores of other drugs, including mescaline, barbituates, benzedrine, cannabis indica, to name a few.

The U.S. was highly concerned over the heavy losses of freighters and other ships in the North Atlantic, all victims of German U-boats. Information about German U-boat strategy was desperately needed and it was believed that the information could be obtained through drug-influenced interrogations of German naval P.O.W.s, in violation of the Geneva Accords.

DEAD MEN TALKING

Tetrahydrocannabinol acetate, a colorless, odorless marijuana extract, was used to lace a cigarette or food substance without detection. Initially, the experiments were done on volunteer U.S. Army and OSS personnel, and testing was also disguised as a remedy for shell shock. The volunteers became known as "Donovan's Dreamers". The experiments were so hush-hush, that only a few top officials knew about them. President Franklin Roosevelt was aware of the experiments. The "truth drug" achieved mixed success.

The experiments were halted when a memo was written: "The drug defies all but the most expert and search analysis, and for all practical purposes can be considered beyond analysis." The OSS did not, however, halt the program. In 1943 field tests of the extract were being conducted, despite the order to halt them. The most celebrated test was conducted by Captain George Hunter White, an OSS agent and ex-law enforcement official, on August Del Grazio, aka Augie Dallas, aka Dell, aka Little Augie, a New York gangster.

Cigarettes laced with the acetate were offered to Augie without his knowledge of the content. Augie, who had served time in prison for assault and murder, had been one of the world's most notorious drug dealers and smugglers. He operated an opium alkaloid factory in Turkey and he was a leader in the Italian underworld on the Lower East Side of New York. Under the influence of the drug,

Augie revealed volumes of information about the underworld operations, including the names of high ranking officials who took bribes from the mob. These experiments led to the encouragement of Donovan. A new memo was issued: "Cigarette experiments indicated that we had a mechanism which offered promise in relaxing prisoners to be interrogated."

When the OSS was disbanded after the war, Captain White continued to administer behavior modifying drugs. In 1947, the CIA replaced the OSS. White's service record indicates that he worked with the OSS, and by 1954 he was a high ranking Federal Narcotics Bureau officer who had been loaned to the CIA on a part-time basis.

White rented an apartment in Greenwich Village equipped with one-way mirrors, surveillance gadgets and disguised himself as a seaman. White drugged his acquaintances with LSD and brought them back to his apartment. In 1955, the operation shifted to San Francisco. In San Francisco, "safe houses" were established under the code name Operation Midnight Climax. Midnight Climax hired prostitute addicts who lured men from bars back to the safehouses after their drinks had been spiked with LSD. White filmed the events in the safehouses. The purpose of these "national security brothels" was to enable the CIA to experiment with the act of lovemaking for extracting information from men.

186

DEAD MEN TALKING

The safehouse experiments continued until 1963 until CIA Inspector General John Earman criticized Richard Helms, the director of the CIA and father of the M.K.-Ultra project. Earman charged the new director John McCone had not been fully briefed on the M.K.-Ultra Project when he took office and that "the concepts involved in manipulating human behavior are found by many people within and outside the Agency to be distasteful and unethical." He stated that "the rights and interest of U.S. citizens are placed in jeopardy". The Inspector General stated that LSD had been tested on individuals at all social levels, high and low, native American and foreign."

Earman's criticisms were rebuffed by Helms, who warned, "Positive operation capacity to use drugs is diminishing owing to a lack of realistic testing. Tests were necessary to keep up with the Soviets." But in 1964, Helms had testified before the Warren Commission investigating the assassination of President John Kennedy, that "Soviet research has consistently lagged five years behind Western research".

Upon leaving government service in 1966, Captain White wrote a startling letter to his superior. In the letter to Dr. Gottlieb, Captain White reminisced about his work in the safehouses with LSD. His comments were frightening. "I was a very minor missionary, actually a heretic, but I toiled wholeheartedly in the vineyards because it was fun, fun, fun," White wrote. "Where else could a red-blooded American boy lie, kill, cheat, steal, rape and pillage with the sanction and blessing of the all-highest?"

The CIA and the Mafia

(Testimony before the 1951 Sub-Committee on Organized Crime and other public sources.)

Though the CIA continued to maintain drug experiments in the streets of America after the program was officially canceled, the United States reaped tremendous value from it. With George Hunter White's connection to underworld figure Little Augie, connections were made with Mafia king-pin Lucky Luciano, who was in Dannemore Prison.

Luciano wanted freedom, the Mafia wanted drugs, and the United States wanted Sicily. The date was 1943. Augie was the go-between between Luciano and the United States War Department.

Luciano was transferred to a less harsh prison and began to be visited by representatives of the Office of Naval Intelligence and from underworld figures, such as Meyer Lansky. A strange alliance was formed between the U.S. Intelligence agencies and the Mafia, who controlled the West Side docks in New York. Luciano regained active leadership in organized crime in America.

DEAD MEN TALKING

The U. S. Intelligence community utilized Luciano's underworld connections in Italy. In July of 1943, Allied forces launched their invasion of Sicily, the beginning push into occupied Europe. General George Patton's Seventh Army advanced through hundreds of miles of territory that was fraught with difficulty, booby trapped roads, snipers, confusing mountain topography, all within close range of 60,000 hostile Italian troops. All this was accomplished in four days, a military "miracle" even for Patton.

Senate Estes Kefauver's Senate Sub committee on Organized Crime asked, in 1951, how all this was possible. The answer was that the Mafia had helped to protect roads from Italian snipers, served as guides through treacherous mountain terrain, and provided needed intelligence to Patton's army. The part of Sicily which Patton's forces traversed had at one time been completely controlled by the Sicilian Mafia, until Benito Mussolini smashed it through the use of police repression.

Just prior to the invasion, it was hardly even able to continue shaking down farmers and shepherds for protection money. But the invasion changed all this, and the Mafia went on to play a very prominent and well-documented role in the American military occupation of Italy.

The expedience of war opened the doors to American drug traffic and Mafia domination. This was the beginning of the Mafia-U.S. Intelligence alliance, an alliance that lasts to this day and helped to support the covert operations of the CIA, such as the Iran-Contra operations.

In these covert operations, the CIA would obtain drugs from South America and Southeast Asia, sell them to the Mafia and use the money for the covert purchase of military equipment. These operations accelerated when Congress cut off military funding for the Contras.

One of the Allies' top occupation priorities was to liberate as many of their own soldiers from garrison duties so that they could participate in the military offensive. In order to accomplish this, Don Calogero's Mafia were pressed into service, and in July of 1943, the Civil Affairs Control Office of the U.S. Army appointed him mayor of Villalba and other Mafia officials as mayors of other towns in Sicily.

As the northern Italian offensive continued, Allied intelligence became very concerned over the extent to which the Italian Communists' resistance to Mussolini had driven Italian politics to the left. Community Party membership had doubled between 1943 and 1944, huge leftist strikes had shut down factories and the Italian underground fighting Mussolini had risen to almost 150,000 men. By mid-1944, the situation came to a head and the U.S. Army terminated arms drops to the Italian Resistance, and started appointing Mafia officials to occupation administration posts. Mafia groups broke up leftists rallies and reactivated black market operations throughout southern Italy.

Lucky Luciano was released from prison in 1946 and deported to Italy, where he rebuilt the heroin trade. The court's decision to release him was made possible by the testimony of intelligence agents at his hearing, and a letter written by a naval officer reciting what Luciano had done for the Navy. Luciano was supposed to have served from 30 to 50 years in prison. Over 100 Mafia members were similarly deported within a couple of years.

Luciano set up a syndicate which transported morphine base from the Middle East to Europe, refined it into heroin, and then shipped it into the United States via Cuba. During the 1950's, Marseilles, in Southern France, became a major city for the heroin labs and the Corsican syndicate began to actively cooperate with the Mafia in the heroin trade. Those became popularly known as the French Connection.

In 1948, Captain White visited Luciano and his narcotics associate Nick Gentile in Europe. Gentile was a former American gangster who had worked for the Allied Military Government in Sicily. By this time, the CIA was already subsidizing Corsican and Italian gangsters to oust Communist unions from the Port of Marseilles.

American strategic planners saw Italy and southern France as extremely important for their Naval bases as a counterbalance to the growing naval forces of the Soviet Union. CIO/AFL organizer Irving Brown testified that by the time the CIA subsidies were terminated in 1953, U.S. support was no longer needed because the profits from the heroin traffic was sufficient to sustain operations.

When Luciano was originally jailed, the U.S. felt it had eliminated the world's most effective underworld leader and the activities of the Mafia were seriously damaged. Mussolini had been waging a war since 1924 to rid the world of the Sicilian Mafia. Thousands of Mafia members were convicted of crimes and forced to leave the cities and hide out in the mountains.

Mussolini's reign of terror had virtually eradicated the international drug syndicates. Combined with the shipping surveillance during the war years, heroin trafficking had become almost nil. Drug use in the United States, before Luciano's release from prison, was on the verge of being entirely wiped out.

Mind Control Experiments Conducted in Our Name

The U.S. government has conducted three types of mind-control experiments: Real life experiences, such as those used on Little Augie and the LSD experiments in the safehouses of San Francisco and Greenwich Village; experiments on prisoners, such as in the California Medical Facility at Vacaville; experiments conducted in both mental hospitals and the Veterans Administration hospitals.

Such experimentation requires money, and the United States government has funneled funds for drug experiments through different agencies, both overtly and covertly.

The Role of the Law Enforcement Assistance Administration

(Reportorial Sources, Including the Washington Post) One of the funding agencies to contribute to the experimentation is the Law Enforcement Assistance Administration (LEAA), a unit of the U.S. Justice Department and one of President Richard Nixon's favorite pet agencies. The Nixon Administration was, at one time, putting together a program for detaining youngsters who showed a tendency toward violence in "concentration" camps.

According to the Washington Post, the plan was authored by Dr. Arnold Hutschnecker. Health, Education and Welfare Secretary Robert Finch was told by John Erlichman, Chief of Staff for the Nixon White House, to implement the program. He proposed the screening of children of six years of age for tendencies toward criminality. Those who failed these tests were to be destined to be sent to the camps. The program was never implemented.

LEAA came into existence in 1968 with a huge budget to assist various U.S. law enforcement agencies. Its effectiveness, however, was not considered too great. After spending $6 billion, the F.B.I. reports general crime rose 31 percent and violent crime rose 50 percent. But little accountability was required of LEAA on how it spent its funds.

LEAA's role in the behavior modification research began at a meeting held in 1970 in Colorado Springs. Attending that meeting were Richard Nixon, Attorney General John Mitchell, John Erlichman, H.R. Haldemann and other White House staffers. They met with Dr. Bertram Brown, director fo the National Institute of Mental Health, and forged a close collaboration between LEAA and the Institute. LEAA was a product of the Justice Department and the Institute was a product of HEW.

LEAA funded 350 projects involving medical procedures, behavior modification and drugs for delinquency control. Money from the Criminal Justice System was being used to fund mental health projects and vice versa. Eventually, the leadership responsibility and control of the Institute began to deteriorate and their scientists began to answer to LEAA alone.

DEAD MEN TALKING

The Role of the National Institute of Mental Health

(Source: Court Records and US Senate Subcommittee on Constitutional Rights)

The National Institute of Mental Health went on to become one of the greatest supporters of behavior modification research. Throughout the 1960's, court calenders became blighted with lawsuits on the part of "human guinea pigs" who had been experimented upon in prisons and mental institutions. It was these lawsuits which triggered the Senate Subcommittee on Constitutional Rights investigation, headed by Senator Sam Erwin. The subcommittee's harrowing report was virtually ignored by the news media.

The Department of Defense

(Source: CIA Documents released under FOIA and Subcommittee Testimony)

Thirteen behavior modification programs were conducted by the Department of Defense. The Department of Labor had also conducted several experiments, as well as the National Science Foundation. The Veterans' Administration was also deeply involved in behavior modification and mind control. Each of these agencies, including LEAA, and the Institute, were named in secret CIA documents as those who provided research cover for the MK-ULTRA program.

Eventually, LEAA was using much of its budget to fund experiments, including aversive techniques and psychosurgery, which involved, in some cases, irreversible brain surgery on normal brain tissue for the purpose of changing or controlling behavior and/or emotions.

Senator Erwin questioned the head of LEAA concerning ethical standards of the behavior modification projects which LEAA had been funding.

Erwin was extremely dubious about the idea of the government spending money on this kind of project without strict guidelines and reasonable research supervision in order to protect the human subjects. After Senator Erwin's denunciation of the funding polices, LEAA announced that it would no longer fund medical research into behavior modification and psychosurgery.

Lobotomies Performed on Black Activists

(Committee Testimony)

Despite the pledge by LEAA's director, Donald E. Santarelli, LEAA ended up funding 537 research projects dealing with behavior modification. There is strong evidence to indicate psychosurgery was still being used in prisons in the 1980's. Immediately after the funding announcement by LEAA, there were 50 psychosurgical operations at Atmore State Prison in Alabama. The inmates became virtual zombies. The operations, according to Dr. Swan of Fisk University, were done on black prisoners who were considered politically active.

Veteran's Administration Practices

(Committee Testimony)

The Veterans' Administration openly admitted that psychosurgery was a standard procedure for treatment and not used just in experiments. The VA Hospitals in Durham, Long Beach, New York, Syracuse and Minneapolis were known to employ these products on a regular basis. VA clients could typically be subject to these behavior alteration procedures against their will. The Erwin subcommittee concluded that the rights of VA clients had been violated.

LEAA also subsidized the research and development of gadgets and techniques useful to behavior modification. Much of the technology, whose perfection LEAA funded, had originally been developed and made operational for use in the Vietnam War.

Private Companies Involved

Companies like Bangor Punta Corporation and Walter Kidde and Co., through its subsidiary Globe Security System, adapted these devices to domestic use in the U.S. ITT was another company that domesticated the warfare technology for potential use on U.S. citizens. Rand Corporation executive Paul Baran warned that the influx back to the United State of the Vietnam War surveillance gadgets alone, not to mention the behavior modification hardware, could bring about "the most effective, oppressive police state ever created".

Some of the Players

One of the fascinating aspects of the scandals that plague the U.S. Government is the fact that so often the same names appear from scandal to scandal. From the origins of Ronald Reagan's political career, as Governor of California, Dr. Earl Brian and Edward Meese played key advisory roles. Dr. Brian's name has been linked to the October Surprise and is a central figure in the government's theft of PROMIS soft ware from INSLAW. Brian's role touches from the Cabazon Indian scandals to United Press International. He is one of those low-profile key figures.

And, alas, his name appears again in the nation's behavior modification and mind control experiments. Dr. Brian was Reagan's Secretary of Health when Reagan was Governor. Dr. Brian was an advocate of state subsidies for a research center for the study of violent behavior. The center was to begin operations by mid-1975, and its research was intended to shed light on why people murder or rape, or hijack aircraft. The center was to be operated by the University of California at Los Angeles, and its primary purpose, ac cording to Dr. Brian, was to unify scattered studies on anti-social violence and possibly even touch on socially tolerated violence, such as football or war. Dr. Brian sought $1.3 million for the center.

It certainly was possible that prison inmates might be used as volunteer subjects at the center to discover the unknowns which triggered their violent behavior. Dr. Brian's quest for the center came at the same time Governor Reagan concluded his plans to phase the state of California out of the mental hospital business by 1982. Reagan's plan is echoed by Governor Pete Wilson today, to place the responsibility of rehabilitating young offenders squarely on the shoulders of local communities. But as the proposal became known more publicly, a swell of controversy surrounded it. It ended in a fiasco. The inspiration for the violence center came from three doctors in 1967, five years before Dr. Brian and Governor Reagan unveiled their plans.

The "Scientific" Basis for Psychosurgery

(Publications of the Participants)

Amidst urban rioting and civil protest, Doctors Sweet, Mark and Ervin of Harvard put forward the thesis that individuals who engage in civil disobedience possess defective or damaged brain cells. If this conclusion were applied to the American Revolution or the Women's Rights Movement, a good portion of American society would be labeled as having brain damage.

In a letter to the Journal of the American Medical Association, they stated: "That poverty, unemployment, slum housing, and inadequate education underlie the nation's urban riots is well known, but the obviousness of these causes may have blinded us to the more subtle role of other possible factors, including brain dysfunction in the rioters who engaged in arson, sniping and physical assault.

"There is evidence from several sources that brain dysfunction related to a focal lesion plays a significant role in the violent and assaultive behavior of thoroughly studied patients. Individuals with electroencephalographic abnormalities in the temporal region have been found to have a much greater frequency of behavioral abnormalities (such as poor impulse control, assaultiveness, and psychosis) than is present in people with a normal brain wave pattern."

Soon after the publication in the Journal, Dr. Ervin and Dr. Mark published their book Violence and the Brain, which included the claim that there were as many as 10 million individuals in the United States "who suffer from obvious brain disease". They argued that the data of their book provided a strong reason for starting a program of mass screening of Americans.

DEAD MEN TALKING

"Our greatest danger no longer comes from famine or communicable disease. Our greatest danger lies in ourselves and in our fellow humans...we need to develop an 'early warning test' of limbic brain function to detect those humans who have a low threshold for impulsive violence...Violence is a public health problem, and the major thrust of any program dealing with violence must be toward its prevention," they wrote.

The Law Enforcement Assistance Administration funded the doctors $108,000 and the National Institute of Mental Health kicked in another $500,000, under pressure from Congress. They believed that psychosurgery would inevitably be performed in connection with the program, and that, since it irreversibly impaired people's emotional and intellectual capacities, it could be used as an instrument of repression and social control.

The doctors wanted screening centers established throughout the nation. In California, the publicity associated with the doctors' report, aided in the development of The Center for the study and Reduction of Violence. Both the state and LEAA provided the funding. The center was to serve as a model for future facilities to be set up throughout the United States.

The Director of the Neurophyschiatric Institute and chairman of the Department of Psychiatry at UCLA, Dr. Louis Jolyon West was selected to run the center. Dr. West is alleged to have been a contract agent for the CIA, who, as part of a network of doctors and scientists, gathered intelligence on hallucinogenic drugs, including LSD, for the super-secret MK-ULTRA program. Like Captain White, West conducted LSD experiments for the CIA on unwitting citizens in the safehouses of San Francisco. He achieved notoriety for his injection of a massive dose of LSD into an elephant at the Oklahoma Zoo, the elephant died when West tried to revive it by administering a combination of drugs.

Dr. West was further known as the psychiatrist who was called upon to examine Jack Ruby, Lee Harvey Oswald's assassin. It was on the basis of West's diagnosis that Ruby was compelled to be treated for mental disorders and put on happy pills. The West examination was ordered after Ruby began to say that he was part of a right-wing conspiracy to kill President John Kennedy. Two years after the commencement of treatment for mental disorder, Ruby died of cancer in prison.

(Note: Dr West is now a member of the Board of Directors of the False Memory Syndrome Foundation.)

DEAD MEN TALKING

The Violence Control Center

(Testimony, FOIA documents, Los Angeles Times, San Francisco Bay Guardian)

After January 11, 1973, when Governor Reagan announced plans for the Violence Center, West wrote a letter to the then Director of Health for California, J. M. Stubblebine:

"Dear Stub:

"I am in possession of confidential in formation that the Army is prepared to turn over Nike missile bases to state and local agencies for non-military purposes. They may look with special favor on health-related applications.

"Such a Nike missile base is located in the Santa Monica Mountains, within a half-hour's drive of the Neuropsychiatric Institute. It is accessible, but relatively remote. The site is securely fenced, and includes various buildings and improvements, making it suitable for prompt occupancy.

"If this site were made available to the Neurophyschiatric Institute as a research facility, perhaps initially as an adjunct to the new Center for the Prevention of Violence, we could put it to very good use. Comparative studies could be carried out there, in an isolated but convenient location, of experimental or model programs for the alteration of undesirable behavior.

"Such programs might include control of drug or alcohol abuse, modification of chronic anti-social or impulsive aggressiveness, etc. The site could also accommodate conferences or retreats for instruction of selected groups of mental-health related professionals and of others (e.g., law enforcement personnel, parole officers, special educators) for whom both demonstration and participation would be effective modes of instruction.

"My understanding is that a direct request by the Governor, or other appropriate officers of the State, to the Secretary of Defense (or, of course, the President), could be most likely to produce prompt results."

Some of the planned areas of study for the Center included:

Studies of violent individuals.

Experiments on prisoners from Vacaville and Atascadero, and hyperkinetic children.

Experiments with violence-producing and violent inhibiting drugs.

Hormonal aspects of passivity and aggressiveness in boys.

Studies to discover and compare norms of violence among various ethnic groups.

Studies of pre-delinquent children.

It would also encourage law enforcement to keep computer files on pre-delinquent children, which would make possible the treatment of children before they became delinquents.

The purpose of the Violence Center was not just research. The staff was to include sociologists, lawyers, police officers, clergymen and probation officers. With the backing of Governor Reagan and Dr. Brian, West had secured guarantees of prisoner volunteers from several California correctional institutions, including Vacaville. Vacaville and Atascadero were chosen as the primary sources for the human guinea pigs. These institutions had established a reputation, by that time, of committing some of the worst atrocities in West Coast history. Some of the experimentations differed little from what the Nazis did in the death camps.

Dr. Earl Brian, Governor Ronald Reagan's Secretary of Health, was adamant about his support for mind control centers in California. He felt the behavior modification plan of the Violence Control Centers was important in the prevention of crime.

The Violence Control Center was actually the brain child of William Herrmann as part of a pacification plan for California. A counter insurgency expert for Systems Development Corporation and an advisor to Governor Reagan, Herrmann worked with the Stand Research Institute, the RAND Corporation, and the Hoover Center on Violence. Herrman was also a CIA agent who is now serving an eight year prison sentence for his role in a CIA counterfeiting operation. He was also directly linked with the Iran-Contra affair according to government records and Herrmann's own testimony.

In 1970, Herrmann worked with Colston Westbrook as his CIA control officer when Westbrook formed and implemented the Black Cultural Association at the Vacaville Medical Facility, a facility which in July experienced the death of three inmates who were forcibly subjected to behavior modification drugs. The Black Cultural Association was ostensibly an education program designed to instill black pride identity in prisons, the Association was really a cover for an experimental behavior modification pilot project designed to test the feasibility of programming unstable prisoners to become more manageable.

Westbrook worked for the CIA in Vietnam as a psychological warfare expert, and as an advisor to the Korean equivalent of the CIA and for the Lon Nol regime in Cambodia. Between 1966 and 1969, he was an advisor to the Vietnamese Police Special Branch under the cover of working as an employee of Pacific Architects and Engineers.

DEAD MEN TALKING

His "firm" contracted the building of the interrogation/torture centers in every province of South Vietnam as part of the CIA's Phoenix Program. The program was centered around behavior modification experiments to learn how to extract information from prisoners of war, a direct violation of the Geneva Accords.

Westbrook's most prominent client at Vacaville was Donald DeFreeze, who be tween 1967 and 1969, had worked for the Los Angeles Police Department's Public Disorder Intelligence unit and later became the leader of the Symbionese Liberation Army. Many authorities now believe that the Black Cultural Association at Vacaville was the seedling of the SLA. Westbrook even designed the SLA logo, the cobra with seven heads, and gave De Freeze his African name of Cinque. The SLA was responsible for the assassination of Marcus Foster, superintendent of School in Oakland and the kidnapping of Patty Hearst.

As a counterinsurgency consultant for Systems Development Corporation, a security firm, Herrmann told the Los Angeles Times that a good computer intelligence system "would separate out the activist bent on destroying the system" and then develop a master plan "to win the hearts and minds of the people". The San Francisco-based Bay Guardian, recently identified Herrmann as an international arms dealer working with Iran in 1980, and possibly involved in the October Surprise. Herrmann is in an English prison for counterfeiting. He allegedly met with Iranian officials to ascertain whether the Iranians would trade arms for hostages held in Lebanon.

The London Sunday Telegraph confirmed Herrmann's CIA connections, tracing them from 1976 to 1986. He also worked for the FBI. This information was revealed in his London trial.

In the 1970's, Dr. Brian and Herrmann worked together under Governor Reagan on the Center for the Study and Reduction of Violence, and then, a decade later, again worked under Reagan. Both men have been identified as working for Reagan with the Iranians.

The Violence Center, however, died an agonizing death. Despite the Ervin Senate Committee investigation and condemnation of mind control, the experiments continued. But when the Watergate scandal broke in the early 1970's, Washington felt it was too politically risky to continue to push for mind control centers.

Top doctors began to withdraw from the proposal because they felt that there were not enough safeguards. Even the Law Enforcement Assistance Agency, which funded the program, backed out, stating, the proposal showed "little evidence of established research ability of the kind of level necessary for a study of this cope".

DEAD MEN TALKING

Eventually it became known that control of the Violence Center was not going to rest with the University of California, but instead with the Department of Corrections and other law enforcement officials. This information was released publicly by the Committee Opposed to Psychiatric Abuse of Prisoners. The disclosure of the letter resulted in the main backers of the program bowing out and the eventual demise of the center.

Dr. Brian's final public statement on the matter was that the decision to cut off funding represented "a callous disregard for public safety". Though the Center was not built, the mind control experiments continue to this day.

The Victims of MK-ULTRA

(Court Records, Senate Testimony and FOIA Documents)

The Central Intelligence Agency held two major interests in use of LSD. to alter normal behavior patterns. The first interest centered around obtaining information from prisoners of war and enemy agents, in contravention of the Geneva Accords. The second was to deter the effectiveness of drugs used against the enemy on the battlefield.

The MK-ULTRA program was originally run by a small number of people within the CIA known as the Technical Services Staff (TSS). Another CIA department, the Office of Security, also began its own testing program. Friction arose and then infighting broke out when the Office of Security commenced to spy on TSS people after it was learned that LSD was being tested on unwitting Americans.

Not only did the two branches disagree over the issue of testing the drug on the unwitting, they also disagreed over the issue of how the drug was actually to be used by the CIA. The office of Security envisioned the drug as an interrogation weapon. But the TSS group thought the drug could be used to help destabilize another country, it could be slipped into the food or beverage of a public official in order to make him behave foolishly or oddly in public. One CIA document reveals that L.S.D. could be administered right before an official was to make a public speech.

Realizing that gaining information about the drug in real life situations was crucial to exploiting the drug to its fullest, TSS started conducting experiments on its own people. There was an extensive amount of self-experimentation. The Office of Security felt the TSS group was playing with fire, especially when it was learned that TSS was prepared to spike an annual office Christmas party punch with LSD, the Christmas party of the CIA. L.S.D. could produce serious insanity for periods of eight to 18 hours and possibly longer.

DEAD MEN TALKING

One of the "victims" of the punch was agent Frank Olson. Having never had drugs before, L.S.D. took its toll on Olson. He reported that, every automobile that came by was a terrible monster with fantastic eyes, out to get him personally. Each time a car passed he would huddle down against a parapet, terribly frightened. Olson began to behave erratically. The CIA made preparation to treat Olson at Chestnut Lodge, but before they could, Olson checked into a New York hotel and threw himself out from his tenth story room. The CIA was ordered to cease all drug testing.

Mind control drugs and experiments were torturous to the victims. One of three inmates who died in Vacaville Prison in July of 1991 was scheduled to appear in court in an attempt to stop forced administration of a drug, the very drug that may have played a role in his death.

Joseph Cannata believed he was making progress and did not need forced dosages of the drug Haldol. The Solano County Coroner's Office said that Cannata and two other inmates died of hyperthermia, extremely elevated body temperature. Their bodies all had at least 108 degrees temperature when they died. The psychotropic drugs they were being forced to take will elevate body temperature.

Dr. Ewen Cameron, working at McGill University in Montreal, used a variety of experimental techniques, including keeping subjects unconscious for months at a time, administering huge electroshocks and continual doses of L.S.D.

Massive lawsuits developed as a result of this testing, and many of the subjects who suffered trauma had never agreed to participate in the experiments. Such CIA experiments infringed upon the much-honored Nuremberg Code concerning medical ethics. Dr. Camron was one of the members of the Nuremberg Tribunal.

L.S.D. research was also conducted at the Addiction Research Center of the U.S. Public Health Service in Lexington, Kentucky. This institution was one of several used by the CIA. The National Institute of Mental Health and the U.S. Navy funded this operation. Vast supplies of L.S.D. and other hallucinogenic drugs were required to keep the experiments going.

Dr. Harris Isbell ran the program. He was a member of the Food and Drug Administration's Advisory Committee on the Abuse of Depressant and Stimulants Drugs. Almost all of the inmates were black. In many cases, L.S.D. dosage was increased daily for 75 days.

Some 1500 U.S. soldiers were also victims of drug experimentation. Some claimed they had agreed to become guinea pigs only through pressure from their superior officers. Many claimed they suffered from severe depression and other psychological stress.

One such soldier was Master Sergeant Jim Stanley. L.S.D. was put in Stanley's drinking water and he freaked out. Stanley's hallucinations continued even after he returned to his regular duties. His service record suffered, his marriage went on the rocks and he ended up beating his wife and children. It wasn't until 17 years later that Stanley was informed by the military that he had been an L.S.D. experiment. He sued the government, but the Supreme Court ruled no soldier could sue the Army for the LSD experiments. Justice William Brennen disagreed with the Court decision. He wrote, "Experimentation with unknowing human subjects is morally and legally unacceptable."

Private James Thornwell was given L.S.D. in a military test in 1961. For the next 23 years he lived in a mental fog, eventually drowning in a Vallejo swimming pool in 1984. Congress had set up a $625,000 trust fund for him. Large scale L.S.D. tests on American soldiers were conducted at Aberdeen Proving Ground in Maryland, Fort Benning, Georgia, Fort Leavenworth, Kansas, Dugway Proving Ground, Utah, and in Europe and the Pacific. The Army conducted a series of L.S.D. tests at Fort Bragg in North Carolina. The purpose of the tests were to ascertain how well soldiers could perform their tasks on the battlefield while under the influence of L.S.D.

At Fort McClellan, Alabama, 200 officers in the Chemical Corps were given L.S.D. in order to familiarize them with the drug's effects. At Edgewood Arsenal, soldiers were given L.S.D. and then confined to sensory deprivation chambers and later exposed to a harsh interrogation sessions by intelligence people. In these sessions, it was discovered that soldiers would cooperate if promised they would be allowed to get off the L.S.D.

In Operation Derby Hat, foreign nationals accused of drug trafficking were given L.S.D. by the Special Purpose Team, with one subject begging to be killed in order to end his ordeal. Such experiments were also conducted in Saigon on Viet Cong POWs.

One of the most potent drugs in the U.S. arsenal is called BZ or quinuclidinyl benzilate. It is a long-lasting drug and brings on a litany of psychotic experiences and almost completely isolates any person from his environment. The main effects of BZ last up to 80 hours compared to eight hours for L.S.D. Negative after-effects may persist for up to six weeks.

DEAD MEN TALKING

Psychological Warfare Drugs

(Court Records, FOIA Documents,

General Accounting Office investigations)

The BZ experiments were conducted on soldiers at Edgewood Arsenal for 16 years. Many of the "victims" claim that the drug permanently affected their lives in a negative way. It so disorientated one paratrooper that he was found taking a shower in his uniform and smoking a cigar. BZ was eventually put in hand grenades and a 750 pound cluster bomb. Other configurations were made for mortars, artillery and missiles. The bomb was tested in Vietnam and CIA documents indicate it was prepared for use by the U.S. in the event of large-scale civilian uprisings.

In Vacaville, psychosurgery has long been a policy. In one set of cases, experimental psychosurgery was conducted on three inmates, a black, a Chicano and a white person. This involved the procedure of pushing electrodes deep into the brain in order to determine the position of defective brain cells, and then shooting enough voltage into the suspected area to kill the defective cells. One prisoner, who appeared to be improving after surgery, was released on parole, but ended up back in prison. The second inmate became violent and there is no information on the third inmate.

Vacaville also administered a "terror drug", Anectine, as a way of "suppressing hazardous behavior". In small doses, Anectine serves as a muscle relaxant; in huge does, it produces prolonged seizure of the respiratory system and a sensation "worse than dying". The drug goes to work within 30 to 40 seconds by paralyzing the small muscles of the fingers, toes, and eyes, and then moves into the the intercostal muscles and the diaphragm. The heart rate subsides to 60 beats per minute, respiratory arrest sets in and the patient remains completely conscious throughout the ordeal, which lasts two to five minutes. The experiments were also used at Atascadero.

Several mind altering drugs were originally developed for non-psychoactive purposes. Some of these drugs are Phenothiazine and Thorzine. The side effects of these drugs can be a living hell. The impact includes the feeling of drowsiness, disorientation, shakiness, dry mouth, blurred vision and an inability to concentrate. Drugs like Prolixin are described by users as "sheer torture" and "becoming a zombie".

The Veterans Administration Hospital has been shown by the General Accounting Office to apply heavy dosages of psychotherapeutic drugs. One patient was taking eight different drugs, three antipsychotic, two antianxiety, one antidepressant, one sedative and one anti-Parkinson. Three of these drugs were being given in dosages equal to the maximum recommended.

Another patient was taking seven different drugs. One report tells of a patient who refused to take the drug. "I told them I don't want the drug to start with, they grabbed me and strapped me down and gave me a forced intramuscular shot of Prolixin. They gave me Artane to counteract the Prolixin and they gave me Sinequan, which is a kind of tranquilizer to make me calm down, which over calmed me, so rather than letting up on the medication, they then gave me Ritalin to pep me up."

Prolixin lasts for two weeks. One patient describes how the drug does not calm or sedate nerves, but instead attacks from so deep inside you, you cannot locate the source of the pain. "The drugs turn your nerves in upon yourself. Against your will, your resistance, your resolve, are directed at your own tissues, your own muscles, reflexes, etc.." The patient continues, "The pain grinds into your fiber, your vision is so blurred you cannot read. You ache with restlessness, so that you feel you have to walk, to pace. And then as soon as you start pacing, the opposite occurs to you, you must sit and rest. Back and forth, up and down, you go in pain you cannot locate. In such wretched anxiety you are overwhelmed because you cannot get relief even in breathing."

Doctor Jose Delgado:

"Man does not have the right to develop his own mind."

(Congressional Record, New York Times)

"We need a program of psychosurgery for political control of our society. The purpose is physical control of the mind. Everyone who deviates from the given norm can be surgically mutilated.

"The individual may think that the most important reality is his own existence, but this is only his personal point of view. This lacks historical perspective.

"Man does not have the right to develop his own mind. This kind of liberal orientation has great appeal. We must electrically control the brain. Some day armies and generals will be controlled by electric stimulation of the brain."

These were the remarks of Dr. Jose Delgado as they appeared in the February 24, 1974 edition of the Congressional Record, No. 262E, Vol. 118.

Despite Dr. Delgado's outlandish statements before Congress, his work was financed by grants from the Office of Naval Research, the Air Force Aero-Medical Research Laboratory, and the Public Health Foundation of Boston.

Dr. Delgado was a pioneer of the technology of Electrical Stimulation of the Brain (ESB). The New York Times ran an article on May 17, 1965 entitled Matador

DEAD MEN TALKING

With a Radio Stops Wild Bull. The story details Dr. Delgado's experiments at Yale University School of Medicine and work in the field at Cordova, Spain. The New York Times stated:

"Afternoon sunlight poured over the high wooden barriers into the ring, as the brave bull bore down on the unarmed matador, a scientist who had never faced fighting bull. But the charging animal's horn never reached the man behind the heavy red cape. Moments before that could happen, Dr. Delgado pressed a button on a small radio transmitter in his hand and the bull braked to a halt. Then he pressed another button on the transmitter, and the bull obediently turned to the right and trotted away. The bull was obeying commands in his brain that were being called forth by electrical stimulation by the radio signals to certain regions in which fine wires had been painlessly planted the day before."

According to Dr. Delgado, experiments of this type have also been performed on humans. While giving a lecture on the Brain in 1965, Dr. Delgado said, "Science has developed a new methodology for the study and control of cerebral function in animals and humans."

Russian Experiments in Hypnotism and Radio Control of the Mind

(Scientific papers and books)

The late L.L. Vasiliev, professor of physiology at the University of Leningrad wrote in a paper about hypnotism: "As a control of the subject's condition, when she was outside the laboratory in another set of experiments, a radio set was used. The results obtained indicate that the method of using radio signals substantially enhances the experimental possibilities." The professor continued to write, "I.F. Tomaschevsky (a Russian physiologist) carried out the first experiments with this subject at a distance of one or two rooms, and under conditions that the participant would not know or suspect that she would be experimented with. In other cases, the sender was not in the same house, and someone else observed the subject's behavior. Subsequent experiments at considerable distances were successful. One such experiment was carried out in a park at a distance. Mental suggestions to go to sleep were complied with within a minute."

The Russian experiments in the control of a person's mind through hypnosis and radio waves were conducted in the 1930s, some 30 years before Dr. Delgado's bull experiment. Dr. Vasiliev definitely demonstrated that radio transmission can produce stimulation of the brain. It is not a complex process. In fact, it need not be implanted within the skull or be productive of stimulation of the brain, itself. All that is needed to accomplish the radio control of the brain is a twitching muscle. The subject becomes hypnotized and a muscle stimulant is implanted. The subject, while still under hypnosis, is commanded to respond when the muscle stimulant is activated, in this case by radio transmission.

Lincoln Lawrence wrote a book entitled Were We Controlled? Lawrance wrote, "If the subject is placed under hypnosis and mentally programmed to maintain a determination eventually to perform one specific act, perhaps to shoot someone, it is suggested thereafter, each time a particular muscle twitches in a certain manner, which is then demonstrated by using the transmitter, he will increase this determination even more strongly. As the hypnotic spell is renewed again and again, he makes it his life's purpose to carry out this act until it is finally achieved. Thus are the two complementary aspects of Radio-Hypnotic Intracerebral Control (RHIC) joined to reinforce each other, and perpetuate the control, until such time as the controlled behavior is called for. This is done by a second session with the hypnotist giving final instructions. These might be reinforced with radio stimulation in more frequent cycles. They could even carry over the moments after the act to reassure calm behavior during the escape period, or to assure that one conspirator would not indicate that he was aware of the co-conspirator's role, or that he was even acquainted with him."

US Experiments in Radio Control of the Mind

(Public Statements of the Principals)

RHIC constitutes the joining of two well known tools, the radio part and the hypnotism part. People have found it difficult to accept that an individual can be hypnotized to perform an act which is against his moral principles. Some experiments have been conducted by the U.S. Army which show that this popular perception is untrue.

The chairman of the Department of Psychology at Colgate University, Dr. Estabrooks, has stated, "I can hypnotize a man without his knowledge or consent into committing treason against the United States." Estabrooks was one of the nation's most authoritative sources in the hypnotic field.

The psychologist told officials in Washington that a mere 200 well trained hypnotists could develop an army of mind-controlled sixth columnists in wartime United States. He laid out a scenario of an enemy doctor placing thousands of patients under hypnotic mind control, and eventually programming key military officers to follow his assignment. Through such maneuvers, he said, the entire U.S. Army could be taken over. Large numbers of saboteurs could also be created using hypnotism through the work of a doctor practicing in a neighborhood or foreign born nationals with close cultural ties with an enemy power.

Dr. Estabrooks actually conducted experiments on U.S. soldiers to prove his point. Soldiers of low rank and little formal education were placed under hypnotism and their memories tested. Surprisingly, hypnotists were able to control the subjects' ability to retain complicated verbal information. J. G. Watkins followed in Estabrooks steps and induced soldiers of lower rank to commit acts which conflicted not only with their moral code, but also the military code which they had come to accept through their basic training. One of the experiments involved placing a normal, stable army private in a deep trance. Watkins was trying to see if he could get the private to attack a superior officer, a cardinal sin in the military. While the private was in a deep trance, Watkins told him that the officer sitting across from him was an enemy soldier who was going to attempt to kill him. In the private's mind, it was a kill or be killed situation. The private immediately jumped up and grabbed the officer by the throat. The experiment was repeated several times, and in one case the man who was hypnotized and the man who was attacked were very close friends. The results were always the same. In one experiment, the hypnotized subject pulled out a knife and nearly stabbed another person.

Watkins concluded that people could be induced to commit acts contrary to their morality if their reality was distorted by the hypnotism. Similar experiments were conducted by Watkins using WACs exploring the possibility of making military personnel divulge military secrets. A related experiment had to be discontinued because a researcher, who had been one of the subjects, was exposing numerous top-secret projects to his hypnotist, who did not have the proper security clearance for such information. The information was divulged before an audience of 200 military personnel.

Dr. Watson's Experiments on Babies

In man's quest to control the behavior of humans, there was a great breakthrough established by Pavlov, who devised a way to make dogs salivate on cue. He perfected his conditioning response technique by cutting holes in the cheeks of dogs and measured the amount they salivated in response to different stimuli. Pavlov verified that "quality, rate and frequency of the salivation changed depending upon the quality, rate and frequency of the stimuli."

Though Pavlov's work falls far short of human mind control, it did lay the groundwork for future studies in mind and behavior control of humans. John B. Watson conducted experiments in the United States on an 11-month-old infant. After allowing the infant to establish a rapport with a white rat, Watson began to beat on the floor with an iron bar every time the infant came in contact with the rat. After a time, the infant made the association between the appearance of the rat and the frightening sound, and began to cry every time the rat came into view. Eventually, the infant developed a fear of any type of small animal. Watson was the founder of the behaviorist school of psychology.

"Give me the baby, and I'll make it climb and use its hands in constructing

DEAD MEN TALKING

buildings or stone or wood. I'll make it a thief, a gunman or a dope fiend. The possibilities of shaping in any direction are almost endless. Even gross differences in anatomical structure limits are far less than you may think. Make him a deaf mute, and I will build you a Helen Keller. Men are built, not born,"

Watson proclaimed. His psychology did not recognize inner feelings and thoughts as legitimate objects of scientific study, he was only interested in overt behavior.

Though Watson's work was the beginning of man's attempts to control human actions, the real work was done by B.F. Skinner, the high priest of the behaviorists movement. The key to Skinner's work was the concept of operant conditioning, which relied on the notion of reinforcement, all behavior which is learned is rooted in either a positive or negative response to that action. There are two corollaries of operant conditioning" Aversion therapy and desensitization.

Aversion therapy uses unpleasant reinforcement to a response which is undesirable. This can take the form of electric shock, exposing the subject to fear producing situations, and the infliction of pain in general. It has been used as a way of "curing" homosexuality, alcoholism and stuttering. Desensitization involves forcing the subject to view disturbing images over and over again until they no longer produce any anxiety, then moving on to more extreme images, and repeating the process over again until no anxiety is produced. Eventually, the subject becomes immune to even the most extreme images. This technique is typically used to treat people's phobias. Thus, the violence shown on T.V. could be said to have the unsystematic and unintended effect of desensitization.

Skinnerian behaviorism has been accused of attempting to deprive man of his free will, his dignity and his autonomy. It is said to be intolerant of uncertainty in human behavior, and refuses to recognize the private, the ineffable, and the unpredictable. It sees the individual merely as a medical, chemical and mechanistic entity which has no comprehension of its real interests.

Skinner believed that people are going to be manipulated. "I just want them to be manipulated effectively," he said. He measured his success by the absence of resistance and counter control on the part of the person he was manipulating. He thought that his techniques could be perfected to the point that the subject would not even suspect that he was being manipulated.

Dr. James V. McConnel, head of the Department of Mental Health Research at the University of Michigan, said, "The day has come when we can combine sensory deprivation with the use of drugs, hypnosis, and the astute manipulation of reward and punishment to gain almost absolute control over an individual's behavior. We want to reshape our society drastically."

206

DEAD MEN TALKING

The Navy's Murderers

(Statements of Lt. Commander Thomas Narut, The London Times)

A U.S. Navy psychologist claims that the Office of Naval Intelligence had taken convicted murderers from military prisons, used behavior modification techniques on them, and then relocated them in American embassies throughout the world. Just prior to that time, the U.S. Senate Intelligence Committee had censured the CIA for its global political assassination plots, including plots against Fidel Castro. The Navy psychologist was Lt. Commander Thomas Narut of the U.S. Regional Medical Center in Naples, Italy. The information was divulged at an Oslo NATO conference of 120 psychologists from the eleven nation alliance.

According to Dr. Narut, the U.S. Navy was an excellent place for a researcher to find "captive personnel" whom they could could use as guinea pigs in experiments. The Navy provided all the funding necessary, according to Narut.

Dr. Narut, in a question and answer session with reporters from many nations, revealed how the Navy was secretly programming large numbers of assassins. He said that the men he had worked with for the Navy were being prepared for commando-type operations, as well as covert operations in U.S. embassies worldwide. He described the men who went through his program as "hit men and assassins" who could kill on command.

Careful screening of the subjects was accomplished by Navy psychologists through the military records, and those who actually received assignments where their training could be utilized, were drawn mainly from submarine crews, the paratroops, and many were convicted murderers serving military prison sentences. Several men who had been awarded medals for bravery were drafted into the program.

The assassins were conditioned through "audio-visual desensitization". The process involved the showing of films of people being injured or killed in a variety of ways, starting with very mild depictions, leading up to the more extreme forms of mayhem. Eventually, the subjects would be able to detach their feelings even when viewing the most horrible of films. The conditioning was most successful when applied to "passive-aggressive" types, and most of these ended up being able to kill without any regrets. The prime indicator of violent tendencies was the Minnesota Multiphasic Personality Inventory. Dr. Narut knew of two Navy programming centers, the neuropsychiatric laboratory in San Diego and the U.S. Regional Medical Center in Italy, where he worked.

During the audio-visual desensitization programming, restraints were used to force the subject to view the films. A device was used on the subjects eyelids to prevent him from blinking. Typically, the preliminary film was on an African youth

207

being ritualistically circumcised with a dull knife and without any anesthetic. The second film showed a sawmill scene in which a man accidentally cut off his fingers.

In addition to the desensitization films, the potential assassins underwent programming to create prejudicial attitude in the men, to think of their future enemies, especially the leaders of these countries, as sub-human. Films and lectures were presented demeaning the culture and habits of the people of the countries where it had been decided they would be sent.

After his NATO lecture, Dr. Narut disappeared. He could not be located. Within a week of so after the lecture, the Pentagon issued an emphatic denial that the U.S. Navy had "engaged in psychological training or other types of training of personnel as assassins." They disavowed the programming centers in San Diego and Naples and stated they were unable to locate Narut, but did provide confirmation that he was a staff member of the U.S. Regional Medical Center in Naples.

Dr. Alfred Zitani, an American delegate to the Oslo conference, did verify Narut's remarks and they were published in the Sunday Times.

Sometime later, Dr. Narut surfaced again in London and recanted his remarks, stating that he was "talking in theoretical and not practical terms." Shortly thereafter, the U.S. Naval headquarters in London issued a statement indicating that Dr. Narut's remarks at the NATO conference should be discounted because he had "personal problems". Dr. Narut never made any further public statements about the program.

During the NATO conference in Oslo, Dr. Narut had remarked that the reason he was divulging the information was because he believed that the information was coming out anyway. The doctor was referring to the disclosure by a Congressional subcommittee which were then appearing in the press concerning various CIA assassination plots. However, what Dr. Narut had failed to realize at the time, was that the Navy's assassination plots were not destined to be revealed to the public at that time.

Electromagnetic Control of Human Behavior

(Published scientific papers and press reports)

There were three scientists who pioneered the work of using an electromagnetic field to control human behavior. Their work began 25 years ago. These three were Dr. Jose Delgado, psychology professor at Yale University; Dr. W. Ross Adey, a physiologist at the Brain Research Institute at UCLA; and Dr. Wilder Penfield, a Canadian.

Dr. Penfield's experiments consisted of the implantation of electrodes deep into the cortexes of epilepsy patients who were to undergo surgery; he was able to drastically improve the memories of these patients through electrical stimulation. Dr. Adey implanted transmitters in the brains of cats and chimpanzees that could send signals to a receiver regarding the electrical activity of the brain; additional radio signals were sent back into the brains of the animals which modified their behavior at the direction of the doctor. Dr. Delgado was able to stop and turn a charging bull through the use of an implanted radio receiver.

Other experiments using platinum, gold and stainless steel electrode implants enabled researchers to induce total madness in cats, put monkeys into a stupor, or to set human beings jerking their arms up and down. Much of Delgado's work was financed by the CIA through phony funding conduits masking themselves as charitable organizations.

Following the successes of Delgado's work, the CIA set up their own research program in the field of electromagnetic behavior modification under the code name Sleeping Beauty. With the guidance of Dr. Ivor Browning, a laboratory was set up in New Mexico, specializing in working with the hypothalamus or "sweet spot" of the brain. Here it was found that stimulating this area could produce intense euphoria.

Dr. Browning was able to wire a radio receiver-amplifier into the "sweet spot" of a donkey which picked up a five-micro-amp signal, such that he could create intense happiness in the animal. Using the jolts of happiness as an "electronic carrot", Browning was able to send the donkey up a 2000 foot New Mexico mountain and back to its point of origin. When the donkey was proceeding up the path toward its destination, it was rewarded; when it deviated, the signal stopped. "You've never seen a donkey so eager to keep on course in your whole life," Dr. Browning exclaimed.

The CIA utilized the electronic carrot technique in getting trained pigeons to fly miniature microphone-transmitters to the ledge of a KGB safe house where the devices monitored conversations for months. There was a move within the CIA to conduct further experiments on humans, foreigners and prisoners, but officially the White House vetoed the idea as being unethical.

In May 1989, it was learned by the CIA that the KGB was subjecting people undergoing interrogation to electromagnetic fields, which produced a panic reaction, thereby bringing them closer to breaking down under questioning. The subjects were not told that they were being placed under the influence of these beams. A few years earlier, Dr. Ross Adey released photographs and a fact sheet concerning what he called the Russian Lida machine. This consisted of a small transmitter emitting 10-hertz waves which makes the subject susceptible to hypnotic suggestion. The device utilized the outmoded vacuum-tube design. Ameri-

DEAD MEN TALKING

can POWs in Korea have indicated that similar devices had been used for interrogation purposes in POW camps.

The ELF Connection

The general, long term goal of the CIA was to find out whether or not mind control could be achieved through the use of a precise, external, electromagnetic beam. The electrical activity of the brain operates within the range of 100 hertz frequency. This spectrum is called ELF or Extremely Low Frequency range. ELF waves carry very little ionizing radiation and very low heat, and therefore do not manifest gross, observable physical effects on living organisms. Published Soviet experiments with ELFs reveal that there was a marked increase in psychiatric and central nervous system disorders and symptoms of stress for sailors working close to ELF generators.

In the mid-1970s, American interest in combining EMR techniques with hypnosis was very prominent. Plans were on file to develop these techniques through experiments on human volunteers. The spoken word of the hypnotist could be conveyed by modulated electromagnetic energy directly into the subconscious parts of the human brain without employing any technical devices for receiving or transacting the messages and without the person exposed to such influence having a chance to control the information input consciously.

In California, it was discovered by Dr. Adey that animal brain waves could be altered directly by ELF fields. It was found that monkey brains would fall in phase with ELF waves. These waves could easily pass through the skull, which normally protected the central nervous system from outside influence.

In San Leandro, Dr. Elizabeth Rauscher, director of Technic Research Laboratory, has been doing ELF/brain research with human subjects for some time. One of the frequencies produces nausea for more than an hour. Another frequency, she calls it the marijuana frequency, gets people laughing. "Give me the money and three months," she says, "and I'll be able to affect the behavior of eighty percent of the people in this town without their knowing it."

The Devastating Mental and Physical Effect of Microwaves

(Soviet Research, State Department Admissions, Public Record)

In the past, the Soviet Union has invested large sums of time and money investigating microwaves. In 1952, while the Cold War was showing no signs of thawing, there was a secret meeting at the Sandia Corporation in New Mexico between U.S. and Soviet scientists involving the exchange of information regarding the biological hazards and safety levels of EMR. The Soviets possessed the greater preponderance of information, and the American scientists were unwill-

210

ing to take it seriously. In subsequent meetings, the Soviet scientists continued to stress the seriousness of the risks, while American scientists downplayed their importance.

Shortly after the last Sandia meeting, the Soviets began directing a microwave beam at the U.S. embassy in Moscow, using embassy workers as guinea pigs for low-level EMR experiments. Washington, D.C. was oddly quiescent, regarding the Moscow embassy bombardment.

Discovered in 1962, the Moscow signal was investigated by the CIA, which hired a consultant, Milton Zaret, and code named the research Project Pandora. According to Zaret, the Moscow signal was composed of several frequencies, and was focused precisely upon the Ambassador's office. The intensity of the bombardment was not made public, but when the State Department finally admitted the existence of the signal, it announced that it was fairly low.

There was consensus among Soviet EMR researchers that a beam such as the Moscow signal was destined to produced blurred vision and loss of mental concentration. The Boston Globe reported that the American ambassador had not only developed a leukemia-like blood disease, but also suffered from bleeding eyes and chronic headaches. Under the CIA's Project Pandora, monkeys were brought into the embassy and exposed to the Moscow signal; they were found to have developed blood composition anomalies and unusual chromosome counts. Embassy personnel were found to have a 40 percent higher than average white blood cell count. While Operation Pandora's data gathering proceeded, embassy personnel continued working in the facility and were not informed of the bombardment until 10 years later. Embassy employees were eventually granted a 20 percent hardship allowance for their service in an unhealthful post. Throughout the period of bombardment, the CIA used the opportunity to gather data on psychological and biological effects of the beam on American personnel.

The U.S. government began to examine the affects of the Moscow signal. The job was turned over to the Defense Advanced Research Projects Agency (DARPA). DARPA is now developing electromagnetic weaponry. The man in charge of the DARPA program, Dr. Jack Verona, is so important and so secretive that he doesn't even return President George Bush's telephone calls.

The American public was never informed that the military had planned to develop electromagnetic weapons until 1982, when the revelation appeared in a technical Air Force magazine.

The magazine article stated, "....specifically generated radio-frequency radiation (RFR) fields may pose powerful and revolutionary anti-personnel military trends." The article indicated that that it would be very easy to use electromagnetic fields to disrupt the human brain because the brain, itself, was an electrically mediated organ. It further indicated that a rapidly scanning RFR system would have a stunning or killing capability over a large area. The system was developable.

Navy Captain Dr. Paul E. Taylor read a paper at the Air University Center for Aerospace Doctrine, Research and Education, at Maxwell Air Force Base, Alabama. Dr. Taylor was responsible for the Navy's Radiation Laboratory and had been studying radiation effects on humans. In his paper, Dr. Taylor stated, "The ability of individuals to function (as soldiers) could be degraded to such a point that would be combat ineffective." The system was so sophisticated that it employed microwaves and millimeter waves and was transportable by a large truck.

Lawrence Livermore National Laboratory in the South Bay, are working on the development of a "brain bomb". A bomb could be dropped in the middle of a battlefield which would produce microwaves, incapacitating the minds of soldiers within a circumscribed area.

Applications of microwave technology in espionage were available for over 25 years. In a meeting in Berkeley of the American Association for the Advancement of Science as early as 1965, Professor J. Anthony Deutsch of New York University, provided an important segment of research in the field of memory control. In layman terms, Professor Deutsch indicated that the mind is a transmitter and if too much information is received, like too many vehicles on a crowded freeway, the brain ceases to transmit. The Professor indicated that an excess of acetyl choline in the brain can interfere with the memory process and control. He indicated excess amounts of acetyl choline can be artificially produced, through both the administration of drugs or through the use of radio waves. The process is called Electronic Dissolution of Memory (EDOM). The memory transmission can be stopped for as long as the radio signal continues.

As a result, the awareness of the person skips over those minutes during which he is subjected to the radio signal. Memory is distorted, and time-orientation is destroyed.

According to Lincoln Lawrence, author of Were We Controlled, EDOM is now operational. "There is already in use a small EDOM generator/transmitter which can be concealed on the body of the person.

Contact with this person, a casual handshake or even just a touch, transmits a tiny electronic charge plus an ultra-sonic signal tone which for a short period will disturb the time-orientation of the person affected....it can be a potent weapon for hopelessly confusing evidence in the investigation of a crime "

DEAD MEN TALKING

Microwave Transmission of Voices Direct to the Brain

Thirty years ago, Allen Frey discovered that microwaves of 300 to 3000 megahertz could be "heard" by people, even if they were deaf, if pulsed at a certain rate. Appearing to be originating just in back of the head, the sound boomed, clicked, hissed or buzzed, depending upon the frequency. Later research has shown that the perception of the waves take place just in front of the ears. The microwaves causes pressure waves in the brain tissue, and this phenomenon vibrates the sound receptors in the inner ear through the bone structure. Some microwaves are capable of directly stimulating the nerve cells of the auditory pathways.

This has been confirmed with experiments with rats, in which the sound registers 120 decibels, which is equal to the volume of a nearby jet during takeoff. Aside from having the capability of causing pain and preventing auditory communication, a more subtle effect was demonstrated at the Walter Reed Army Institute of Research by Dr. Joseph C. Sharp. Dr. Sharp, himself, was the subject of an experiment in which pulsed microwave audiograms, or the microwave analog of the sound vibrations of spoken words, were delivered to his brain in such a way that he was able to understand the words that were spoken. Military and undercover uses of such a device might include driving a subject crazy with inner voices in order to discredit him, or conveying undetectable instructions to a programmed assassin.

But the technology has been carried even a step further. It has been demonstrated by Dr. Ross Adey that microwaves can be used to directly bring about changes in the electrical patterns of different parts of the brain. His experiments showed that he could achieve the same mind control over animals as Dr. Delgado did in the bull incident. Dr. Delgado used brain implants in his animals, Dr. Adey used microwave devices without preconditioning. He made animals act and look like electronic toys.

Nazi Mind Control Experiments

(Report from the US Naval Technical Mission)

At the conclusion of World War Two, American investigators learned that Nazi doctors at the Dachau concentration camp in Germany had been conducting mind control experiments on inmates. They experimented with hypnosis and with the drug mescaline.

Mescaline is a quasi-synthetic extract of the peyote cactus, and is very similar to LSD in the hallucinations which it produces. Though they did not achieve the degree of success they had desired, the SS interrogators in conjunction with the Dachau doctors were able to extract the most intimate secrets from the prisoners when the inmates were given very high doses of mescaline.

There were fatal mind control experiments conducted at Auschwitz. The experiments there were described by one informant as "brainwashing with chemicals". The informant said the Gestapo wasn't satisfied with extracting information by torture. "So the next question was, why don't we do it like the Russians, who have been able to get confessions of guilt at their show trials?" They tried various barbiturates and morphine derivatives. After prisoners were fed a coffee-like substance, two of them died in the night and others died later.

The Dachau mescaline experiments were written up in a lengthy report issued by the U.S. Naval Technical Mission, whose job it was at the conclusion of the war to scour all of Europe for every shred of industrial and scientific material that had been produced by the Third Reich. It was as a result of this report that the U.S. Navy became interested in mescaline as an interrogation tool. The Navy initiated Project Chatter in 1947, the same year the Central Intelligence Agency was formed. The Chatter format included developing methods for acquiring information from people against their will, but without inflicting harm or pain. At the conclusion of the war, the OSS was designated as the investigative unit for the International Military Tribunal, which was to become known as the Nuremberg Trials. The purpose of Nuremberg was to try the principal Nazi leaders. Some Nazis were on trial for their experiments, and the U.S. was using its own "truth drugs" on these principal Nazi prisoners, namely Goring, Ribbentrop, Speer and eight others. The Justice in charge of the tribunal had given the OSS permission to use the drugs.

The Dachau doctors who performed the mescaline experiments also were involved in aviation medicine. The aviation experiments at Dachau fascinated Heinrich Himmler. Himmler followed the progress of the tests, studied their findings and often suggested improvements. The Germans had a keen interest in several medical problems in the field of flying, they were interested in preventing pilots from slowly becoming unconscious as a result of breathing the thin air of the high altitudes and there was interest in enhancing night vision.

The main research in this area was at the Institute of Aviation in Munich, which had excellent laboratories. The experiments in relationship to the Institute were conducted at Dachau. Inmates had been immersed in tubs of ice water with instruments placed in their orifices in order to monitor their painful deaths. Dr. Hubertus Strughold, who ran the German aviation medicine team, confirmed that he had heard humans were used for the Dachau experiments. Hidden in a cave in Hallein were files recording the Dachau experiments.

DEAD MEN TALKING

Nazi Altitude and Cold Endurance Experiments

On May 15, 1941, Dr. Sigmund Rascher wrote a letter to Himmler requesting permission to use the Dachau inmates for experiments on the physiology of high altitudes. Rascher lamented the fact that no such experiments have been done using human subjects. "The experiments are very dangerous and we cannot attract volunteers," he told Himmler. His request was approved.

Dachau was filled with Communists and Social Democrats, Jews, Jehovah's Witnesses, Gypsies, clergymen, homosexuals, and people critical of the Nazi government. Upon entering Dachau, prisoners lost all legal status, their hair was shaved off, all their possessions confiscated, they were poorly fed, and they were used as slaves for both the corporations and the government. The SS guards were brutal and sadistic. The idea to test subjects at Dachau was really the brain child of Erich Hippke, chief surgeon of the Luftwaffe.

Between March and August of 1942 extensive experiments were conducted at Dachau regarding the limits of human endurance at high altitudes. These experiments were conducted for the benefit of the German Air Force. The experiments took place in a low-pressure chamber in which altitudes of up to 68,000 feet could be simulated. The subjects were placed in the chamber and the altitude was raised, many inmates died as a result. The survivors often suffered serious injury. One witness at the Nuremberg trails, Anton Pacholegg, who was sent to Dachau in 1942, gave an eyewitness account of the typical pressure test:

"The Luftwaffe delivered a cabinet constructed of wood and metal. It was possible in the cabinet to either decrease or increase the air pressure. You could observe through a little window the reaction of the subject inside the chamber. The purpose of these experiments was to test human energy and the subject's capacity...to take large amounts of pure oxygen, and then to test his reaction to a gradual decrease in oxygen. I have personally seen through the observation window of the chamber when a prisoner inside would stand a vacuum until his lungs ruptured. Some experiments gave men such pressure in their heads that they would go mad and pull out their hair in an effort to relieve the pressure. They would tear their heads and face with their fingers and nails in an attempt to maim themselves in their madness. They would beat the walls with their hands and head and scream in an effort to relieve pressure in their eardrums. These cases of extreme vacuums generally ended in the death of the subjects."

The former prisoner also testified, "An extreme experiment was so certain to result in death that in many instances the chamber was used for routine execution purposes rather than an experiment." A minimum 200 prisoners were known to have died in these experiments.

DEAD MEN TALKING

The doctors directly involved with the research held very high positions: Karl Brandt was Hitler's personal doctor; Oskar Schroeder was the Chief of the Medical Services of the Luftwaffe; Karl Gebhardt was Chief Surgeon on the Staff of the Reich Physician SS and Police and German Red Cross President; Joachim Mrugowsky was Chief of the Hygienic Institute of the Waffen SS; Helmut Poppendick was a senior colonel in the SS and Chief of the Personal Staff of the Reich Physicians SS and Police; Siegfried Ruff was Director of the Department of Aviation Medicine.

The first human guinea pig was a 37 year old Jew in good health. Himmler invited 40 top Luftwaffe officers to view a movie of an inmate dying in the pressure chamber. After the pressure chamber tests, the cold treatment experiments began. The experiments consisted of immersing inmates in freezing water while their vital signs were monitored. The goal was to discover the cause of death. Heart failure was the answer. An inmate described the procedures:

"The basins were filled with water and ice was added until the water measured 37.4 F and the experimental subjects were either dressed in a flying suit or were placed in the water naked. The temperature was measured rectally and through the stomach. The lowering of the body temperature to 32 degrees was terrible for experimental subjects. At 32 degrees the subject lost consciousness. They were frozen to 25 degrees. The worst experiment was performed on two Russian officer POWs. They were placed in the basin naked. Hour after hour passed, and while usually after a short time, 60 minutes, freezing had set in, these two Russians were still conscious after two hours. After the third hour one Russian told the other, 'Comrade, tell that officer to shoot us.' The other replied, 'Don't expect any mercy from this Fascist dog.' Then they shook hands and said goodbye. The experiment lasted at least five hours until death occurred.

"Dry freezing experiments were also carried out at Dachau. One subject was put outdoors on a stretcher at night when it was extremely cold. While covered with a linen sheet, a bucket of cold water was poured over him every hour. He was kept outdoors under sub-freezing conditions. In subsequent experiments, subjects were simply left outside naked in a court under freezing conditions for hours. Himmler gave permission to move the experiments to Auschwitz, because it was more private and because the subjects of the experiment would howl all night as they froze. The physical pain of freezing was terrible. The subjects died by inches, heartbeat became totally irregular, breathing difficulties and lung endema resulted, hands and feet became frozen white." As the Germans began to lose the war, the aviation doctors began too keep their names from appearing in Himmler's files for fear of future recriminations.

The Nazi doctors who experimented on the inmates of prison camps during

DEAD MEN TALKING

World War Two were tried for murder at the Nuremberg Tribunal. The accused were educated, trained physicians, they did not kill in anger or in malice, they were creating a science of death. Ironically, in 1933, the Nazi's passed a law for the protection of animals. The law cited the prevention of cruelty and indifference to animals as one of the highest moral values of a people, animal experimentation was unthinkable, but human experimentations were acceptable. The victims of the crime of these doctors numbered into the thousands.

US Contempt for International Human Experimentation Protocols

In 1953, while the Central Intelligence Agency was still conducting mind control and behavior modification on unwitting humans in this country, the United States signed the Nuremberg Code, a code born out of the ashes of war and human suffering. The document was a solemn promise never to tolerate such human atrocities again. The Code maintains three fundamental principles:

1.The subjects of any experimentation must be volunteers who thoroughly understand the purpose and the dangers of the experiments.

2.They must be free to give consent and the consent must be without pressure and they must be free to quit the experiments at any time.

3.The experiments must be likely to yield knowledge which is valuable to everyone. The knowledge must be such that it could not be gained in any other way.

The experiments must be conducted by only the most competent doctors, and they must exercise extreme care.

The Nazi aviation experiments met none of these conditions. Most inmates at Dachau knew that the experiments in the pressure chamber were fatal. From the very beginning, control of the experiments was largely in the hands of the SS, which was later judged to be a criminal organization by the Nuremberg Tribunal.

Despite our lessons from Nuremberg and the death camps, the CIA, U.S. Navy and the U.S. Army Chemical Corps targeted specific groups of people for experimentation who were not able to resist, prisoners, mental patients, foreigners, ethnic minorities, sex deviants, the terminally ill, children and U.S. military personnel and prisoners of war.

They violated the Nuremberg Code for conducting and subsidizing experiments on unwitting citizens. The CIA began its mind control projects in 1953, the very year that the U.S. signed the Nuremberg Code and pledged with the international community of nations to respect basic human rights and to prohibit experimentation on captive populations without full and free consent.

DEAD MEN TALKING

Dr. Cameron, a CIA operative, was one of the worst offenders against the Code, yet he was a member of the Nuremberg Tribunal, with full knowledge of its testimony. In 1973, a three judge court in Michigan ruled, "experimental psychosurgery, which is irreversible and intrusive, often leads to the blunting of emotions, the deadening of memory, the reduction of affect, and limits the ability to generate new ideas. Its potential for injury to the creativity of the individual is great and can infringe on the right of the individual to be free from interference with his mental process.

"The state's interest in performing psychosurgery and the legal ability of the involuntarily detained mental patient to give consent, must bow to the First Amendment, which protects the generation and free flow of ideas from unwarranted interference with one's mental processes."

Citing the Nuremberg Code, the court found that "the very nature of the subject's incarceration diminishes the capacity to consent to psychosurgery."

In 1973, the Commonwealth of Massachusetts enacted regulations which would require informed written consent from voluntary patients before electroshock treatment could be performed.

Senator Sam Ervin's Committee lashed out bitterly at the mind control and behavior modification experiments and ordered them discontinued, they were not.

The New England Journal of Medicine states, that the consent provisions now in place are "no more than an elaborate ritual." They called it "a device that when the subject is uneducated and uncomprehending, confers no more than a semblance of propriety on human experimentation."

The Nuremberg Tribunal brought to light that some of the most respected figures in the medical profession were involved in the vast crime network of the SS. Only 23 persons were charged with criminal activity in this area, despite the fact that hundreds of medical personnel were involved. The defendants were charged with crimes against humanity. They were found guilty of planning and executing experiments on humans without their consent, in a cruel and brutal manner which involved severe torture, deliberate murder and with the full knowledge of the gravity of their deeds. Only seven of the defendants were sentenced to death and hanged, others received life sentences. Five who were involved in the experiments were not tried. Ernest Grawitz committed suicide, Carl Clauberg was tried in the Soviet Union, Josef Mengele escaped to South America and was later captured by Israeli agents, Horst Schumann disappeared and Siegmund Rascher was executed by Himmler.

DEAD MEN TALKING

US Use of Dachau Data and "Friendly" Nazi Doctors

There were 200 German medical doctors conducting these medical experiments. Most of these doctors were friends of the United States before the war, and despite their inhuman experiments, the U.S. attempted to rebuild a relationship with them after the war. The knowledge the Germans had accumulated at the expense of human life and suffering, was considered a "booty of war", by the Americans and the Russians. The Americans tracked down Dr. Strughold, the aviation doctor who was in charge of the Dachau experiments.

With full knowledge that the experiments were conducted on captive humans, the U.S. recruited the doctors to work for them. General Dwight D. Eisenhower gave his personal approval to exploit the work and research of the Nazi's in the death camps.

Within weeks of Eisenhower's order, many of these notorious doctors were working for the U.S. Army at Heidelberg. Army teams scoured Europe for scientific experimental apparatus such as pressure chambers, compressors, G-force machines, giant centrifuges, and electron microscopes. These doctors were wined and dined by the U.S. Army while most of Germany's post-war citizens virtually starved.

The German doctors were brought to the U.S. and went to work for Project Paperclip. All these doctors had been insulated against war crime charges. The Nuremberg prosecutors were shocked that U.S. authorities were using the German doctors despite their criminal past.

Under the leadership of Strughold, 34 scientists accepted contracts from Project Paperclip, and were moved to Randolph Air Force Base at San Antonio, Texas. The authorization to hire these Nazi scientists came directly for the Joint Chiefs of Staff. The top military brass stated that they wished to exploit these rare minds. Project Paperclip, ironically, would use Nazi doctors to develop methods of interrogating German prisoners of war.

As hostilities began to build after the war between the Americans and the Russians, the U.S. imported as many as 1000 former Nazi scientists.

In 1969, Americans landed on the moon, and two groups of scientist in the control center shared the credit, the rocket team from Peenemunde, Germany, under the leadership of Werner von Braun. These men had perfected the V-2s which were built in the Nordhausen caves where 20,000 slave laborers from prison camp Dora had been worked to death. The second group were the space doctors, lead by 71-year-old Dr. Hubertus Strughold, whose work was pioneered in Experimental Block No. 5 of the Dachau concentration camp and the torture and death of hundreds of inmates. The torture chambers that was used to slowly kill the prisoners of the Nazi's were the test beds for the apparatus that protected Neil Armstrong from harm, from lack of oxygen, and pressure, when he walked on the moon.

BIBLIOGRAPHY: The Napa Sentinel would like to acknowledge the exceptional contribution of radio commentator David Emory and his extensive archives. Other source material included:

Acid Dreams by Martin Lee & Bruce Shlain

From the Belly of the Beast, Jack Henry Abbott

Congressional Record, No. 26, Vol. 118, Feb. 24, 1974: testimony of Jose Delgado

The Glass House Tapes, by Louis Tackwood

The Great Heroin Coup, by Henrik Kruger

"Individual Rights and the Federal Role in Behavior Modification," 93rd Congress, 2nd Session, 1974. Sam Ervin Senate Subcommittee on Constitutional 'Rights

The Last Hero, Wild Bill Donovan, by Anthony Cave Brown

Mind Control, by Peter Schrag

The Mind Stealers, by Samuel Chavkin

"Matador with a radio stops wild bull," New York Times, May 17, 1965

Operation Mind Control, Water Bowart

The Phoenix Program, Douglas Valentine

The Physical Control of the Mind, Jose M. R. Delgado, MD

The Politics of Heroin in Southeast Asia, Alfred McCoy

"Role of Brain Disease in Riots and Urban Violence," by Vernon H. Mark, Frank R. Ervin, and William H. Sweet. Journal of the American Medical Association, September 11, 1967.

San Francisco Bay Guardian, August 28, 1991

"Convict Talks of 1984 Arms Talks With Iran," San Francisco Chronicle, December 29, 1986

San Francisco Chronicle, January 13, 1973

Guy Wright Column, San Francisco Chronicle, July 5, 1987 BR>

DEAD MEN TALKING

Sunday Times, July 1975.

Violence and the Brain, by Vernon H. Mark and Frank R. Ervin

War on the Mind: The Military Uses and Abuses of Psychology, by Peter Watson

Were We Controlled? - by Lincoln Lawrence

"Why Was Patricia Hearst Kidnapped?" by Mae Brussell, The Realist

222

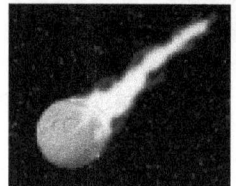

224

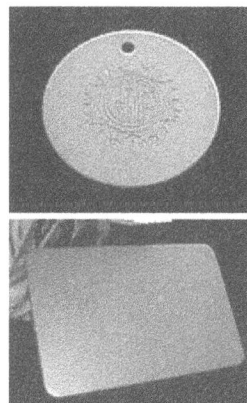

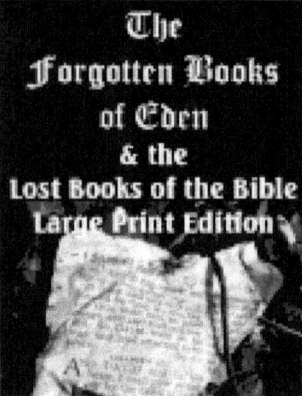

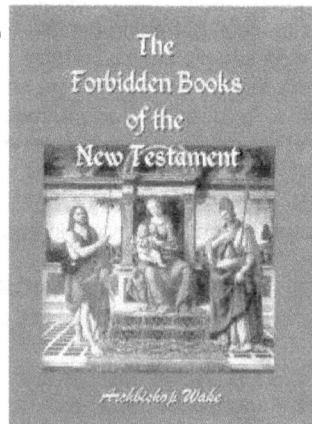

FIRE FROM THE SKY

CIA AND NAZI COLLABORATION EXPOSED! GERMAN SCIENTISTS UTILIZE TESLA TECHNOLOGY TO CONSTRUCT FLYING SAUCERS

Soon after cessation of hostilities closed World War II, hundreds of former Nazi and SS members were secretly smugged into America to work on military and space programs. They were employed by nearly every one of the military-industrial complex companies, developing bombs, missiles, rockets, aircraft and advanced ground vehicles.

Many former Nazis went to work for the CIA, and, indeed, actually formed the foundation of that agency because they kept accurate records of their enemies (Russia), and the CIA purchased this knowledge and contact information from them.

Both the U.S. and USSR made adequate use of Tesla technologies to create weapons and communications devices previously undreamed of, including — if the records are true — aerial disc platforms, or "Flying Saucers." Intelligence records show that German scientists had built and test-flown several different types of flying discs. The complete plans for one type were captured at the BMW auto factory in Prague at the close of the war.

FIRE FROM THE SKY exposes how it all happened and the consequences with which we all must live today. It also explains the circumstances under which UFO researchers and the public have been manipulated into certain belief patterns, including aspects of the abduction phenomenon which utilizes a high degree of mind control.

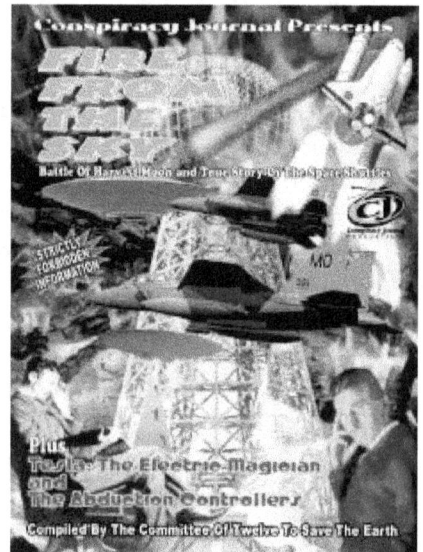

OUR SPECIAL PRICE:
$25.00 + $5.00 S/H

EXCLUSIVE BOOK & AUDIO CD SET

( ) WANT TO KNOW MORE?? EVIL AGENDA OF THE SECRET GOVERNMENT — EXPOSING PROJECT PAPER CLIP AND THE UNDERGROUND UFO BASES OF HITLER'S ELITE.
Tim Swartz reveals how the Controllers have imitated REAL alien abductions and are breeding a Hybrid Zombie Race.
Add $15.00 to your order!

Timothy Beckley
Box 753 · New Brunswick, NJ
08903

PARTIAL LIST OF CONTENTS: In The Begining; USS Thresher and the U-2; Total Russian Defense; Project Paperclip; Operation Sunrise; Project Overcast; German Scientists and Aliens; NICAP; Then Came 1947; Antarctica; Admiral Byrd and Operation Highjump; Hitler Escaped!; Polar Defenses; UFOs: Nazi or Alien?; Russian Space Program; Scalar Weapons Activated; Rudolph Hess and Secret Space Base; Werner Heisenberg; Who Created The Atomic Bomb?; German Submarines in the South Atlantic; German Flying Saucers; Falklands Islands War; The Kennedy/Nazi Connection; Cover and Concealment; Nikola Tesla: The Forgotten Genius; Nikola Tesla— The Greatest Hacker Of All Time & MORE!

228